Present-day Russian Psychology

Present-day
Russian Psychology

A SYMPOSIUM BY SEVEN AUTHORS

Edited by

NEIL O'CONNOR, M.A., Ph.D.

Medical Research Council Psychologist, Institute of Psychiatry,
The Maudsley Hospital, London

PERGAMON PRESS

OXFORD · LONDON · EDINBURGH · NEW YORK
TORONTO · SYDNEY · PARIS · BRAUNSCHWEIG

Pergamon Press Ltd., Headington Hill Hall, Oxford
4 & 5 Fitzroy Square, London W.1

Pergamon Press (Scotland) Ltd., 2 & 3 Teviot Place, Edinburgh 1

Pergamon Press Inc., 44–01 21st Street, Long Island City, New York 11101

Pergamon of Canada Ltd., 6 Adelaide Street East, Toronto, Ontario

Pergamon Press (Aust.) Pty. Ltd., 20–22 Margaret Street,
Sydney, New South Wales

Pergamon Press S.A.R.L., 24 rue des Écoles, Paris 5e

Vieweg & Sohn GmbH, Burgplatz 1, Braunschweig

Printed in Great Britain by A. Wheaton & Co. Ltd., Exeter

(3044/66)

Contents

Editor's Introduction

Previous Surveys and This

This book is unique in that it is the first comprehensive survey of Russian psychological literature written by bilingual psychologists. Other surveys have, of course, appeared in the *Annual Review of Psychology* by such authors as Brožek (1962) and Mintz (1958), one of whom has written a chapter in this book. However, these have of necessity been more limited for space and have served chiefly as brief guides to recent trends. Other more comprehensive surveys, such as those of Simon (1957, 1963) and O'Connor (1961) have provided direct translations of Russian articles. Each of these has served its purpose of making Russian psychology more familiar to English readers. In addition, such books as Gray's *Pavlov's Typology* (1964) have added basic information about one aspect of Soviet psychology, just as Anrep's *Conditioned Reflexes* (1927) did many years ago. We have also had translations of whole books by Luria (1961, 1963) and Vigotsky (1962), which have proved very valuable. One must also pay respectful tribute to the long-term studies of Horsley Gantt (1928, 1944) and Razran (1965), who forged a link between Russian and Western psychology in the 1920's and 1930's and who for so many years have preserved the connection, when most Western psychologists knew Hull but not Pavlov. Nowhere, however, has it been possible to find in one book a comprehensive and sympathetic but critical account of Soviet psychology. The present volume meets this need. It is not simply a survey of Soviet psychological literature by competent linguists who are also psychologists. In addition, each of the contributors has specialized in that aspect of psychology which he writes about below, so that this book may be considered exceptional on this account.

There are, of course, shortcomings. The coverage in a book of this size is limited and no comparative animal or social psychology is included, for example. The main reason is that these subjects are only just beginning in Russia. Some of the chapters may be hard reading for the intelligent layman, and not all the references given will be easily available. In addition, those philosophically inclined readers will notice that the contributors have tried to present some aspects of dialectical materialism. These attempts to apprehend the philosophical underpinning of some Soviet psychology might seem unsophisticated to philosophers and logicians. However, I consider that since some Soviet psychology has been oriented by dialectical materialism, at least in its choice of subject matter and sometimes of method, some comprehension of the elements of "Materialism and Empirio-Criticism", for example, is essential, and the inclusion of these short statements is therefore desirable. It is interesting to note that in the immediate post-war years, Soviet psychological publications were sometimes more philosophical than psychological and the charge could have been made against them that they understood dialectics better than psychology. But just as British psychologists are now attempting to understand the Leninist theory of reflection and the experiments it has inspired, Soviet psychologists themselves are accepting other sources and employing, for example, cybernetic models in their applied industrial studies. Whatever the shifts of emphasis in theory may be, practice in the science of both countries is drawing even closer together than the still somewhat differing theoretical statements would lead us to believe. At least, continued interchange of experimental reports will inevitably make this so and should ultimately produce a theory which is mutually acceptable.

The Contents of this Book

This book contains surveys of psychology and psychiatry which are set out in individual chapters by the authors, whose texts are largely their own, although the editor has made occasional suggestions concerning the history of Russian psychology. No doubt,

Soviet psychologists will find weaknesses in the expositions offered here, but the authors have made every effort to present a balanced picture. The book should thus serve two functions: the first to convey to the intelligent English-speaking reader some idea of the subject matter and quality of Soviet psychology, and the second to invite comment and correction from Russian colleagues. So far as English and American readers are concerned, we would be happy to have encouraged them to go on to read further in following their special interests. A good number of English texts on Russian psychology are quoted. In these respects, it is to be hoped that this book will be a suitable aid, not only to lay readers but to specialists in psychology, who will be able to use it as a first text. Exchange arrangements now make it possible for students to work in Russian laboratories, and before long books of this kind will become unnecessary as knowledge is more widely exchanged between the two countries. In the meantime, however, there is still so much ignorance concerning work in the Soviet Union that the contents of this book should serve as both an introduction and, on two or three subjects, a standard work.

The chapters include a statement on the orienting reflex and the voluntary control of motor behaviour, a survey of recent psychiatry, a look at the use of information theory and its increased popularity, a review of abnormal psychology and psychotherapy, an analysis of psycholinguistic psychology, a review of studies of child development and an account of a personal visit to Russian laboratories. There is no special order about this arrangement of subjects, because the interests and specialities of the authors follow no narrow and confined plan. However, history imposes something of its own order on events and this can be discerned in the subject matter.

Schools of Psychology in the U.S.S.R.

In my previous collection (*Recent Soviet Psychology*, 1961) and elsewhere (1964) I was able to suggest that there were by now three schools of Soviet psychology—one a Pavlovian school, one inspired by Vigotsky and one in Georgia drawing for inspiration on the work of Uznadze. Only a short time has elapsed since this view was put forward, but in that time other trends, already present when I wrote, have emerged more markedly. For example, the emphasis which Soviet health and education authorities put on child care has resulted in a tremendous increase in the number of studies of child development. The work of Zaporozhets and El'Konin, as well as Leont'ev, is especially noteworthy. In addition, Luria, following many studies with defectives, has begun to write about his extensive neurological experience. This has led to publications concerned with localization of function in studies of head injuries. These two newly expanding fields are part of the growth of Soviet psychology. Equally part of it have been studies showing new trends within established disciplines. The best example of this in the present volume is Rabbitt's description of the development of statistical and cybernetic models in Soviet laboratories. The continued lack of involvement with intelligence testing is one of the few remaining basic differences between Soviet and Western psychology, but another important one is the relatively small involvement with rat experiments in Russia. In the United States and to a lesser extent in Britain, the rat has become the experimental animal of choice and rebellion against the rat has scarcely begun. In Russia, on the other hand, the rat does not exist and even the dog is going out of favour. Although there are signs that intelligence testing may be re-examined by Soviet psychologists, the lack of interest in the rat reveals a basic theoretical difference, which is discussed below.

How then can we characterize the growth of present-day Russian psychology? With the increase in the number of psychologists, both in education and in child development, the trend towards an examination of abilities on the one hand and patterns of development on the other has increased. This is no more than to maintain the existence of a trend which I have already discussed in a previous collection. The theory in both these fields remains substantially unchanged in the last ten years. Work in education continues to emphasize Leont'ev's view of abilities and skills, namely, that any one skill can be based on a number of different combinations of abilities, and that different types can none the less be taught the same subject to the same level of skill. Work on child development follows the pattern of Vigotsky's early opinions on the one hand and Zaporozhets's examination of voluntary motor control on the other. The extension of Pavlov's and Ivanov Smolenski's studies by Teplov and Nebilitsyn also in some respect continue the same theoretical standpoint, namely, the analysis of types of nervous system in human subjects, as judged by the effect of drugs on visual and other receptors. In addition, a further continuation may be assumed for the Georgian School of Prangishvili and Natadze.

It might be inferred, therefore, that the categorization of Russian psychology into three theoretical groupings is still the basic position. However, there are indications that at least one other trend exists. This is the trend towards the use of cybernetic and statistical models in Russian physiological and industrial psychology. This trend was recently noted by Zangwill (1964). For the last few years, problems of industrial control have led to a number of attempts by psychologists to master complex communication and management problems. Examples found in Russian journals include the control of entry of trains to a terminal and the location of a fault in a generating station.

Schools versus Techniques

This kind of study, whilst common in post-war psychology in the West, took a few years more before interesting Soviet psychologists. However, there is not so much difference between the two groups by now, except in sheer quantity of work done. There has thus been a considerable *rapprochement*, with the initiative by no means confined to one side. Perhaps the biggest arbitrator in this co-mingling of interests has been the growing attention to technique in both Eastern and Western psychology. Every research worker eventually develops skills and these skills can be more or less sophisticated. It is the degree of sophistication of the techniques of a science which eventually determine its acceptability. Ingenuity of experimentation and a useful integrating insight can and do earn respect, but more and more as the science develops, techniques determine the acceptability of findings and often in themselves make findings possible. This fact is beginning to imbue Soviet work and some of the original insights promoted by national needs or philosophical opinions are undergoing modification. The same is, of course, true of Western psychology. The interchange of such techniques inevitably unifies science, because the techniques generally run ahead of political opinions and fall outside the classical boundaries of theories of government.

This is not to say that philosophical views can no longer aid the development of science but to suggest that as a science develops, it gains its own internal disciplines, which arise from its special subject-matter. As the facts are often similar from country to country, this makes for unity of opinion in the science concerned. Naturally, this is less so in a social than in a physical or biological science and it is notable that in the applied field of education, Soviet and Western psychologists still differ. In general, however, they are approximating more and more.

In one respect, there remains a fundamental cleavage characteristic of philosophical differences. In the U.S.A., Skinner's approach to conditioning rests on premises which make consciousness unnecessary. For Soviet psychology, however, the concept of consciousness is basic, and efforts to eliminate it through such early Watsonian-type theories as Bekhterev's "collective reflexology" have always been rejected. Higher nervous function is a concept developed in the U.S.S.R. and used continually as a phrase in psychological discussions. It might mean, for example, the study of complex behaviour, but generally it does so only in relation to speech. The complexities of emotional or social behaviour are rarely discussed in Russian texts. In a country which still sets store on the effect of history on the psychology of the individual, the lack of a developed social psychology is an interesting social phenomenon. One can only conjecture that an earlier start was not made because the new form of socialist society was thought to be an experiment in itself. Some of the by-products of this larger experiment have shown the need for a more detailed analysis of the forces at work and this is now beginning, although there is much leeway to be made up. Perhaps the lack of a social science is only a temporary phenomenon, but the dispute over consciousness is likely to prove a more lasting difference between the two hemispheres. Pavlov always rejected Watsonian views and Skinner's views will need to become much more technical before philosophical disputes become irrelevant.

Summary

In summary, then, there are still three trends in Soviet psychology: (1) Pavlovian studies of conditioning and central nervous type; (2) studies of verbal behaviour based on Vigotsky's original findings; and (3) Georgian "set" theory based on Uznadze's work. However, a fourth interest has developed and become established, i.e. the application of statistical and cybernetic techniques to problems in fields where decision theory is applicable. There is still an emphasis on consciousness and higher nervous activity, compared with Western schools, but in most other directions, the psychologies of the U.S.S.R. and the U.S.A. are growing closer and closer together. In my opinion, this is in part due to the fact that increasing technical knowledge in psychology is beginning to lift it out of the arena of political speculation and pressure. As a result, one no longer meets pure Marxist psychologists and pure capitalist psychologists, but individuals whose technical problems and skills are similar. This is an inevitably healthy line of development in all pure science—whatever may be said of its applications. Whether we will be able to say the same of Soviet Social Psychology, based as it must be on a different social structure, will depend on two things. These are the development of a science of sociology and social psychology in the U.S.S.R. on the one hand, and on the other, the degree to which Socialist society diverges from our own in expressing its economically and morally different aims.

References

ANREP, G. V. (1927) *Conditioned Reflexes*. London: Oxford Univ. Press.

BROŽEK, J. (1962) Current status of psychology in the U.S.S.R. *Ann. Rev. Psychol.* **13**, 515–66.

GANTT, HORSLEY, W. (1928) (Trans. and Ed.) *I. P. Pavlov: Lectures on Conditioned Reflexes*. London: Lawrence & Wishart.

GANTT, HORSLEY, W. (1944) *Experimental Basis for Neurotic Behaviour*. New York: Hoeber Inc.

GRAY, J. (1964) *Pavlov's Typology*. Oxford: Pergamon Press.

LURIA, A. R. (1961) *The Role of Speech in the Regulation of Normal and Abnormal Behaviour*, J. Tizard (Ed.). Oxford: Pergamon Press.

LURIA, A. R. (1963) *Restoration of Function after Brain Injury*. O. L. Zangwill (Ed.). Pergamon Press and MacMillan, New York.

MINTZ, A. (1958) Recent developments in the U.S.S.R. *Ann. Rev. Psychol.* **9**, 453–504.

O'CONNOR, N. (1961) *Recent Soviet Psychology*. Oxford: Pergamon Press.

RAZRAN, G. (1965) Russian physiologist's psychology and American experimental psychology: A historical and a systematic collation and look into the future. *Psychol. Bull.* **63**, 42–64.

SIMON, B. (1957) *Psychology in the Soviet Union*. London: Routledge and Kegan Paul.

SIMON, B. and SIMON, J. (1963) *Educational Psychology in the U.S.S.R.* London: Routledge and Kegan Paul.

VYGOTSKY, L. S. (1962) *Thought and Language*, E. Hanfmann and G. Vakar (Trans. and Eds.). New York: M.I.T. and John Wiley.

ZANGWILL, O. L. (1965) *Psychology* (1) *Current Approaches in "The State of Soviet Science"*. Massachusetts: M.I.T. Press.

Contributors

J. A. GRAY, Ph.D., Lecturer in Psychology, University of Oxford, and Fellow of University College, Oxford.

B. H. KIRMAN, M.D., D.P.M., Consultant Psychiatrist, Fountain and Carshalton Hospital Group.

P. M. A. RABBITT, Ph.D., Research Worker, Medical Research Council, Applied Psychology Unit, Cambridge.

R. LYNN, Ph.D., Lecturer in Psychology, University of Exeter.

D. I. SLOBIN, M.A., Ph.D., Assistant Professor of Psychology, University of California, Berkeley.

L. RAHMANI, Ph.D., Clinical Psychologist, Kfar Shaul Village, Government Mental Hospital, Jerusalem.

JOSEF BROŽEK, Ph.D., Professor of Psychology, Lehigh University, Pa.

CHAPTER 1

Attention, Consciousness and Voluntary Control of Behaviour in Soviet Psychology: Philosophical Roots and Research Branches

JEFFREY A. GRAY

Institute of Experimental Psychology, University of Oxford

SOVIET psychology is not well known in the West. To some extent this is undoubtedly due to the language barrier. However, there are other barriers which, though less obvious, are at least as important as the linguistic one. It is not an uncommon experience for someone to read an English translation of the work of an eminent Soviet psychologist and feel almost as baffled as if he were reading an unknown tongue. And this is only marginally due to the admittedly poor quality of many translations. The real difficulty is the unfamiliarity of the whole Soviet approach to problems in psychology; for this approach has grown out of a very different intellectual tradition from the Anglo-Saxon one. I want here to outline some of the most important features of this tradition and to show how it has led to certain valuable programmes of research. I hope this will serve the double purpose of making the pattern of Soviet psychology more generally intelligible to the Western reader and of making us aware, by contrast, of some features of our own intellectual tradition which, without our realizing it, have shaped the development of our research endeavours and explanatory systems in psychology.

To sum up those features of Soviet psychology which distinguish it most from its Anglo-Saxon counterpart, the former emphasizes

1

the *active* part played by the subject (and especially the conscious human subject) in *structuring* his own environment and his own experience, in contrast to the traditional (though perhaps weakening) Anglo-Saxon insistence on a *passive* organism, in which associations are formed by the interplay of processes (such as temporal contiguity, and the occurrence of rewards and punishments) assuring successful *adaptation to* the environment. The reader with an interest in philosophy may have noticed in this formulation a parallel to the classical philosophical controversies between the British empiricist school (e.g. Locke, Hume, J. S. Mill), for whom the mind was a *tabula rasa* awaiting the impressions of repeated experience, and those continental philosophers, such as Leibnitz, Kant and Schopenhauer, who believed that our experience is shaped in important ways by the structure and activities of the mind. This parallel is certainly not an accidental one—both Soviet philosophy and Soviet psychology have European roots rather than Anglo-Saxon ones; and it is, I believe, the persistence of long-standing philosophical differences on the two sides of the English Channel which, more than anything else, accounts for the difficulties which the English or American reader encounters when he reads Soviet psychology.

Dialectical Materialism, Behaviourism and Consciousness

The philosophical differences between the Soviet and Anglo-Saxon attitudes to psychological research and explanation have, however, been sharpened by the adoption of Marxist-Leninism as the official philosophy of the Soviet Union. This philosophy, while growing out of the general continental tradition which culminated in the Hegelian dialectic and thus already opposed in important ways to the British tradition, has added new points of difference. Moreover, the official status of Marxist-Leninism has had the result that philosophy intrudes in scientific research and writing in a way which is totally unexpected for a Western scientist. It is a shock to discover in a text ostensibly concerned with the empirical investigation of psychology that there are frequent references to Marx, Engels, Lenin and even—not so long ago—Stalin. One's first reaction is to dismiss this as a necessary obeisance in the direction of the political powers-that-be—as no doubt, in part, it is; and, in any case, one feels that philosophy has no place in the conduct of scientific research. However, a more sympathetic consideration of the use to which these philosophers are put reveals that there is something of more importance, and perhaps even of real value, going on. In the first place, the Russian habit of making the philosophical background plain for all to see is not such a bad one; above all, it becomes clear that, with different philosophical assumptions, there would be different research and different favoured forms of explanation—and this connection is not to be broken simply by keeping the philosophical assumptions out of sight (and out of mind) as the Anglo-Saxon psychologist tries to do. Secondly, there is a good case to be made for the particular assumptions of Marxist philosophy as a reasonable starting point for a scientific psychology—provided, of course, that we are ready to abandon them if our data suggest that other assumptions would make a better starting point. In particular, it can be argued that Marxist assumptions are more consistent with the results of recent psychological and neurophysiological research than are the assumptions contained in the extreme associationist-behaviourist point of view identified with the names of J. B. Watson and C. L. Hull; and that the recent retreat from this extreme position in Anglo-American psychology has made it possible to attempt a *rapprochement* between the views of human nature held in the East and the West. Those assumptions of Marxism which are most pertinent to this thesis are concerned with the role of consciousness in the organization and control of behaviour.

As a materialistic monism, Marxism has as its chief philosophical assumption that there is only one "stuff" in the world, described as "matter in motion" and studied by the physical sciences. Consciousness, however (to which the essentially dualist philosophy of much Western thought would ascribe a non-material status) is not simply denied. On the contrary, it is allotted an extremely important role, both as part of the subject-matter to be studied by psychology and in the control of the behaviour of the individual organism. From the point of view of Marxist philosophy, consciousness is described as a "property of highly organized matter"—in particular, of that system of highly organized matter which we call the human brain (but also of animal brains, although important distinctions are drawn between the two cases). To account (philosophically, not scientifically) for the emergence of this property, the Marxist invokes the "law of transition from quantity to quality", which claims that new qualities emerging in nature are to be understood as the result of a gradual accumulation of small quantitative changes. Thus, if the temperature of water is gradually lowered (a quantitative change), it eventually reaches a point at which it suddenly changes into ice, which has many qualities different from those of water. In rather the same way, it is thought that the gradual accumulation of quantitative changes in the complexity with which organic matter is organized eventually leads to a situation in which the new property of consciousness emerges.

Whether or not this account of the relations between an organism and conscious sensation is found philosophically satisfying, it has the advantage of including consciousness within the realm of phenomena which may be studied scientifically and *excluding* that kind of philosophical mind–body interactionism to which many Western scientists still probably subscribe. Such interactionism, to take an extreme example, can lead to the suggestion, endorsed by Eccles in *The Neurophysiological Basis of Mind*, that "mind could control the behaviour of matter within the limits imposed by Heisenberg's Principle of Uncertainty" (p. 278). It is absurdities of this kind which lead the Marxist to condemn the behaviourist position as "vulgar materialism" (a term of considerable abuse in the Soviet vocabulary) and to lump it together with *idealism*. This juxtaposition can be quite startling the first time a behaviourist meets it. It takes some time to realize that a genuine and (as it seems to me) valid criticism of behaviourism is intended. The point is that, if we concern ourselves with behaviour only and regard the phenomena of conscious experience as beyond the pale of scientific

discourse, then the way is open for the idealist (i.e. the philo-
sopher who is prepared to allow the existence of non-physical
entities in the world) to claim these phenomena for his own—as
Eccles does in the passage cited. For one who is committed to the
attempt to include all observable phenomena within the framework of a single network of scientific laws this is an unsatisfactory
situation. Thus, the Marxist position that consciousness is to be
treated as a datum and explained in terms of physical laws has
much to recommend it. And, indeed, Western scientists, as they
come closer to the problems posed by the fact of consciousness,
are increasingly adopting a similar position.

It should, however, be added that the acceptance of consciousness as a datum by Soviet psychologists is not due only to their
Marxist ideology. In part, I believe, it is also due to the fact that
Russian psychology never underwent a behaviourist revolution.
The reason for this, in turn, is not far to seek—there was no need
for one. Forty-seven years before Watson raised the behaviourist
standard in his 1913 paper, "Psychology as the Behaviourist views
it", we find the Russian physiologist, I. Sechenov, writing in his
book, *Reflexes of the Brain*: "All the endless diversity of the
external manifestations of the activity of the brain can be finally
regarded as one phenomenon—that of muscular movement." And
this was no isolated statement; it formed part of a complete
behaviourist programme in which emotions were to be treated as
heightened reflex activity and thought as inhibited reflexes. Thus
the luxuriant growth of introspective psychology with which
Watson was contending had never taken root on Russian soil, and
the way was clear for Pavlov to follow where Sechenov had led. It
might be expected, then, that Watson's revolution, when it came,
would merely bring American psychology into line with its Russian
counterpart. But, as is the way with revolutions, Watson's went
too far, and, in abandoning introspection as a method, it also abandoned consciousness as both datum and problem. In Russia, on the
other hand, the physiological materialism espoused by Sechenov
and later by Pavlov was never driven into the situation of pre-
tending that the scientific problem of consciousness does not exist.

Another way in which the tradition started by Sechenov lives on in present-day Soviet psychophysiology is in the insistence, taken over from the French nineteenth-century school of physiology associated with the name of Claude Bernard, that the job of physiology is to describe and explain the functional unity of the intact organism, not merely to analyse the physico-chemical activity of each of its separate organs. Pavlov's pioneering work in analysing the conditioned reflex mechanisms by which the intact organism is able to adapt its behaviour to a changing environment is clearly in this tradition. And, I believe, the readiness of Soviet physiologists and psychologists to call in central mechanisms to account for perceptual data, when the Anglo-Saxon worker would sooner seek for an explanation in the structure and functioning of the peripheral receptors, is another example of the same tendency. It is pertinent here to note that recent neurophysiological evidence suggests that we have probably overstressed the importance of peripheral factors in perception in the West; we may soon see, therefore, a growth of interest in the vast store of theory and data emphasizing the role of central perceptual mechanisms accumulated by Soviet workers (see, for example, London, 1954).

It is time to return to the Marxist view of consciousness. In doing so, we should note that the marriage which took place after the October Revolution between Marxist materialism and the physiological materialism initiated by Sechenov, though forced, was by no means ill-matched. Emphasis on the primacy of the physiological basis of behaviour and subjective experience, together with an acceptance of consciousness as datum, accord well with the Marxist metaphysics of consciousness as we have seen it so far; and the insistence on the role of central mechanisms which ensure the functional unity of the intact organism fits neatly with a further aspect of the Marxist theory of consciousness which we have not yet brought out in sufficient detail—namely, that consciousness is regarded not as a purely passive awareness of environmental stimuli, as so often in the Anglo-American tradition of both philosophy and psychology, but as a highly active process which

plays an important role in the organization and control of behaviour. Thus it has been suggested by a leading Soviet psychologist,
A. N. Leontiev (1959), that the functional value of consciousness
which has led to its evolutionary development in the animal kingdom is that it enables the organism to respond not merely to
stimulation which is of vital significance to survival in its own
right, but also to stimuli which may perhaps signal the imminent
occurrence of *other* vitally important stimuli. With further increase
in the complexity of animal organisms during phylogenesis, and
especially with the development at the human level of social interaction and the "second signal system" (i.e. language, regarded in
Pavlovian theory as a system of signals of signals), there is a
corresponding increase in the scope and importance of consciousness, so that its functional value in Man is to free him "from the
constraint of the immediate situation, and to permit him to direct
his actions towards goals and tasks beyond that situation" (Bauer,
1952, p. 132). Furthermore, "it is through the development of
consciousness and through the acquisition of needs and interests
that lie beyond the immediate situation that behaviour becomes
voluntary" (Bauer, *loc. cit.*).

It should not be thought, however, that this doctrine of the
active role of consciousness in any way nullifies the general determinist approach of both Marxist philosophy and Soviet psychology. For the conscious goals that play such an important part in
the direction of voluntary actions are themselves held to be determined by the individual's previous experience acting in accordance
with biological and sociological laws of behaviour. The apparent
difficulty of both allowing an active role to consciousness and pre-
serving a determinist approach to the study of behaviour arises
only if one considers consciousness to be in some way outside the
physical world, and, as we have seen, for the Marxist this cannot
be the case. Thus there is no more difficulty in accepting the fact
that consciousness can alter behaviour than in accepting, for
example, the fact that activity in the reticular formation of the
brain stem (known to be crucial for consciousness) also alters
behaviour; in both cases, we may presume that the phenomena in

question form part of a causal chain, determined by preceding members of the chain and contributing to the determination of succeeding members of the chain. Moreover, as we have already seen, there is no intention to imply that consciousness is the privilege of Man alone; Anokhin (1961), for example, has extended the Pavlovian conditioned reflex schema to include an internal representation of the "intention" which he believes to precede the performance of an act by a dog in a standard conditioning situation. However, it *is* held that in Man the extent to which stimuli transcending the immediate environment are able to direct characteristically voluntary behaviour is so immensely increased by the development of society and language that a qualitative difference between animal and human consciousness has emerged; and this difference is usually marked by the use of two different words— *psikhika* (mind or psyche) for animal consciousness and *soznaniye* (cognition or consciousness) for human consciousness.

There is a second gloss which may be put on the distinction between the Anglo-American treatment of consciousness as *passive* and the Soviet treatment of it as *active*, and this is that, for the Soviet psychologist, consciousness is shaped by the results of action on the world rather than by the passive receipt of stimulation. This view, which is a fundamental tenet of Marxist philosophy, has some rather far-reaching consequences. It is clear that at different times in the history of mankind and in different societies at any one time both the environment in which the child develops and the possibilities for action on that environment will be radically different. To fully appreciate the scope of this comment it must be understood that, as Vygotsky (1962) has stressed, the most important part of the environment for the development of the individual human being is the specifically human *social* environment, including all the tools fashioned by previous generations for operating on the non-social environment. Moreover, these tools include the extremely important linguistic and conceptual tools contained in the particular language learned by the growing child. This class of tools is important not only for the increased flexibility with which a linguistic animal is able to react to its environment, but also for the ability it affords to *direct one's own behaviour*—an aspect of language emphasized by Pavlov and more recently studied in some detail, as we shall see, by Luria. These reflections lead the Russian psychologist to the conclusion that, if consciousness acquires its particular properties as a result of action on the environment, then the nature of consciousness must be very different in different epochs and in societies of different levels of economic and cultural development. Carried to the extreme, this view can become a little startling, as when Leontiev (1959) discusses at great length the particular characteristics of consciousness developed in "Soviet Man" by fifty years of socialism However, used more discretely, it achieves a certain plausibility. If it is the case, as the Russians believe, that the function of consciousness is to enable the organism to take action appropriate to goals not present in the environment at the time of action, then it is clear that this function must have undergone considerable widening in scope since the first attempt at social groupings and linguistic communication was made by primitive Man.

Social and Historical Roots of Behaviour

So far, we have considered the Marxist influence on Soviet psychology almost exclusively as it concerns the concept of consciousness. There are other important ways, however, in which this influence makes itself apparent. As is well known, Marxism is intensely concerned with the social determinants of behaviour; and the foregoing discussion of the differences which different societies are expected to produce in the nature of human consciousness is a good example of this concern. Indeed, Soviet accounts of the development of human behaviour (e.g. Vygotsky, 1962; Leontiev, 1959) lay such stress on the role of the social environment that psychology becomes virtually coextensive with what in the West we call "social psychology". Perhaps in consequence of this tendency to see social factors everywhere (but also, perhaps, in consequence of possible political complications), the type of investigation which is specifically regarded in the West as social psychology (e.g. the investigation of interactions between members of groups, or the conduct of social surveys) is almost totally neglected in the Soviet Union.

Finally, we cannot leave this discussion of the Marxist influence on Soviet psychology without mentioning that Marxism, above all else, emphasizes the *historical* approach in the sciences. In the case of psychology, the historical approach becomes the study of the phylogenetic evolution of behaviour, on the one hand, and, on the other, the study of behaviour as it develops during onto-genesis. And it can be no accident that (if we exclude the etho-logical literature, which is largely concerned with innate, as distinct from learned, behaviour) both these branches of psychology are very much more advanced in the Soviet Union than they are in England and America. According to Razran (1965): "Russian laboratories have to date yielded a vast amount of experimental data—approximately five hundred experiments—on comparative conditioning in phylogeny and ontogeny, with special emphasis on compound-stimulus conditioning in animals and language ac-quisition or verbal conditioning in young children." In contrast, there are hardly any such experiments in the English language literature; although the work of Bitterman (1965) on phylogenetic comparisons of instrumental learning speed and that of the Kendlers (Kendler and Kendler, 1962) on changes in discrimina-tion learning during the development of the child suggest that a new interest in both these fields is now developing. It should be noted, furthermore, that the greater interest of Soviet psychology in the evolution of behaviour goes hand in hand, as is natural, with a greater tendency to consider the functional value of behaviour; for, in general, it is presumably true to say that only behaviour which confers some additional chance of survival can be inherited and so developed during phylogenesis. We have already had occasion to refer to a good example of this approach, namely Leontiev's (1959) hypothesis that consciousness has developed be-cause of the ability it confers on animals to respond to stimuli which, while not themselves of vital significance for survival, may act as signals of other stimuli which *are* vital. In sum, then, the

Soviet Union is well on the way to creating a genuine comparative psychology; whereas what goes by this name in the West has often been no more than the testing of hypotheses concerning Man by observations made on rats.

The Orienting Reflex and Conditioning

Having completed this brief survey of some of the more important intellectual roots of contemporary Soviet psychology, we may now consider some of the research which has grown from them.

Some of the most important work done in the Soviet Union over the last decade has been concerned with what Pavlov called the orienting reflex—i.e. the responses called forth by presentation of a novel stimulus. This programme of research illustrates virtually all the features of Soviet psychology which we have discussed. It is in sharp contrast to the behaviourist school associated with the name of Hull, for which the acquisition of new behaviour depends only on the correct relations of temporal contiguity and reinforcement holding between stimulus and response. Instead, Russian research on orienting reflexes emphasizes the extremely important role played by active, selective attention in enabling the organism to adapt its behaviour to the demands of a changing environment. It is interesting to note that, while a number of Western workers in the field of learning theory (e.g. Goodwin and Lawrence, 1955; Sutherland, 1959; Broadbent, 1958) have also realized the necessity of supplementing the Hullian account of learning with some provision for the selection of stimulus input by the organism, the method of going about supplying this lack has been very different from the one favoured by the Russian workers on the orienting reflex. Whereas the Western workers have constructed "black-box" models (e.g. Broadbent's "filter theory" or Sutherland's "stimulus analysing mechanisms") which, it is hoped, will predict the observed forms of behaviour, the Russians, starting from a much more physiological point of view, have set out to objectify the process of attention by direct physiological measurement. I am not suggesting that, in principle, either of these methods of approach is to be preferred to the other. On the contrary, I believe that an alliance between the two methods may lead to far greater dividends than either could produce in isolation. In particular, it is possible that, by measurement of some of the responses which the Russians have described under the name "orienting reflexes", some of the Western models of selective attention could be investigated in a more direct manner than hitherto.

Let us, then, examine the results achieved by the Russians in their investigation of the orienting reflex. The following account of these results is based on a number of chief sources, many of which are now available in English (Sokolov, 1960, 1963; Razran, 1961; Lynn, 1966), although others can only be obtained in Russian (Vinogradova, 1961; Voronin *et al.*, 1958; Sokolov, 1959).

The term "orienting reflex" (OR) embraces a number of separate responses, which we may call "component responses of the OR". Operationally, a component response of the OR may be defined as any response which is elicited by the first presentations of a novel stimulus and which, with repeated presentation of the stimulus, ceases to be elicited by it (a process described as "habituation"). It has further been found that all orienting responses, once habituated, will recur (i.e. "dehabituation" will take place) if the stimulus is changed in any way, whether qualitatively or quantitatively. Dehabituation also occurs if an "extra-stimulus" is presented to the subject—i.e. the introduction of a second novel stimulus into the experimental situation results in the reappearance of orienting responses to a previously habituated stimulus. Furthermore, a process similar to the spontaneous recovery manifested by an extinguished *conditioned* reflex also occurs in the case of the habituated OR—i.e. if a period of time is allowed to elapse which is long compared to the intervals between stimulus presentations during the process of habituation, then the orienting responses recur when the stimulus is presented after this lapse of time. One further defining characteristic of orienting responses should be noted: in general, they are not specific to the modality of the stimulus (although the relative rapidity with which the various component responses of the OR are habituated does depend to some extent on modality). Taken together, these regularities may be assumed to define the orienting reflex; and it may usually be assumed that if a response is described as "orienting" in the Russian literature, then it has been shown to behave in these ways.

What, then, are the component responses of the OR which have been isolated to date? Historically, attention was first drawn to the OR in Pavlov's conditioning experiments. It was found that the performance of a conditioned reflex (CR) was disrupted by any unusual stimulus occurring during the course of the experiment (a process described by Pavlov as "external inhibition"). This disruption of conditioning was accompanied by motor behaviour on the part of the dog which seemed to indicate that it was "paying attention" to the novel stimulus—i.e. turning of head and eyes towards the source of stimulation, pricking up of ears, adoption of an unmoving posture, etc. Thus, these motor responses were the first to be christened "orienting reflexes". (Though one should notice that the process of external inhibition itself may also be regarded as a component of the OR, since it shows exactly the same regularities as the other component responses.) In more recent years attention has been turned towards some of the less obvious components of the OR. These responses include somatic, vegetative, and electrographic changes, as well as, most importantly, alterations in the sensitivity of the sensory systems. Using the operational criteria already outlined, the following components of the OR have been identified:

(1) Motor components: turning of head and eyes towards the source of stimulation; pricking up of ears; sniffing; interruption of ongoing activity; general increase in muscle tension as measured by the electromyogram.

(2) Autonomic components: a fall in the electrical resistance of the skin on the palms of the hands and soles of the feet (known as the psychogalvanic response or galvanic skin response—PGR or GSR); vascular changes consisting of vasodilation in the head and vasoconstriction in the peripheral limbs; changes in respiratory rate and heart rate, both of which are rather variable, sometimes taking the form of an increase in rate, sometimes that of a decrease.

(3) Sensory changes: pupil dilation; a fall in the absolute visual and auditory thresholds; an increase in the ability of both the retina and the cerebral cortex to "follow" (i.e. respond discretely to each member of) a train of visual stimuli closely spaced in time.

(4) Changes in the electroencephalogram (EEG): desynchronization and acceleration of the resting rhythms (alpha-rhythm, rolandic rhythm) of the EEG if these are present; reappearance of the alpha-rhythm if there are slow waves present in the EEG.

(5) Changes in the performance of conditioned reflexes: the phenomenon of external inhibition has already been described; in addition, it seems likely that the phenomenon of "disinhibition", in which a novel stimulus causes the reappearance of a conditioned reflex which is undergoing extinction, may also be closely connected with the OR.

The function of the responses which make up the OR appears to be, in the main, that of improving the perceptual capacities of the organism and its ability to process incoming information. This is fairly obvious in the case of the motor orienting responses listed under (1) above and the sensory changes listed under (3). Inhibition of ongoing motor activity and of conditioned reflexes seems likely to have the same effect, in that the organism in this way can concentrate on analysis of the novel stimulus. It is possible that the vascular changes also subserve the same function, inasmuch as a redistribution of the blood supply from the body to the head should enable the central nervous system to maintain the higher levels of activity that would presumably be required for the complex analysis of incoming stimuli. There is some evidence suggesting that the EEG changes may also represent an increased perceptual capacity: Fuster (1958) has shown that stimulation of the reticular formation of the brain stem via implanted electrodes (a procedure known to desynchronize the resting EEG rhythms) produces more accurate visual choice responses in the monkey; and Lansing *et al.* (1959) have demonstrated a close correlation in human subjects between the amount of desynchronization ("alpha-blocking") induced by a warning stimulus and the speed of response to a subsequent stimulus. Some of the other component responses of the OR are less easily interpreted in this way. The change in the electrical resistance of the skin (GSR) remains enigmatic in spite of the great use to which it has been put in psychological experiments in both East and West. Darrow (1936) and Sokolov (1963, p. 56) have suggested that it is accompanied by a rise in cutaneous sensitivity, but there is little evidence to support this hypothesis. Some of the changes in respiration—particularly the initial arrest of respiration which is sometimes reported, especially if it is preceded by a sharp inspiration—may conceivably increase olfactory sensitivity. However, it seems likely that some of the orienting responses serve a different function—that of increasing the organism's readiness for rapid and energetic action, should this be necessary. This is most obviously seen in the case of the generalized increase in muscle tension, but may also apply to those respiratory and cardiac changes which take the form of an increase in rate of activity. It is also possible that the GSR falls into this category, for Darrow (1936) has suggested that the function of the increased perspiration which accompanies this response is to improve grip—obviously important for both fight and flight in an ungloved and unshod organism.

The reader may have noticed among the list of component responses of the OR a number of responses which have been extensively studied in the West, but usually in isolation from one another; the GSR and the alpha-blocking response, for example, would fall in this category. That the Russians have demonstrated that these responses all show the same regularities and probably all serve similar purposes in the organization of behaviour is, I think, an excellent—and highly profitable—example of their tendency to seek for functional unities in behaviour. The importance of their success in isolating the OR as a functional unit of this kind becomes clearer when we look at the work they have done on the role of the OR in conditioning.

As we have seen, the first interactions between the OR and conditioned reflexes to be observed in Pavlov's laboratories were of an antagonistic kind—the elicitation of an OR during the performance of a CR was found to inhibit the latter. More recently, however, it has been shown that the OR plays a very important positive role in the elaboration of a CR, as well as in the adaptation of the CR to various changes in the sequence of stimuli to which the subject is exposed. In the first place, it has been found that it is much harder to form a conditioned reflex if the stimulus which is to be turned into a conditioned stimulus (CS) is first presented alone repeatedly until the orienting reflex to it is thoroughly habituated. On the other hand, a completely novel stimulus is also not the most suitable for use as a CS. In fact, the optimal stimulus to use as a CS turns out to be one which has been presented alone for a sufficient number of times at the beginning of the experiment for the initial orienting responses to have diminished in intensity without, however, having disappeared completely. Moreover, if a stimulus to which the OR has previously been habituated *is* used as a CS, it is reported that successful conditioning only takes place after the would-be CS has once more begun to elicit orienting responses. Secondly, it has been shown that there is a recurrence of ORs at every point in a conditioning experiment at which the relations between the stimuli to which the subject is exposed are changed. Thus the OR is elicited when the CS is first presented in conjunction with the unconditioned stimulus (UCS) and continues to be elicited during the initial stages of the series of joint presentations of CS and UCS. Gradually, the OR declines in magnitude and eventually disappears. It is to be noted that during this stage of habituation of the OR (and similarly during habituation of the OR in later stages of a conditioning experiment, there is a reciprocal relation between the OR and the CR: as the latency of the CR decreases and its stability increases (i.e. as performance of the CR becomes more highly predictable or automatic), so the intensity of the OR decreases. Thus, while it appears to be essential for successful conditioning that ORs should occur, during their actual elicitation they interfere with the smooth performance of the CR. When the habituation of the orienting reflex is complete and the conditioned reflex is being performed almost automatically, any change in the experimental situation serves to re-elicit the OR and to increase the latency and diminish the magnitude of the CR. With repetition of the changed conditions of stimulation, the process of habituation of the orienting reflex together with stabilization of the conditioned reflex takes place once more. Thus it appears that a conditioning experiment cannot be regarded as simply a passive business in which the experimenter causes "associations" to be formed or destroyed in the experimental subject. At each change in the conditions of stimulation an active process of attention is evoked in the subject, whose function appears to be that of maximizing the organism's capacity to process the information contained in the new environmental circumstances while delaying action until it is clear what the most appropriate action is.

There is one feature of the interaction between the OR and conditioned reflexes which is worth noticing as it is rather unexpected. We saw earlier that the effect of a novel stimulus upon an established CR is to inhibit it ("external inhibition"). This seems functionally a very sensible arrangement—it may clearly conduce to the survival of an animal in its natural environment that it should stop what it is doing to concentrate its attention upon a novel stimulus, one which may, for example, signal the approach of a predator. What is rather less obviously a useful arrangement is the phenomenon of "disinhibition", in which a CR which has recently been subjected to a process of inhibition (whether by the procedure of experimental extinction, the establishment of conditioned inhibition, or of inhibition of delay) proves to be re-elicited if the CS is presented shortly after the subject has been exposed to a novel stimulus. It is as though the nervous system has built into it an arrangement which, upon warning of possible danger, causes the organism to revert to whatever it was doing *last*—i.e. to cease responding if responding was the most recent thing learnt in the particular environment, but to *resume* responding if the most recent thing learnt was to *cease* responding. However, it seems from some of Pavlov's writings that the phenomenon of disinhibition occurs mainly in a state of drowsiness; and, in this state, a number of other odd phenomena relating to both orienting reflexes and conditioned reflexes have been described in Russian laboratories, as we shall now see.

The relation between habituation of the orienting reflex and the onset of sleep is still unclear. It has often been claimed that repetitive presentation of a stimulus until and after habituation of the OR has taken place hastens the onset of sleep; but, to the writer's knowledge, the demonstrations (e.g. Gastaut and Bert, 1961) that sleep sets in very quickly when subjects are repeatedly exposed to a stimulus which has neither vital nor signal value for them have never been accompanied by the crucial control experiments in which subjects would be left in an unvarying environment *without* repetitive stimulation. Whether or not repetitive stimulation actually hastens sleep, it is clear that sleep does occur under these conditions. Now Sokolov and his colleagues (Sokolov, 1963) have recently shown that, when a stimulus is repeatedly presented to human subjects well after habituation of the OR has taken place, there is a sudden reappearance of orienting responses at a time when the subject shows behavioural and EEG signs of drowsiness. In these experiments, the response components of the OR observed were the GSR, alpha blocking, and vascular responses; but earlier demonstrations of the same phenomenon had been made in Pavlov's laboratories using motor orienting responses in the dog (experiments of Rozhanskii and Babkin, reviewed by Vinogradova, 1961). Sokolov has called this paradoxical phenomenon "overextinction" of the orienting reflex, and, as we shall see, he has sought in it support for his theory of the neurophysiological mechanism mediating both execution and habituation of the orienting reflex. It is tempting to suppose that "overextinction" of the OR is connected with the phenomenon of disinhibition which we met in the last paragraph, and also with the strange phenomena described by Pavlov as the "hypnotic" phases of conditioning. As the name implies, these phases in the performance of a CR also occur during drowsiness; they take the form either that the response to a weak conditioned stimulus (usually relatively small) is greater than the response to a strong stimulus (usually large)—this is known as the "paradoxical phase"; or that a normally inhibitory stimulus *elicits* a response while a normally positive stimulus *fails* to do so—the "ultra-paradoxical phase". The fact that these various odd phenomena—disinhibition, over-extinction of the OR, and the paradoxical and ultra-paradoxical phases of conditioning—all occur during drowsiness illustrates once more the intimate connection between mechanisms of conditioning and mechanisms of attention.

One more aspect of the interrelations between ORs and CRs which should be mentioned concerns the possibility of forming a *conditioned* OR. By this is meant that, if one stimulus is regularly followed by another, neither stimulus being of biological importance to the experimental organism, then the first stimulus comes to elicit orienting responses which are appropriate to the second. For example, it has been reported that, when children were exposed to a sound regularly followed by a light, they soon began to turn their head and eyes towards the light-source upon presentation of the sound (experiments of Kasatkin *et al.* and of Mirzoyants, described by Sokolov, 1963, p. 151). With repeated presentation of the combination of sound and light, the latency of the conditioned OR shortened and the reflex became more stable— exactly as occurs with normal CRs. However, with still further repetition of the combination of stimuli the conditioned OR disappeared. In this respect, of course, the conditioned OR differs from normal CRs, which do not usually undergo extinction with repetition (although this does occur under some circumstances). However, the reason for this difference is obvious: the "reinforcing" value of the stimulus presented second in conditioned OR experiments (i.e. its ability to maintain performance of the conditioned response) depends on its *novelty*; thus, with repeated presentation, it must lose this reinforcing value, with the consequent extinction of the conditioned OR which is in fact observed. Similar observations have been made with slightly different techniques and using animals as well as human subjects.

The Physiology of the Orienting Reflex

It would not be possible to leave this discussion of Soviet work on the orienting reflex without mentioning Sokolov's important hypothesis concerning the neurophysiological mechanisms which control this reflex. This hypothesis depends to a large extent on data relating to the habituation of the OR. The crucial fact which emerges from these data is the extreme specificity of the habituation process. By this is meant the fact that, if the ORs to a particular stimulus are habituated by repeated presentation of this stimulus, then almost any change in the stimulus, or in the environmental background to the stimulus, is sufficient to reinstate the habituated responses. To be sure, some degree of generalization of habituation to neighbouring stimuli on both quantitative and qualitative continua is observed—i.e. if the ORs are first habituated to a stimulus, S_1, and another stimulus, S_2, is then presented, there is a failure to observe orienting responses to S_2 if it is very similar to S_1; and, as the similarity of S_2 to S_1 decreases, so the intensity of the ORs elicited by S_2 increases. However, the extent of the generalization of habituation observed is very much less than the generalization reported for conditioned responses. Furthermore, it is not simply change in the quality of the stimulus (e.g. a change in pitch of an auditory stimulus or in the colour of a visual stimulus) which causes a reappearance of habituated ORs. The same phenomenon of dehabituation is observed with changes in stimulus intensity (whether an increase or a decrease in intensity is involved); in stimulus duration (again, whether an increase or a decrease); in stimulus patterning (for example, if a sequence of tones is presented in the order 1–2–3 until the ORs are habituated and are then presented in the order 3–2–1); and in the temporal regularity of presentation of the stimulus (including complete omission of a stimulus at a time when, on the basis of a preceding regularity of presentation, it would be expected to occur). Lynn (1966) has argued convincingly that these data cannot be explained by a "one-stage" model of the mechanisms involved; by which he means a model in which the same part of the system is responsible for analysing stimulus inputs and organizing response outputs. The most usual form taken by such a one-stage model is to suppose that the tissues in the central nervous system which are excited by any particular stimulus or combination of stimuli gradually become refractory to further excitation with repeated presentation of the same stimuli. A model of this type has the advantage that there is no need to postulate any special memory mechanism for analysing present inputs and comparing them with past inputs. However, as Lynn points out, such a mechanism could not account for the recurrence of ORs when, for example, stimulus intensity is reduced, the patterning of a combination of stimuli is changed, or a stimulus is omitted at its usual place in a regular temporal sequence. Nor could it account for the dehabituation caused by an "extra-stimulus". Thus it appears necessary to devise a model of the orienting reflex in which one system does the job of stimulus analysis and is able to control another system which organizes the actual production of orienting responses; although this commits us to postulating an extremely complex mechanism which is able to store information concerning the quality, intensity, duration, spatial and temporal patterning, and combination of stimuli recently encountered in a particular environment and then match present stimulation against this set of stored inputs to see whether it is "the same" or "different".

It is a "two-stage" model of this kind which Sokolov has proposed to account for the data on habituation and dehabituation of the OR. Rightly, in my view, he has realized that the complexities of analysis involved could only be performed in the massive neuronal network which constitutes the cerebral cortex, and it is here that he has placed his "modelling mechanism". The system for production of the orienting responses themselves he has placed in the reticular formation of the brainstem, a system known to be crucial for the maintenance of consciousness. A schematic diagram of Sokolov's hypothesis is presented in Fig. 1. According to this hypothesis the cortex forms a "neuronal model" of all the important features of the stimulation experienced in a particular environment. An incoming stimulus is projected to both the cortex (pathway 1) and the reticular formation (pathway 2): if it does not match an existing neuronal model in the cortex, the reticular formation is left to get on with the job of organizing orienting responses (pathway 7); if it does match an existing model, the cortex sends out an inhibitory message which prevents the stimulus from being received in the reticular formation (pathway 3). The

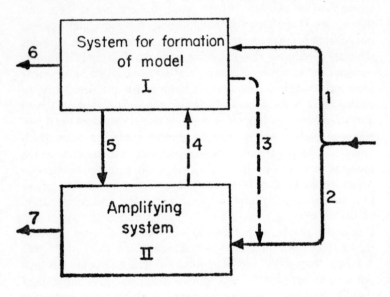

FIG. 1

cortex is also supplied with an excitatory pathway (No. 5) by which it can activate the reticular formation. (It is not clear why Sokolov felt the necessity to postulate this pathway as well as pathway 3, for it would seem that a message along pathway 5 should have the same effect as the absence of a message along pathway 3.) Pathway 4 represents the activating effect of the reticular formation on the cortex, known to exist as the result of a large number of neurophysiological studies, and indicated by the desynchronization and acceleration of the rhythms of the EEG which we have already encountered as one of the components of the OR. Pathway 6 is the route along which the cortex organizes a conditioned reflex, when the incoming stimulus does match an existing neuronal model, but one which, rather than corresponding to an "indifferent stimulus", corresponds to a conditioned stimulus.

Sokolov's hypothesis is consistent with a fair amount of existing data. It is known that stimulation of the reticular formation by implanted electrodes can produce many of the component responses of the OR, including the EEG changes just mentioned, the GSR, pupil dilation, and respiratory, vascular and cardiac changes. It is also known that the cortex is able to exert both excitatory and inhibitory influences on the reticular formation. Furthermore, an incoming stimulus is received at the cortex, as indicated by evoked electrical changes, before it is received in the reticular formation; so that it is possible, as Sokolov suggests, that the cortex has time to analyse the stimulus and, if necessary, prevent the passage of the stimulus input to the reticular formation by activating pathway 3. Furthermore, there is one crucial piece of evidence which suggests that the cortex does indeed play the inhibitory role in habituation of the OR which is allotted to it by Sokolov: decortication renders habituation of the OR impossible (experiments of Zeleny on dogs and of Popov on pigeons and cats, reviewed by Vinogradova, 1961; also, Jouvet and Michel, 1959). One more piece of evidence cited by Sokolov in favour of his hypothesis is the phenomenon of "overextinction" of the OR, which we have already encountered. Sokolov explains this phenomenon by saying that, when the subject becomes drowsy, the efficiency of the cortex in matching stimulus inputs against past inputs drops to the point at which it fails to organize the necessary inhibitory outflow along pathway 3, with a consequent return of orienting responses. It is consistent with this explanation that any procedure which fully arouses the subject during the phase of overextinction abolishes this phenomenon.

In general, it seems probable that Sokolov's hypothesis is on the right lines. However, it certainly cannot account for all the data.

For example, the phase of overextinction is eventually followed, if the stimulus continues to be presented, by complete sleep (and so, presumably, lowered cortical efficiency) and the disappearance of ORs again; and Sokolov offers no way of explaining this. He also does not attempt to explain the *conditioned* OR, when a stimulus which does match an existing neuronal model nevertheless produces an OR; nor the fact that verbal instructions to a human subject to "pay attention" to a stimulus have the same result. Nevertheless, it seems likely that what is needed to account for these additional facts is an extension of Sokolov's theory, rather than a complete alteration of it.

One very important point should be noted. Even if Sokolov's model proves to be incorrect, there are significant implications which would attach to the adoption of *any* two-stage model; and we have seen that it is likely that only a two-stage model can account for all the data on habituation and dehabituation of the orienting reflex. Such a model implies that highly complex processes of stimulus analysis, storing of past inputs, and matching of present stimulation against these stored inputs must go on even in an apparently very simple form of learning—learning not to attend to a repeated stimulus which has neither biologically vital nor signal signification.

As is to be expected, the Russians have not ignored the phylogenetic development of the OR. Orienting responses have been described in tortoises, fish and birds, as well as at many levels of the mammalian scale. From this work, Lynn (1966) has extracted the following tentative generalizations. As one goes up the phylogenetic scale, the OR becomes more pronounced, especially in its somatic components. Habituation of the OR also comes to take place more rapidly; thus, whereas the rabbit shows habituation after 6–15 presentations of visual or auditory stimuli, pigeons require from 15–40 presentations and carp from 53–172 (Vedyaev and Karmanova, 1958). Another feature of phylogenetic development is that the OR can be elicited sooner after birth in more highly developed animals. Finally, it is found that dehabituation of the OR by a change in the experimental situation (the actual stimuli presented remaining the same) can be obtained in dogs and pole cats, but not in pigeons and fish (Vedyaev and Karmanova, 1958), nor is it commonly observed in mammalian infants (Bronstein *et al.*, 1958). These observations suggest that phylogenetic development has led to an increase in the flexibility with which the OR responds to change and regularity in the environment. Such increased flexibility in the course of phylogenetic development is consistent with the vital role allotted to the cerebral cortex (which, of course, is known to increase enormously in importance with progress up the phylogenetic scale) in Sokolov's neurophysiological model of the mechanisms governing the OR.

Some of the data gathered by the Russians on the *ontogenetic* development of the OR are also consistent with the important role allotted by Sokolov to the cortex. Thus, although the autonomic components of the OR appear to be present (although not necessarily in a mature form) in the newly born, the motor components (which adjust the animal's posture so as to facilitate investigation of novel stimuli) are almost completely absent in newborn mammals, first appearing in the puppy and infant rabbit, for example, at about 45 days of age (Obraztsova *et al.*, 1958). Similar observations have been made in human infants by Degtyar (cited by Lynn, 1966). The close connection between orienting reflexes and learning which we have commented on earlier is further emphasized by a number of reports that successful conditioning and instrumental learning become possible only when the motor components of the OR make their appearance; and Vinogradova (1961) has suggested that the mature OR is in fact a necessary precondition for such learning. Another important feature of the ontogenetic development of the OR is that orienting responses are much more resistant to habituation with repetition of the stimulus in young animals than in adults. It is supposed by the Russian workers (Vinogradova, 1961) that this change is connected with the maturation of the cerebral cortex. This, if true, is also consistent with Sokolov's model of the OR; however, the evidence for differential rates of habituation in young and mature animals is not altogether convincing as yet, since there does not appear to have been any control for the probable differences in *novelty* of stimulation when the same stimulus is presented to subjects of different ages.

We have examined the Soviet work on the orienting reflex at some length both because of its intrinsic importance and for the light it throws on the general tendencies of Soviet psychological thought discussed earlier in this article. There is other research which illustrates these tendencies equally well and is of no less importance, but, unfortunately, space is lacking for more than a brief enumeration of the salient features of these programmes of research.

Consciousness and its Biological Significance

Earlier, I emphasized the Soviet concern with the importance of consciousness. While the work on the orienting reflex has obvious connections with this concern, they are, perhaps, of a tangential nature. More directly related to the function and nature of consciousness is the work of A. N. Leontiev. In his doctoral dissertation of 1940 (published in Leontiev, 1959), this leading Soviet psychologist posed a problem which a psychologist trained in the behaviourist school of thought might well regard as unscientific in principle, let alone capable of genuine empirical investigation, namely: what were the reasons for the development of consciousness during the course of zoological evolution, i.e. what survival value did consciousness confer? In answer to this question, Leontiev proposed the hypothesis that consciousness allows organisms to respond to stimuli which, while they are not of crucial importance for survival in themselves, may act as signals of other stimuli which do have such importance. We cannot follow here the arguments which led Leontiev to adopt this point of view. What is perhaps of most interest is the method he chose to test this apparently untestable hypothesis and the very intriguing results which he obtained.

Leontiev argued that, if consciousness develops so as to enable the organism to respond to stimuli of important signal significance, then a human subject, when placed in a situation in which a stimulus of which he is not normally conscious regularly precedes stimulation of some biological importance, should develop awareness of that stimulus. To test this prediction, he set up an experiment in which an electric shock to the hand was regularly preceded by a light stimulus shone on the palm of the hand; the subject, however, did not know anything about the light, and, since it was too weak to produce any sensation of heat, he was at first quite unaware of any stimulation on the palm at all. The subject held down a key, which he was instructed to release as soon as he felt an electric shock. In one condition, he was told simply that he was taking part in an experiment whose purpose was to measure sensitivity to electric shocks. Under these conditions, even after 400 trials, there was no sign of an anticipatory reaction (which would be a sign of developing sensitivity to the light regularly preceding the shock). In a second condition, subjects were informed that, a few seconds before the shock came on, the palm of their hands would be stimulated by "a very weak influence, not easily discernible" and that, if they took their hand from the key during the presentation of this "influence" they would avoid the electric shock. It will be seen that these instructions may be expected to set up an actively attentive attitude in the subject, while not giving him any clue as to the nature of the "influence" he is to expect. Four subjects were tested under these conditions: all of them learned to respond to the light, removing their hand from the key during the action of the light but before the onset of the shock. And, most importantly from the point of view of Leontiev's hypothesis, all of them came to experience odd sensations, which they found difficult to describe ("like a little wind", "a trembling", "a streaming sensation"), in the palm of their hands. Control experiments eliminated the possibility that the subjects were responding to heat, and further experiments not only replicated the original findings but also showed that the subjects could learn to discriminate between red light and green light (Leontiev, 1959). Thus it appears that Leontiev has succeeded in demonstrating that, when a light stimulus directed to the palm of the hand has signal value, human subjects can develop conscious awareness of the sensations produced by such a stimulus. Naturally, evidence of this nature is too indirect to offer any real support for Leontiev's hypothesis that, in general, conscious awareness has developed during the course of evolution because it enables the organism to respond to stimuli of possible signal value. Nevertheless, there can be no doubt of the importance of the actual experimental work this hypothesis has led to, and of the light it throws on the nature of consciousness. Fortunately, there are signs that this line of research is being taken up by Western workers who have heard of the Russian results (e.g. Youtz, 1963).

The Marxist emphasis on the role of active transactions with the environment in shaping consciousness also finds an echo in some of Leontiev's other research. For example, in an investigation of pitch perception in Man, he showed that discrimination of pitch can be improved by a factor of six to eight by giving the subject practice in *singing* the appropriate notes. Thus an apparently "pure" receptor function such as that of hearing depends at least to some extent on the subject's motor activities. Similar demonstrations of the importance of motor activity in shaping perception have recently become available in the Western literature on sensory adaptation to the wearing of distorting lenses; for example, Held and Freedman (1963) report that such adaptation is possible with active movement on the part of the subject but not when the subject is passively moved by the experimenter. However, more recent Western work (Howard *et al.*, 1965) suggests that the crucial variable may not be the degree of active movement on the part of the subject, but the amount of information available to the subject concerning the incorrectness of his perceptions.

If we keep to the subject of perception, there are whole areas of research carried out in the Soviet Union since the 1930's which until recently have had little counterpart in the West and which show very clearly the Russian tendency to seek for central factors in perception and thus venture into fields which a Western research worker would regard as most unlikely to prove fruitful. One of the most important of these fields is that of sensory interaction, i.e. the effect of stimulation in one sense modality on perception in another modality—an effect which can clearly only be of central origin. In a thorough review of the Soviet literature on this subject (containing over 500 references!), London (1954) remarks that "this research appears to demonstrate that all modalities undergo various modifications of sensory response on appropriate application of an accessory stimulus". Although the amount of Western work on this subject is incomparably less, such research as has been carred out (e.g. Zajonc and Dorfman, 1964) leaves no doubt as to the reality of the phenomenon. Moreover, our increased knowledge of the physiology of the central nervous system (in particular, of the non-specific activating systems of the brainstem and thalamus) makes it clear that there exist in the brain mechanisms which could produce such interactions between sensory inputs of different modalities (e.g. Granit, 1955; Magoun, 1963; Hernández-Peón, 1961).

The increase in our neurophysiological knowledge also confers added plausibility on Russian claims, made repeatedly since Dolin's original demonstration of the phenomenon in 1936, that it is possible to establish conditioned changes in sensory thresholds. For example, if a strong light is presented to a subject who has been in the dark for some time, there is a decrease in visual sensitivity for a short period after the flash of light. If such a light-flash is preceded regularly by, for example, an auditory stimulus, then it is reported that, after a number of pairings of the two stimuli, the auditory stimulus presented alone also elicits a fall in sensitivity (see Gray, 1964, for a review of work utilizing this conditioned change in sensitivity). Other conditioned changes in sensory thresholds of a similar nature have also been observed. In the West, however, virtually nothing is known of this phenomenon. Thus we see once more how the greater Russian willingness to postulate central mechanisms in control of behaviour, including perception, has led them into research paths which are very different from those which have been taken in the West.

The Voluntary Control of Motor Behaviour

One final illustration of our general thesis concerns Soviet research into mechanisms of voluntary control of behaviour. We saw earlier the intimate connection in Soviet thought between consciousness and the voluntary direction of behaviour. A direct demonstration of the role of awareness in the development of control over reactions mediated by the autonomic nervous system has been contributed by Lisina (1958) working in Zaporozhets's laboratory. She studied the vasoconstriction response which is produced by electric shock, and determined to see whether she could get her subjects instead to show vaso*dilation*, if this response were rewarded by cancellation of the shock. She found that this was not possible under normal conditions and attributed this failure to the fact that there is simply not enough sensory feedback from the vasodilation response for the subject to become aware of what aspect of his behaviour is controlling the offset of the shock. To test this hypothesis, Lisina introduced a visual feedback by having the subject watch a pointer which moved in one direction to indicate the subject's own vasoconstriction responses and in the other to indicate vasodilation (without, however, informing the subject of the connection between the movements of the pointer and the vasomotor changes). Under these conditions, the subjects of the experiment successfully learned to control the shock by producing vasodilation responses. In other words, they gained voluntary control over this "autonomic" response. It should be noted, however, that the "consciousness" involved in this experiment was not consciousness of the relation between the vasomotor responses and the electric shock, for, even when they had learnt to control their vasomotor responses, the subjects did not know that the pointer had anything to do with this particular aspect of their own behaviour. Thus it appears that the crucial factor for control over responses mediated by the autonomic nervous system is that they should be given sufficient additional sensory feedback properties, rather than that the subject should "understand" what he is doing. In fact, most subjects, having noted the relation between particular positions of the pointer and the cessation of the electric shock, and realizing that the pointer had *something* to do with their own bodies, adopted some such strategy as altering their breathing or relaxing their muscles—procedures which, since they were accompanied by vasodilation, had the appropriate effects on the pointer and on the shock. However, by the end of the experiment, these procedures were no longer necessary, and subjects reported that they could control the pointer as they liked—although they still did not know how they were doing it! Incidentally, Brener (1964) has recently made very similar observations using heart rate plus additional auditory or visual feedback at Birkbeck College, London.

But the most important Soviet research on the voluntary control of behaviour is the work on the development of the regulatory function of language which has been conducted under the direction of A. R. Luria. This work illustrates not only the Soviet concern with voluntary behaviour, but also the great interest in developmental psychology in the Soviet Union. The combination of these two interests (inspired by the example of a great Soviet psychologist of the 1930's, L. S. Vygotsky) has led to some extremely profitable results. Much of Luria's work is now available in English (Luria, 1960, 1961, 1963a, 1963b; Luria and Yudovich, 1959), and we may therefore confine ourselves here to the briefest description of the main lines of his work. By means of some simple, but very ingenious, experiments he and his colleagues have succeeded in demonstrating the extremely important role played by language in the regulation of behaviour—a function of language which until recently (e.g. O'Connor and Hermelin, 1963; Kendler and Kendler, 1962) has been almost totally neglected in the West. Their success in demonstrating this regulatory role has been largely due to their adoption of a developmental approach, for, in the adult, linguistic operations are so completely internalized that there is usually no overt evidence that complex forms of voluntary behaviour are under any form of verbal control at all. In the growing child, however, it is possible to trace the stages by which verbal stimuli gradually become dominant in the control of behaviour.

Luria's basic experimental situation is a simple one. The child has to do one of two things—press a rubber bulb or refrain from pressing it—in response to various signals, usually lights of different colours. Using this and other situations, Luria (1961) has shown how words spoken to a child by an adult are at first (when the child is about $1\frac{1}{2}$ to 2 years old) capable only of initiating a response, but not of causing the child to refrain from or alter an ongoing response. At a later stage of development (about $3\frac{1}{2}$ years), the adult is able both to initiate and restrain the child's responses by appropriate verbal stimuli, but only if these are spoken *each time* the visual signals are presented. At this stage, moreover, the child begins to be able to use words in the same way (i.e. speaking them each time he has to respond or refrain from responding) so as to regulate his own motor behaviour. However, he cannot yet respond appropriately when he is given generalized instructions (e.g. "press the bulb whenever there is a red light, but don't press when there is a green light") before the experiment begins. Furthermore, the control exerted over his behaviour by verbal stimuli is in large measure due to the *stimulus* aspect of the words used, rather than their *meaning*. Thus, to the words "Go! Go!" (whether spoken by an adult or by the child himself) the child of $3\frac{1}{2}$ can press a bulb twice in quick succession, but to the words "You (or I) must press twice", he cannot—even though he understands the meaning of the word "twice". It is only in the next stage of development (age $4\frac{1}{2}$ to $5\frac{1}{2}$) that the control exerted by speech over the child's motor behaviour depends definitely on the meaning of words, rather than on their stimulus aspect. And it is in this stage that the child is able to organize his behaviour appropriately when given generalized instructions before the experiment begins. This is made possible by the interiorization of speech which also occurs during this stage. Thus, although the child who has been given prior instructions will respond appropriately and *silently* on an easy task, if the task is made more difficult, he will be observed to *speak* the relevant instructions aloud at critical moments. Finally, with still further development, the child approximates to the ability of the adult to formulate general verbal instructions for himself and use these instructions to guide his own behaviour.

In this way, then, Luria and his colleagues have succeeded in demonstrating some of the extremely complex developmental history which underlies the ability of the adult human being to behave, in Pavlov's words, as "the highest self-regulating system". Confirmation of the special nature of the regulatory role of speech —and an indication of the neurophysiological substratum of this function of language—comes from data on the effects of brain lesions. Luria (1960) reports that lesions to the frontal lobes— which produce no obvious symptoms of aphasia—apparently have a disruptive effect specifically on the use of speech to regulate behaviour. Thus (experiments of Khomskaya), patients with lesions of this kind cannot follow instructions to press a bulb gently in response to a green light and strongly in response to a red light —even though they appear to understand the instructions. Nor are they helped by speaking the words "gently" or "strongly" at the same time as they attempt to make the corresponding response: they speak the correct *words* in response to the appropriate signals, but press on the bulb with equal strength under both conditions. Thus, such a frontal lobe patient does not have the ability to use speech to regulate his own motor behaviour which has been attained by a normal 5-year-old child—although in all other respects his speech remains typical of a mature adult. It should be noted that patients with parietal lesions do not show any disturbance in the regulatory role of speech when tested in the same way (Luria, 1960).

A recent experiment reported by Khomskaya (1965) throws further light on the function of the frontal lobes in verbal behaviour—a function which, until these Russian data became available, was hardly suspected. In the normal adult, orienting responses which have been habituated by repeated stimulation may be reinstated immediately by verbal instructions which confer a signal value on the stimulus (e.g. instructions to count the number of stimuli or that the stimulus will be followed by an electric shock). Similarly, the ORs may be just as quickly eliminated by cancellation of the instructions. Khomskaya reports that neither the reinstatement nor the elimination of the OR by verbal instructions can be so easily obtained in patients with lesions of the frontal lobes, although lesions of the parietal and temporal lobes leave the normal pattern of response virtually undisturbed. Thus it appears possible that the role of speech in directing motor behaviour is intimately connected with the verbal direction of orienting responses—a conclusion which can also be drawn from Zaporozhets's (1961) important work on the voluntary control of behaviour in children—and that both functions are crucially dependent on neural systems located in the frontal lobes. Such a view of the role of the frontal lobes would be consistent with much of the data from animal experiments (e.g. Rosvold and Mishkin, 1961) suggesting that this part of the brain is necessary for the successful switching of attention to stimuli which, either intrinsically or as the result of learning, are not easily able to capture attention. Such switching of attention is typically accomplished in the human being by means of verbal mediating stimuli. It would also be consistent with the clinical observations (see Willett, 1960) suggesting that patients with frontal lesions are deficient in the ability to "plan for the future", an ability which clearly involves the direction of one's own behaviour by self-produced verbal stimuli.

The work of Luria and his colleagues on the verbal control of behaviour—Man's most distinctively human characteristic—brings this brief and very selective review of current Soviet research in psychology to a fitting close. I hope I have been successful in showing how this research has not been chosen at random, but has grown out of a philosophical background which emphasizes different aspects of behaviour from those given most attention in the West. The great philosophical problem for a consistent monist materialism, such as Marxist-Leninism, is to incorporate conscious experience within the same causal network which is applied to the data with which the natural sciences deal. It is to the Russians' very great credit that they have never tried (as our own Behaviourist school did) to pretend that this problem does not exist. Nor have they minimized the very real differences between, at the one extreme, purely reflex behaviour and, at the other, behaviour which is under fully conscious voluntary control. On the contrary, as a revolutionary philosophy, Marxism has emphasized above all Man's ability to interfere actively in his environment and, by changing that, to change himself. It can be no accident that these philosophical preoccupations have been paralleled by the particular kind of research which has grown up in the Soviet Union. This research has tried to demonstrate the exceptional importance of active attention in conditioning and learning, while establishing the concept of attention on a firm physiological basis.   It has defended a functional view of consciousness which would give it a very real role to play in the guidance of behaviour, while making it possible to account for the development of consciousness during phylogeny according to the principle of natural selection. It has emphasized the importance of active transaction with the environment in the shaping of sensation and perception, along with the existence of central perceptual mechanisms capable of subserving such transaction. And it has tried to illuminate the complex developmental history and the physiological systems which underly Man's voluntary control of his own behaviour.

Acknowledgement

My thanks are due to Dr. Susanna Millar for her critical comments on the manuscript.

References

ANOKHIN, P. K. (1961) A new conception of the physiological architecture of conditioned reflex. In: J. F. Delafresnaye (Ed.)., *Brain Mechanisms and Learning*. Oxford: Blackwell, pp. 189–227.

BAUER, R. A. (1952) *The New Man in Soviet Psychology*. Cambridge, Mass.: Harvard Univ. Press.

BITTERMAN, M. E. (1965) The evolution of intelligence. *Sci. Amer.* **212,** 92–100.

BRENER, J. (1964) The characteristics of heart rate during various conditioning procedures. Unpublished Ph.D. Thesis, University of London.

BROADBENT, D. E. (1958) *Perception and Communication*. London: Pergamon Press.

BRONSTEIN, A. I., ITINA, N. A., KAMENETSKAYA, A. G., and SYTOVA, V. A. (1958) Orientirovochnyye reaktsii novorozhdennykh detei [Orienting responses in new-born children]. In: Voronin, L. G. et al. (Eds.), Orientiro-vochnyi Refleks i Orientirovochnaya-issledovatel'skaya Deyatel'nost' [The Orienting Reflex and Exploratory Behaviour]. Moscow, Akad. Pedag. Nauk R.S.F.S.R., pp. 237–42.

DARROW, C. W. (1936) The galvanic skin reflex (sweating) and blood-pressure as preparatory and facilitative functions. Psychol. Bull. 33, 73–94.

DOLIN, A. O. (1936) Novyye fakty k fiziologicheskomu ponimaniyu assotsiatsii u cheloveka [New material for the physiological understanding of association in Man]. Arkh. biol. Nauk, 42 (1–2).

ECCLES, J. C. (1953) The Neurophysiological Basis of Mind. Oxford: Clarendon Press.

FUSTER, J. M. (1958) Effects of stimulation of brain stem on tachistoscopic perception. Science, 127, 150.

GASTAUT, H. and BERT, J. (1961) Electroencephalographic detection of sleep induced by repetitive sensory stimuli. In: Wolstenholme, G. E. W. and O'Connor, M. (Eds.), The Nature of Sleep. Ciba Foundation Symposium. London: Churchill, pp. 260–71.

GOODWIN, W. R. and LAWRENCE, D. H. (1955) The functional independence of two discrimination habits associated with a constant stimulus situation. J. comp. physiol. Psychol. 48, 437–43.

GRANIT, R. (1955) Receptors and Sensory Perception. New Haven, Conn.: Yale Univ. Press.

GRAY, J. A. (1964) Strength of the nervous system as a dimension of personality in man: a review of work from the laboratory of B. M. Teplov. In: Gray, J. A. (Ed.), Pavlov's Typology. Oxford: Pergamon, pp. 157–287.

HELD, R. and FREEDMAN, S. J. (1963) Plasticity in human sensorimotor control. Science 142, 455–61.

HERNÁNDEZ-PEÓN, R. (1961) Reticular mechanisms of sensory control. In: Rosenblith, W. A. (Ed.), Sensory Communication. New York: M.I.T. and Wiley, pp. 497–520.

HOWARD, I. P., CRASKE, B. and TEMPLETON, W. B. (1965) Visuo-motor adaptation to discordant ex-afferent stimulation. J. exp. Psychol. 70, 189–91.

JOUVET, M. and MICHEL, F. (1959) Aspects électroencéphalographiques de l'habituation de la réaction d'éveil. J. Physiol. (Paris) 51, 489–90.

KENDLER, H. H. and KENDLER, T. S. (1962) Vertical and horizontal processes in problem solving. Psychol. Rev. 69, 1–16.

KHOMSKAYA, YE., D. (1965) Regulyatsiya vegetativnykh komponentov orientirovochnogo refleksa s pomoshch'yu rechevykh instruktsii prirazlichnykh lokal'nykh porazheniyakh mozga [The verbal regulation of vegetative components of the orienting reflex in patients with differently located brain lesions]. Vopr. Psikhol. 11 (1), 55–65.

LANSING, R. W., SCHWARTZ, E. and LINDSLEY, D. B. (1959) Reaction time and EEG activation under alerted and non-alerted conditions. J. exp. Psychol. 58, 1–7.

LEONTIEV, A. N. (1959) Problemy Razvitiya Psikhiki [Problems of Mental Development]. Moscow: Akad. Pedag. Nauk R.S.F.S.R.

LISINA, M. I. (1958) Rol' orientirovki v prevrashchenii reaktsii iz neproiz-vol'nykh v proizvol'nyye [The role of orientation in converting involuntary to voluntary responses]. In Voronin, L. G. *et al.* (Eds.), *Orientirovochnyi Refleks i Orientirovochno-issledovatel'skaya Deyatel'nost'* [The Orienting Reflex and Exploratory Behaviour]. Moscow, Akad. Pedag. Nauk R.S.F.S.R., pp. 339–44.

LONDON, I. D. (1954) Research on sensory interaction in the Soviet Union. *Psychol. Bull.* **51**, 531–68.

LURIA, A. R. (1960) Verbal regulation of behaviour. In: Brazier, M. A. B. (Ed.), *The Central Nervous System and Behaviour, Transactions of the Third Conference.* Josiah Macy Jr. Foundation, pp. 359–421.

LURIA, A. R. (1961) *The Role of Speech in the Regulation of Normal and Abnormal Behaviour.* Oxford: Pergamon Press.

LURIA, A. R. (Ed.) (1963a) *The Mentally Retarded Child.* Oxford: Pergamon Press.

LURIA, A. R. (1963b) *Restoration of Function after Brain Injury.* Oxford: Pergamon Press.

LURIA, A. R. and YUDOVICH, F. IA. (1959) *Speech and the Development of Mental Processes in the Child.* London: Staples Press.

LYNN, R. (1966) *Arousal, Attention and the Orientation Reaction.* Oxford: Pergamon Press.

MAGOUN, H. W. (1963) *The Waking Brain*, 2nd ed. Springfield, Ill.: Thomas.

OBRAZTSOVA, G. A., POMAZANSKAYA, L. F., STEL'MAKH, L. N. and TRO-SHIKHIN, V. A. (1958) Ob orientirovochoi reaktsii na indifferentnyye i uslovnyye razdrazhiteli u sobaki i krolika v ontogeneze [Orienting responses to indifferent and conditioned stimuli in the dog and the rabbit during ontogenesis]. In Voronin, L. G. *et al.* (Eds.), *Orientirovochnyi Refleks i Orientirovochno-issledovatel'skaya Deyatel'nost'* [The Orienting Reflex and Exploratory Behaviour]. Moscow: Akad. Pedag. Nauk R.S.F.S.R., pp. 248–53.

O'CONNOR, N. and HERMELIN, B. (1963) *Speech and Thought in Severe Sub-normality: an Experimental Study.* Oxford: Pergamon Press.

RAZRAN, G. (1961) The observable unconscious and the inferable conscious in current Soviet psychophysiology: interoceptive conditioning, semantic con-ditioning and the orienting reflex. *Psychol. Rev.* **68**, 81–147.

RAZRAN, G. (1965) Evolutionary psychology: levels of learning—and percep-tion and thinking. In: Wolman, B. B. and Nagel, E. (Eds.), *Scientific Psychology.* New York: Basic Books, pp. 207–53.

ROSVOLD, H. E. and MISHKIN, M. (1961) Non-sensory effects of frontal lesions on discrimination learning and performance. In: Delafresnaye, J. F. (Ed.), *Brain Mechanisms and Learning.* Oxford: Blackwell, pp. 555–67.

SECHENOV, I. M. (1935) Reflexes of the brain. In: *Selected Works of I. M. Sechenov.* Moscow: State Publishing House for Biological and Medical Literature, pp. 263–336.

SOKOLOV, YE. N. (Ed.) (1959) *Orientirovochnyi Refleks i Voprosy Vysshei Nervnoi Deyatel'nosti* [The Orienting Reflex and Problems of Higher Nervous Activity]. Moscow: Akad. Pedag. Nauk R.S.F.S.R.

SOKOLOV, YE. N. (1960) Neuronal models and the orienting reflex. In: Brazier,

M. A. B. (Ed.), *The Central Nervous System and Behavior. Transactions of the Third Conference*. Josiah Macy Jr. Foundation, pp. 187–276.

SOKOLOV, YE. N. (1963) *Perception and the Conditioned Reflex*. Oxford: Pergamon Press.

SUTHERLAND, N. S. (1959) Stimulus analysing mechanisms. In: *Proceedings of a Symposium on the Mechanization of Thought Processes*, Vol. 2. London: H.M. Stationery Office, pp. 575–609.

VEDYAEV, F. P. and KARMANOVA, I. G. (1958) K sravnitel'noi fiziologii orientirovochnogo refleksa [On the comparative physiology of the orienting reflex]. In: Voronin, L. G. *et al.* (Eds.), *Orientirovochnyi Refleks i Orientirovochno-issledovatel'skaya Deyatel'nost'* [*The Orienting Reflex and Exploratory Behaviour*]. Moscow: Akad. Pedag. Nauk R.S.F.S.R., pp. 201–4.

VINOGRADOVA, O. S. (1961) *Orientirovochnyi Refleks i yego Neirofiziologicheskiye Mekhanizmy* [*The Orienting Reflex and its Neurophysiological Mechanisms*]. Moscow: Akad. Pedag. Nauk R.S.F.S.R.

VORONIN, L. G., LEONTIEV, A. N., LURIA, A. R., SOKOLOV, YE. N., and VINOGRADOVA, O. S. (Eds.) (1958) *Orientirovochnyi Refleks i Orientirovochno-issledovatel'skaya Deyatel'nost'* [*The Orienting Reflex and Exploratory Behaviour*]. Moscow: Akad. Pedag. Nauk R.S.F.S.R.

VYGOTSKY, L. S. (1962) *Thought and Language*. New York: Wiley.

WATSON, J. B. (1913) Psychology as the behaviorist views it. *Psychol. Rev.* **20**, 158–77. Reprinted in Dennis, W., *Readings in the History of Psychology*, 1948, pp. 457–71.

WILLETT, R. (1960) The effects of psychosurgical procedures on behaviour. In: Eysenck, H. J. (Ed.), *Handbook of Abnormal Psychology*. London: Pitman, pp. 566–610.

YOUTZ, R. P. (1963) Aphotic digital color sensing—a case under study. Paper read to Psychonomic Society, 29 August 1963.

ZAJONC, R. B. and DORFMAN, D. D. (1964) Perception, drive and behavior theory. *Psychol. Rev.* **71**, 273–90.

ZAPOROZHETS, A. V. (1961) The origin and development of conscious control of movements in Man. In: O'Connor, N. (Ed.), *Recent Soviet Psychology*. Oxford: Pergamon Press.

CHAPTER 2

Psychotherapy in the Soviet Union

BRIAN H. KIRMAN

Queen Mary's Hospital, Carshalton, Surrey

PSYCHOTHERAPY is usually taken to mean the influencing of the clinical condition of a patient by means of a direct and personal contact between the therapist and the subject of the therapy. When psychotherapy is discussed, formal direct and purposeful sessions are what the participants in the discussion usually have in mind. However, informal supportive psychotherapy has always been part of the stock-in-trade of the good physician. Many people other than the medical adviser play a psychotherapeutic role. It is, therefore, difficult to draw the line between a formal therapeutic relationship and others which provide counsel, sympathy, moral support, understanding, serve a confessional role, or otherwise make up the relation between the individual and the society in which he lives. It is generally recognized that the need for psychiatric help is conditioned in part by the nature of society. It seems likely that this would be particularly the case in regard to the neuroses. However, even in regard to the psychoses, Kerbikov (1964) speaks about the danger that in using the ever-increasing number of available drugs, the physician will shift the responsibility from himself to the medicine. He points out that the long-term prognosis of such an illness as schizophrenia does not appear to have been influenced in the Soviet Union by use of "psychotropic" drugs. On the other hand, cases of schizophrenia adequately followed up proved, in the experience of the Ryazan dispensary, to need readmission to hospital only one-third as often as others without the benefit of after-care. In taking up this position, Kerbikov is not pressing so much for formal psychotherapy in major psychoses, but is rather pleading for the psychiatrist to avoid "automation" in psychiatry and to devise a régime suited to the individual patient in all his complexity. Such a régime must clearly include, as an important ingredient, therapeutic personal relationships. Kerbikov believes that this is barely feasible in many Western countries in hospital, owing to the very large numbers of patients in charge of one doctor, by contrast with the relatively generous medical staffing of most Soviet psychiatric hospitals. He also believes that pressure by drug firms may favour standard methods of treatment, with neglect of the personal relationship.

Some Similarities in Problems and Methods

The above remarks emphasize differences which can be expected in a new type of society, with a nationalized drug industry and health service and with altered social relationships and professional outlook. It is easy, however, to over-emphasize differences. There is much in common between the problems facing the psychiatrist in Great Britain and in the Soviet Union. In considering differences stemming from a new system of social organization, it should be remembered that new social forms are only now being slowly and somewhat tentatively evolved, the process having been interrupted by the Second World War and its aftermath, quite apart from earlier difficulties. Whereas attitudes in the West to "psychotropic"† drugs may be influenced by sales pressure, in the Soviet Union an important difficulty until recently was the shortage of a number of drugs. It is only during the last few years that it has been possible to set aside large sums of money for the development of the chemical industry in the U.S.S.R.

† This is a term which has been much used recently, particularly in literature issued by drug houses in relation to tranquillizers and antidepressant drugs— the term implies that the drug in question has the effect of restoring normal mental activity either in depression when antidepressants may be indicated or in schizophrenia and related conditions when "tranquillizers" may be used.

Alcoholism

An example of a common problem is that of alcoholism, which figures more prominently in Soviet psychiatric literature than in the British. Winn (1962) states: "Alcoholism is obviously on the increase and calls for a more vigorous and advanced study." In the collection of papers which he edits and which were read at the 1956 conference on psychotherapy in Moscow, there is a section dealing with the treatment of alcoholism and smoking. The three papers devoted to alcoholism all relate to suggestion and hypnosis. Lukomsky of Archangel bases his report on the treatment of over 300 chronic alcoholics and advocates the combination of hypnosis and suggestion with conditioning to apomorphine.† Where apomorphine is contra-indicated, he uses a vomiting reponse developed during a hypnotic session, assisted by weak olfactory and gustatory stimuli, but without apomorphine and based on verbal suggestion. The more specific treatment is preceded by a general explanatory and exploratory session. Consolidation of the results is left to the patient's relatives and the community. In considering this last point, it should be remembered that Soviet society, with its emphasis on the role of the collective, tends to be tightly knit, even when urban. Supervision of rehabilitation can therefore be organized either from the place of work or on a neighbourhood basis.

Gordova and Kovalev report from Kursk on the treatment of 150 chronic alcoholics, 114 of whom were between the ages of 21–30 at the onset of the alcoholism. They treated twenty-eight patients with hypnosis, and sixty-two with hypnosis and apomorphine, whilst sixty had only apomorphine. The hypnotic sessions were conducted in groups of four or five persons, twice a week for 30 minutes; altogether there were from five to twelve such sessions. There were individual talks before each treatment. The

† This is a substance chemically related to morphine but with a powerful effect on the vomiting centre when given by injection; subjectively it produces nausea and creates a sensation like that in sea sickness. It is this effect which can serve as a unconditioned stimulus in the treatment of alcoholism whilst the smell and taste of alcohol are the conditioned stimulus.

sessions themselves were conducted in a special room, slightly darkened. Hypnosis was induced by verbal suggestion, accompanied by the sound of a ticking clock. The results of the different methods of treatment are shown in the following table.

TABLE 1. RESULTS OF TREATMENT OF 150 CHRONIC
ALCOHOLICS BY THREE DIFFERENT METHODS

Method of treatment	N	Subsequent abstention in months		
		3	4–12	12+
Hypnosis	20	30%	15%	55%
Hypnosis and apomorphine	40	33%	17%	50%
Apomorphine	40	50%	33%	17%

It was noted that the effectiveness of hypnotic treatment depended on the number of sessions; no fewer than nine to twelve was considered desirable.

Some Practical Limitations

Kerbikov (1961) points to some problems concerning the organization and teaching of psychiatry. He indicates that for some considerable time to come, it will be the general practitioner (i.e. polyclinic doctor or regional doctor) who will deal with "minor" and "borderline" psychiatry. He further suggests that in line with Gannushkin's teaching, the instruction of the medical student should be based largely on this type of case, though he should also have a good working knowledge of well-defined mental illness. Kerbikov is concerned at the fact that the instruction of the medical student in psychiatry is largely devoted to the major psychoses and is influenced by the researches which happen to be in train in the units where instruction is imparted. He considers that reform of the programme of instruction is indicated, with emphasis on the sort of problems which are likely to be met with by the general practitioner. In particular, the psychiatrist should be able to impart to the medical student an ability to envisage the patient as a whole in his social milieu. In effect, such a reform would help to re-establish and re-emphasize the psychotherapeutic role of the doctor and would help to put the care and treatment of the major psychoses in perspective, against the needs of the very numerous section of the population with symptoms of neurosis and maladjustment.

There are in the Soviet Union seventy-nine medical schools, with a curriculum which is uniform throughout the Union. Psychiatry is taught during the course of the fifth year and neurological diseases during the fourth. The departments of neurology and psychiatry are separate. Students are examined for each of these subjects. One hundred hours of instruction are allocated to each of them, divided into 40% lectures and 60% practical instruction. In the course of their practical work, students take part in the treatment of patients in hospital, in out-patient and at follow-up clinics in the psychiatric dispensary, and accompany the physician on home visits in cases of psychiatric emergency. About two-thirds of the cases seen by the student are of major psychosis and only about one-third are of neurosis or personality disorder. It would appear therefore that, at present, the opportunity for the student to familiarize himself with psychotherapeutic techniques must be limited.

Available Resources

As Rokhlin (1959) says, it is a mistake to assess a psychiatric service merely on the number of beds available in hospitals. It is necessary to take into account other types of psychiatric institutions, dispensaries and day hospitals and to consider new developments in Soviet psychiatric hospitals. He stresses that a very important factor is the number of physicians and junior medical personnel. In 1913 the Tsarist empire had 480 psychiatrists; in 1936 there were 1392 in the U.S.S.R. and in 1955, 4086. The staffing figures in 1954 for Soviet psychiatric hospitals were:

1 psychiatrist for 28 patients, 1 nurse for 6 and 1 attendant for 3.
The bed figures were:

Year	1911	1923	1940	1957
Beds	47,975	12,950	83,895	115,430

Rokhlin compares American, Canadian and Australian doctor–
patient ratios in psychiatry unfavourably with those in the Soviet
Union. He states that in the U.S.S.R., passive treatments and the
belief that mental diseases are incurable have been replaced by
active medical work, imbued with a vigorous striving for therapeutic effect. He points out that treatment is not confined to the
use of drugs but includes work therapy, psychotherapy, physiotherapy, medical gymnastics, and appropriate environmental and
social prophylactic measures.

One of the principles which is recognized in the Soviet Union,
as indeed in a number of other countries, is the need to decentralize
the psychiatric services and to bring them closer to the community.
Rokhlin quotes the example of the Moscow region where, in addition to the Yakovenko hospital with 1500 beds, sixteen inter-
district psychiatric institutions have been set up in recent times.
These are small psychiatric hospitals for new cases and several
colonies, mainly of an agricultural type. This dispersion has the
effect of making treatment available locally to a large section of
the population with "temporary mental disorders . . . in cases of
alcoholic, infectious, hysterical, epileptic and other psychoses".

Another principle which finds expression in the Soviet Union, as
in contemporary psychiatry elsewhere, is that of unity with general
medicine. This is effected in part through the establishment of
psychiatric departments in general hospitals. The first such department was set up by Gannushkin in the Botkin Hospital in Moscow
and the Ukrainian Republic has had a good deal of experience in
setting up such departments of late. This arrangement leads to
exchange of experience between the psychiatrist and his colleagues
in other branches of medicine and makes psychiatric assistance
available to patients in other departments.

The Psychiatric Dispensary

The changes described above should facilitate provision of psychotherapy where this is indicated, including its use for in-patients. It is, however, in the "dispensary" or out-patient clinic that such treatment is most likely to be available. The psychiatric dispensaries which appeared after the 1917 revolution were mainly located in Moscow and Leningrad. By 1957 there was wider pro-vision with 2467 psychiatric clinics in general dispensaries and 119 special psychiatric dispensaries. In these clinics, attention is focused on: "lesser mental disorders, incipient and light forms of mental diseases and neuroses". Visits are paid to patients' homes by doctors and nurses from the dispensary and each doctor is respon-sible for a certain area of the region which the dispensary serves.

Psychotherapeutic Theory

In pre-revolutionary times, Russian psychiatry had a strong physiological and anatomical bias under the influence of such men as Korsakov and Pavlov. In recent years, this trend has been emphasized and combined with a social approach to psychiatric problems. Pavlov's prime interest, which motivated his research into adaptive behaviour, was the possibility of treatment of mental illness, with particular reference to psychotherapy. He hoped to achieve unity with objective science in this field and to analyse the mode of operation of psychological stimuli. In this he was largely successful, but the implications of his work for psychotherapy have not been fully developed, either inside or outside the Soviet Union.

Pavlov was much concerned with the opposing nervous pheno-mena of excitation and inhibition. He studied external, internal†

---

† Pavlov divided inhibition in the nervous system with particular reference to conditioned responses into external and internal for certain purposes. For example, a sudden unexpected noise in the environment will prevent the appearance of a conditioned reflex; an experimental dog which had been con-ditioned to salivate at the sight of a particular object might fail to do so if a loud bell were suddenly rung immediately after the object had been shown to the dog—this is external inhibition. On the other hand, if the object is

and reciprocal inhibition† in dogs and in other animals, as well as in humans. He developed his view of "protective inhibition" to include pathological processes such as catatonic stupor, normal phenomena such as sleep, and induced states such as hypnosis. He noted and measured the development of inhibition consequent on prolonged repetition of an unreinforced stimulus. He remarked also that internal inhibition which was so produced tended to become generalized in some animals, leading to a state resembling natural sleep. He considered that this phenomenon was of the same nature as the hypnotic trance, which depends in most techniques largely on repetitive, monotonous, unreinforced stimuli, which are usually both verbal and non-verbal. Hypnosis is a recognized technique of psychotherapy in the Soviet Union and is indeed the only one picked out by Rokhlin in his booklet as an illustration of Soviet psychotherapy. He considers that post-hypnotic suggestion is very valuable as a therapeutic measure and illustrates this by quoting a 27-year-old woman with hysterical paralysis who was brought to the Kuibyshev Clinic on a stretcher and who was cured after seven hypnotic sessions.

Rokhlin also quoted Pavlov in giving reasons why psychoanalytical theory is not popular in the Soviet Union. He states that this method of treatment has fallen into disrepute because of its mysticism and overemphasis of the role of the sexual urge. He believes that psychoanalysis exaggerates the importance of

---

repeatedly shown to the dog without reinforcement, i.e. if the dog is not fed after being shown the object, the salivary response will become less and less until it is finally extinguished and there is no longer any salivation when the object is demonstrated—this is internal inhibition which may spread until the animal goes to sleep.

† It is a basic law of nervous activity that if there is excitation in one part of the nervous system other parts, particularly adjacent parts, show reduced activity, become inhibited—this is reciprocal inhibition. This reciprocity is seen at all levels of the nervous system and is essential for normal co-ordination of muscle groups. It applies both to unconditioned and conditioned responses and includes the concept of external inhibition. For example, if a bitch is placed near to a dog this may have the effect of inhibiting unconditioned responses to potentially harmful stimuli and may interfere with acquired or conditioned responses.

instinctual drives in the determination of human behaviour in general, leading to an underestimation of the importance of the social and economic conditions of the society in which the individual lives. He emphasizes that man is a product of social education. Furthermore, he considers that Freudian teaching is unduly pessimistic and can be used as an apologia for war and overt aggression in society.

Rokhlin considers that the psychotherapeutic approach should not be limited to the formal interview but should permeate the whole of the patient's treatment. Reassurance, persuasion and advice to the patient and to members of his family are particularly mentioned, including—"regular chats between physician and patient, a friendly cordial word and a display of solicitude".

The Word as a Physiological and Therapeutic Factor

This is the title of a monograph by Platonov, which was first published in Russian in 1930. The second edition appeared in Russian in 1955 and an English version in 1959. In psychotherapy the facial expression of the therapist, his physical attitude, his gestures, his approach, perhaps even the way he dresses and other details of his appearance are factors in the total situation and in production of rapport and therapeutic effect. However, the main vehicle for exchange remains the word. Even with play therapy in young children, an important aspect is the development of verbal relationships, however simple, between patient and therapist. The attainment of verbal understanding and expression may indeed be largely equated with the peculiarly human aspects of consciousness and memory, and is essential to the development of conscious social attitudes.

When a dualist philosophy is used or assumed, there is tendency to create an artificial division between physiological and psychological processes. Phenomena which are termed psychological then tend to be thought of as subjective and describable in words. It was, however, one of the main contributions of Pavlov and his colleagues to consider the word as a physiological agent and to achieve the union of the objective and the subjective, so enabling man to study his own psychological reactions objectively. In Pavlov's own words: "Owing to the entire preceding life of the human adult a word is connected with all the external and internal stimuli coming to the cerebral hemispheres, signals all of them, replaces all of them and can, therefore, evoke all the actions and reactions of the organism which these stimuli produce."

Pavlovian Physiology

The Pavlovian view thus enables social exchanges and the phenomena of the therapeutic interview to be expressed in physiological terms and to be analysed, in the same way as educational processes, in terms of conditioning. Thus (Pavlov, 1941)

> . . . the temporary nervous connection is a universal physiological phenomenon both in the animal world and in our own. And at the same time it is likewise a mental phenomenon, which psychologists call an association, no matter whether it is a combination of various actions or impressions, or that of letters, words and thoughts. What reason might there be for drawing any distinction between what is known to a physiologist as a temporary connexion and to a psychologist as an association? Here we have a perfect coalescence, a complete absorption of one by the other, a complete identification. Psychologists seem likewise to have acknowledged this, for they (or at any rate some of them) have made statements that experiments with conditioned reflexes have provided associative psychology, i.e. such psychology as believes association to be the foundation of mental activity, with a firm basis. This is the more so because by means of an established conditioned stimulus it is possible to form a new conditioned stimulus; and of late it has been convincingly proven on an animal (a dog) that even two indifferent stimulations, repeated one after the other, become inter-connected, one causing the appearance of the others.

For a long period of time, work on conditioning made only limited impact on Western psychology and still less on psychiatry. Of recent years, interest in the Pavlovian approach has grown and many conditioning techniques are now in general and accepted use, e.g. the Hallpike peepshow method for audiometry in children. Moreover, a variety of psychotherapeutic techniques based on conditioning have developed, one example of which is "behaviour therapy" (Eysenck, 1960). Bridger (1964), in discussing techniques of therapeutic conditioning, points out that "since the neurotic symptom is produced by acting in the first signalling system, therapy must involve not only words but direct experience". However, there are still many who look upon study of conditioning as providing an understanding of simple adaptation and learning, excluding higher levels of intellectual activity and excluding also emotional responses. As shown above, Pavlov himself, his colleagues and contemporary Soviet psychology do not view the matter in this light. Work on conditioning provides an explanation of simple reactions, such as the flow of saliva into the dog's mouth at the sight of the person who feeds him or the sucking movements which the baby makes at a certain stage of development when he sees the breast. The conditioning process is seen generally, however, as the fundamental activity in the adaptation, through the brain, of the organism to the outside world. Conditioning is based on reinforcement, that is on the formation of a link with unconditioned responses, i.e. with inborn drives or instincts. Thus, the response to an unconditioned stimulus which may be described as arousing pain, hate, fear, anger, love or tenderness, may be highly abstract and verbal, as in poetry. Similarly, a highly abstract conditioned stimulus such as a line of verse may act like an unconditioned stimulus, producing a primitive type of reaction, which again may be described in emotional terms. Therefore, the whole gamut of the exchanges and changes which may be effected at the psychotherapeutic interview can be contained within the body of Pavlovian teaching.

The Therapeutic Interview

The above observations apply to the ordinary conscious therapeutic interview, where use is made of suggestions, explanation and the inhibition of pathological reactions by repetition of appropriate stimuli without reinforcement. Platonov, in the work mentioned above, is particularly concerned with the use of hypnotic suggestion and again uses as an example the treatment of an

c

hysterical reaction in a patient who had been exposed to danger in a threatened train accident. The patient was brought to a railway polyclinic with hysterical attacks, in between which he said that he could see a picture of a wreck before his eyes. His resistance to hypnosis was overcome with some difficulty, but this was accomplished and he improved after each hypnotic session during which he was reassured. Calm and forgetfulness of his experience were suggested to him. After the sixth session, the attacks stopped. After recurrence of the attacks the patient was sent to hospital, where he had six further sessions of treatment. He was discharged from hospital and went back to his former job as assistant locomotive engineer, subsequently qualifying as full engineer and remaining well under observation for 3 years, during which time he drove his locomotive.

Platonov also describes the use of hypnosis for anxiety states and phobias of obsessional type, as well as for compulsive urges. In describing a case of kleptomania, however, he refers to a different method of treatment, which will be more familiar to contemporary Western psychiatrists. The case was that of a young woman whose father had remarried when she was a girl and who had had difficulty with her stepmother, including the withholding of various trinkets given to her by her own mother, who had died when the patient was 8 years old. Platonov states that the origin and mechanism of the formation of her compulsive urge were explained to the patient and her anxiety about the future was relieved. She remained well after seven sessions of psychotherapy. These sessions were conducted "in the waking and drowsy states", so it would appear that in some of them at least, a hypnotic technique was used. However, the patient was a medical practitioner and this may have been one of the considerations that led to the use of explanation rather than suggestion as the main therapeutic instrument.

Insight by the Patient

The explanation advanced by Platonov in this case, and presumably offered to and accepted by the patient, was on classical

Pavlovian lines, as understood by him. Certain features of this therapeutic process, however, might stand and be accepted by psychiatrists with quite different theoretical orientations. First, there is an assumption that she was not aware of the pathogenesis of her compulsion and that this was operating at an unconscious level. Secondly, there is the assumption that it would be possible to get her to accept a logical explanation of the genesis of her kleptomania and thirdly, there is an assumption that this process of making her fully conscious of the psychopathology would benefit her. It may also be assumed that the success of the treatment would partly depend on the establishment of a satisfactory therapeutic relationship between patient and physician.

It will be seen that in this case, something more radical than suggestion under hypnosis was attempted and achieved. When using the hypnotic method and relying on suggestion, the therapist is offering to the patient a ready-made solution to a particular problem, whereas the explanatory technique attempts to get the patient to take an active rather than a passive role in the therapy, which is again more in line with much current psychotherapeutic orientation in Britain and America. In this type of approach, one may be forgiven for wondering whether the accuracy of the explanation offered is as important as its acceptability to the patient. However that may be, these cases serve as illustration of the way in which different therapeutic techniques can be based on Pavlovian teaching. Throughout Platonov's writing, the emphasis is on the neurosis, the pathological symptoms, as learned behaviour. This is a useful and constructive approach to the problem, removing as it does much of the mystique from therapeutic techniques and equating them with remedial education. On the negative side, whilst providing a basic and acceptable understanding of psychological processes in terms of neurophysiology, Pavlovian work does not afford a very useful explanation as to why one individual faced with a given stress breaks down and another does not. Explanations in terms of "weak" and "strong" nervous systems or inherited temperaments are too general to be very helpful, and are less acceptable in the case of such a social animal as man than in the case of dogs. Indeed, in the particular case mentioned above Platonov, quoting Bechterev, refers to the latter's view that klepto-mania is a conditioned reflex formed under unfavourable social conditions.

Platonov proceeds to explain that:

> the above patient suffered from an obsessive-compulsive neurosis whose pathophysiological basis was due to inertness of the stimulatory process confined to a definite section of the cerebral cortex, against the back-ground of protracted asthenic emotion . . . under the influence of emotion (irradiation of excitation from the subcortex), this point assumed a dominating role.

There has now accumulated a vast body of data on condition-ing, the validity of which is unquestioned. This information has immediate relevance to the learning process, both in normal and abnormal human behaviour patterns. When it comes, however, to a statement of the central processes involved in the development of a neurosis, classical Pavlovian hypotheses seem somewhat un-sophisticated, in the light of contemporary knowledge of the func-tion of the central nervous system. The model of two-dimensional spread and concentration of excitation and inhibition was useful, but the thesis would need now to be restated in terms of a three-dimensional process. Furthermore, it is necessary to think, not so much of "points" as of functional units in the nervous system. It is difficult to think of the anatomical substrate of such a complex piece of behaviour as kleptomania in terms of a "point", but it can be considered as an inert stereotype with a definite anatomical foundation, even though this is highly complex.

Psychoprophylaxis

It is perhaps not legitimate to speak of psychotherapy in a normal process such as childbirth. However, verbal stimuli are used in this connection in much the same way as in the therapeutic situation to produce reassurance, to allay apprehension or to cause a hypnotic state. Whereas this method was particularly developed in the Soviet Union on a Pavlovian basis, it is now widely accepted in this country, in France and elsewhere; it can be very effective in competent hands. Like other methods of suggestion or hypnosis, it involves a considerable expenditure of time and is therefore only capable of general application in a well-staffed service. Platonov puts on record a mother's own account of how she was delivered under hypnosis. Her account ends as follows:

> I had never been under hypnosis before and did not know its effects. I am surprised how simply and naturally it works. Calling to mind the process of labour I cannot say which was suggestion, which was autosuggestion, and which was simply distraction of my attention. It makes me laugh now to hear that it is terrible to submit to "hypnosis".

The case mentioned above was delivered in 1925. Platonov and his colleagues have since reported favourably on the method, on the basis of their experience of 766 cases. Similar methods had been used in Leningrad for 20 years at the date of publication of Platonov's second edition of his monograph: they are used very widely throughout the Soviet Union.

Disinhibition

Platonov, whilst basing the theory of his approach to psychotherapy on Pavlov, concentrates his attention on hypnosis and suggestion as the most valuable tools. Pavlovian work, in fact, suggests a great variety of possible approaches to different symptoms and diseases. Frolov (1938), in his account of Pavlov and his school, refers to the classical incident of the Leningrad flood in his section on experimental neuroses. In fact, the results of this incident might be more properly referred to under the heading of accidental neuroses. However, Pavlov, being the shrewd observer that he was, soon turned them to good account in the laboratory.

The flood took place on 23 September 1924 and water unexpectedly penetrated into the building where the feeding room of the dogs was situated. The animals were kept in compartments with the door near the floor. To rescue each dog, it was necessary to submerge it in order to drag it through the opening, a difficult process which the dogs themselves resisted. All the animals were saved, but as a result of the flood, some quite exceptional consequences were observed in several animals. Pavlov's collaborators, A. Speransky and Rikman, noted that after the flood conditioned reflexes to ordinary stimuli, such as light or sounds, had disappeared. It was as if they had never been formed. Only very gradually, by means of numerous repetitions, was it possible to restore these reflexes. But the matter did not end there. It was found that if a powerful electric bell was used as a conditioned stimulus with one of these dogs, that externally seemed completely normal, the dog (which prior to the flood had given a good reflex to the bell) now reacted to it in quite a different fashion. As soon as the bell sounded, the dog became strongly agitated; it began to glance around as if it wanted to run away. But the most remarkable feature was that all the other conditioned reflexes that had only just been restored now once more disappeared for a long time.

After careful study of the problem, Pavlov arranged a critical experiment. A stream of water was directed into the chamber where the dog was on the stand. As soon as the dog noticed the water, it fell into extreme agitation. It began to pant; it yelped and trembled. This category of phenomena is well known to the psychiatrist and would cover many of the cases which, during the First World War, were referred to as suffering from "shell-shock". The uniqueness of Pavlov's discovery, however, was firstly, that a similar state could be produced in certain animals at will, once the mechanism of inhibition of normal conditioned reflexes by the noxious agent or set of circumstances was understood. More importantly, Pavlov showed how, in animals which had developed intricate patterns of response to appropriate stimuli, these patterns could be interrupted. This understanding of the physiological basis of pathological inhibition with related phenomena of panic, agitation, somatic disturbance, etc. (which are described clinically as anxiety states, hysterical amnesia or under other heads), suggests a variety of methods of treatment. One of these is indicated in the passage quoted from Frolov. Patient work with the affected animals resulted in re-establishment of normal responses. With humans, removal from the offending stimulus or set of stimuli and persistent efforts to obtain normal responses by engaging patients in accustomed activity are often successful. There is still the risk, however, that the patient will be re-exposed to the offending agent or to some other stimulus which will produce a similar effect. In the experiment carried out by Pavlov, there had been such generalization of the effect of the traumatic experience with the water that widespread inhibition and derangement of normal function could be produced, not only to the sight and sound of water itself but to other powerful stimuli, e.g. a loud noise.

The obvious method of treatment suggested by Pavlovian work in such a case is disinhibition by graduated exposure to the offending stimulus, either without reinforcement, thus relying on gradual inhibition of the effect of the inhibiting agent, or else by reinforcing with some positive stimulus and relying on the phenomenon of reciprocal inhibition of the inhibiting stimulus. Thus, if the dog on whom the sight of water had a disruptive effect, inhibiting normal behaviour and working patterns, were very gradually exposed to the sight of small but increasing quantities of water in normal and reassuring circumstances, the ill-effect would gradually disappear in a favourable case and the sight of water would lose its power to inhibit normal conditioned reflexes. In the case of the dog, the effect might be achieved more quickly if the sight of water became a signal for feeding. In the human subject, positive reinforcement might be achieved by verbal and facial reassurance, or by a variety of other means which will readily suggest themselves.

The work quoted above provides also the logical basis for aversion therapy. In this case, the pathological response, rather than being in response to trauma is, on the contrary, one to a positive and pleasurable stimulus, e.g. as in homosexuality or in alcoholism. The therapeutic situation must therefore be so contrived as to convert the positive response into a negative one, i.e. inhibition of the learned response is in this case the object of the treatment, rather than the reason for the treatment. This can be achieved in favourable cases, as mentioned above, in the case of alcoholism by the exhibition of actual reinforcement of a negative character at an appropriate interval in relation to the alcohol, or by the use of hypnosis and suggestion, separately or combined with the actual non-verbal reinforcement.

Choice of Psychotherapy

The above sections illustrate some of the various ways in which logical application of Pavlovian methods may be used for psychotherapy. In the Soviet Union, however, there appears to be a preference for hypnosis and suggestion. Miassischev (1962) discusses the choice of a suitable method of therapy. He emphasizes the importance of the social as well as of the physiological aspects of neurosis. He states that: "Acute psychogenic forms of neurosis are likely to call for hypnotic suggestion." He considers that this may also apply where somatic function is disturbed, but believes that some of these need "deep psychotherapy". Where a patient has an attitude of passive suffering towards his ailment, he suggests beginning with hypnosis but going on to "narco-psychotherapy". He believes that distraction, as recommended by Bechterew, is useful in psychotherapy. In this connection, Miassischev states:

It does not directly affect the pattern of the patient's attitudes, nor does it conspicuously alter his character; but it does remove from the patient's mind, the sources of painful experiences and, to that extent, is justified, both psychologically and physiologically. In successfully distracting the patient's attention from the symptoms of his illness, the physician is able to revive his interest in life and thus enables him to form new associations of ideas. This method provides a ready physiological advantage, in that it creates new centres of stimulation which act, by way of negative irradiation, to weaken the central mechanisms of the pathological condition.

Miassischev believes that group therapy deserves more attention and says that apart from the use of group hypnosis in dealing with alcoholism, it is now used only by a few therapists. He considers that the main fault of group therapy as used by "foreign specialists" is its dependence on Freud's teaching. In this connection, it may be useful to quote the definitions of psychotherapy given respectively by the *Large Soviet Encyclopedia* (1955) and the *Popular Medical Encyclopedia* (1961):

Psychotherapy is treatment by influencing the patient psychologically. The general task of psychotherapy is the creation of favourable conditions for treatment, the production of the correct attitude in the patient to the treatment prescribed for him (drugs, physiotherapy etc.), assistance in restoring harmony and in the prevention of traumatic psychological factors, and in the removal of psychogenic symptoms. It follows that there can be included under psychotherapy in the widest sense of the term the action on the patient of his whole environment, the effect of his physicians and of other medical personnel etc. This form of psychotherapy (often called minor psychotherapy) is accessible to and is essential for the doctor in any specialty: by explaining to the patient questions which are not clear and which worry him, connected with his illness, the doctor prevents incorrect attitudes, evaluations and reactions on the part of the patient to one or another aspect of the illness and helps him to keep to a régime which prevents the progress of the disease and assists a speedy cure. Explanatory sessions may be organized for individuals or groups (in particular in the form of medical, educational talks). Suggestion is a component of persuasion and explanation. Owing to the regulating role of the cerebral cortex suggestion is capable of exerting an extremely favourable influence on the course of different pathological processes. A graphic example of the favourable effect of such explanation, persuasion and suggestion is psychoprophylactic preparation for childbirth, reducing or obviating pain and the fear which is associated with this during delivery. A great importance attaches to psychotherapy in the clinical handling of nervous and medical diseases, especially in dealing with hysterical symptoms, in treating drug addiction etc.

Suggestion, in the form of a course of systematic treatment (in the waking or the hypnotic state) is part of major or special psychotherapy. During this, verbal formulae (sentences and expressions) are employed as stimuli which are designed to suit the symptoms of the disease and, in particular, the personality of the patient. During such suggestion the patient may simply lie quietly with his eyes shut or may be placed in a hypnotic state beforehand, after which suggestion is carried out (during the hypnotic state suggestibility is increased). During both forms of suggestion the word as a stimulus produces a more or less concentrated focus of stimulation in the cerebral cortex with a spread around this of induced inhibition. The word has a powerful effect both during the hypnotic session and afterwards as a result of the development of stable conditioned reflexes. The effect of hypnosis extends not only to the mood and behaviour of the patient, but also to the function of the internal organs, metabolism, etc. Work therapy is closely related to psychotherapy. Free exhibition of psychotherapy does not give the physician the right to underestimate those methods of therapy which are basic for the given disease. Faith of the patient in the doctor and a correct attitude on the part of the latter are decisive factors in successful treatment by suggestion.

A psychotherapeutic approach was characteristic of the great Russian medical scientists, Mukhin, Mudrov, Dyadkovsky, Botkin, Zakharin and others. The basis of the psychotherapeutic approach of these Russian scientists was the theory of psychosomatic unity. The theory of psychotherapy in general and of hypnosis in particular was provided with a physiological foundation through the work of Sechenov on central inhibition by the brain of lower structures in the central nervous system. Sechenov's studies provided the basis for wide scientific study and practical application of psychotherapy by Danilevsky, Manassein, Tokarsky, Bechterev and others.

A qualitatively new stage creating wide perspectives for the development of psychotherapy in the medical clinic, in nervous diseases, in midwifery, in surgery and so forth, was the work of Pavlov. The chief weapon of psychotherapy, i.e. the word, is according to Pavlov's studies, just as effective a stimulus as any other, but for Man, more all-embracing, that is to say, for him it is linked with all stimuli, coming from the external or the internal world. In contrast to the scientific materialist position in psychotherapy is the subjective idealist concept of the nature of suggestion and hypnosis which, as is well known, is widespread in a number of foreign countries. For example the French physician Bernheim looked upon the mechanism of hypnosis as self-suggestion. The French neurologist, Charcot, regarded hypnosis as a pathological state. The Austrian neurologist, Freud, considered that the effect of psychotherapy depended on the disclosure and abreaction of so-called repressed instincts, unconscious desires (sexual), of childhood conflicts which had not been acted out (psychoanalysis).

The *Popular Medical Encyclopedia* states:

Psychotherapy is treatment by influencing the patient psychologically. In the wide sense of the term the whole behaviour of the physician during the process of treatment may be included under psychotherapy, also the influence on the patient of his surroundings, a correct régime in therapeutic institutions and the removal of unfavourable factors which traumatise the patient in his life and at work, rest, new experiences, positive emotions etc. In the narrower sense of the term psychotherapy is treatment by means of explanation, persuasion, *suggestion* and *hypnosis*. Psychotherapy is only effective when the personality of the patient as a whole is carefully studied, together with the history of his life and illness. The very fact of the doctor carefully listening as the patient relates how he fell ill and what he felt, often brings great relief to the patient, especially the neurotic. Psychotherapy is carried out individually and in groups.

Several methods of psychotherapy can be distinguished. The most widely applied is treatment by means of suggestion. Suggestion may be used both in the hypnotic and in the waking state. Explanatory psychotherapy takes the form of repeated sessions with the doctor during the course of which the patient has explained to him the nature and cause of his illness, of the symptoms of which he complains and also has explained the measures which will be taken to deal with his present state, also how the patient should behave and what attitude he should adopt to his illness and treatment. The basis for an optimistic prognosis for the illness and for fitness for work is also explained. Explanation and persuasion always contain, to a greater or lesser extent, an element of suggestion. Depending on the character of the illness explanatory psychotherapy may prove more effective than suggestion (for example in psychasthenia). In other cases it may supplement and be combined with suggestion. Explanatory psychotherapy is based on Pavlov's teaching, according to which the word is for man an all-embracing stimulus, since for him the word is linked with all stimuli coming from the external and internal world. . . .

Soviet psychotherapy based on Pavlov's work includes the principles of protection, activation and correction. Psychotherapy reveals to the patient the causes of his illness, it removes factors which are traumatic and weaken the resistance of the organism, it facilitates the development of adaptation and helps to combat the disease. Psychotherapy is extremely valuable, not only in neuroses (in some of which it is the main form of treatment), but also in conjunction with other forms of treatment in many general disorders.

Technique

It is notoriously difficult to express on paper the techniques used in psychotherapy, and apprenticeship is essential to learning them. Published material is for this reason relatively scanty, in so far as it deals in a practical manner with what actually happens at the therapeutic interview. Partly on this account, reports of work in this field undoubtedly emphasize differences rather than similarities in psychotherapeutic technique between the Soviet Union and methods used in other countries. A great deal of what is taken for granted in the account of therapy is common to all therapists.

Korolev (1962) may be quoted as an example. He reports thirty-six patients whom he saw in the department of psychiatry of the second Moscow medical institute and whose neurosis he attributed to exhaustion and overwork. The majority of these patients were students, many of whom were in employment as well as pursuing their studies. Treatment included prescription of rest, advice as to régime, use of sedatives and "explanatory psychotherapy". The reader is left to fill in for himself the form which this last component might have taken and also to assume from his knowledge of similar clinical problems that it was this element in the treatment which was most effective.

It is interesting to contrast this paucity of reported technical detail in psychotherapy with work in remedial education by Luria and his school and by others in the educational field. Slavina (1957) gives an excellent account of methods and results in dealing with backward pupils, using the example of arithmetic. She shows how it is possible to alter a negative emotional attitude to school work to a positive one by presenting the learning process in the form of a game or play activity. She also shows that by reverting to a concrete method, using counters, it is possible to establish basic number sense and that the transition to abstract work can be made by introducing graded, intermediate steps, e.g. by asking the child to carry out a simple exercise in mental arithmetic with his back turned to the counters, but allowing him to turn round for help to the counters if he gets into difficulties.

If one subscribes to the view which stems from Pavlovian physiology that neuroses are learned behaviour, albeit inefficiently learned from the standpoint of the health of the organism, it seems reasonable to equate remedial education with psychotherapy. Certainly, much of the best-documented Soviet work in this field is carried out under the aegis of the education authorities. Luria and Yudovich (1959) give a detailed and very readable account of their work with a pair of twins, who suffered from developmental retardation and impairment of the evolution of speech. They considered that the twin situation favoured limited and abnormal speech, since the twins were satisfied with each other and had a reduced tendency to communicate with others. Developing Luria's views on the organizing role of language, the authors concluded that the fact that at the age of 5 years the twins could neither master skills nor organize complex play of a kind proper to children of this age was due to their linguistic retardation. They therefore placed the children in separate, parallel groups in a kindergarten. When separated, the primitive speech which had previously distinguished the children gave place to a normal communication system and this was accompanied by the rapid development of constructive play. Special remedial sessions given to one twin produced an improvement in his thought processes, as compared with his brother.

Luria (1963) further develops his views on the organizing role of speech in relation to the mentally retarded child. Among other things, he considered that there is a disturbance in the ability of the nervous processes in mental retardation. This is an aspect which has been much studied by Pavlovian physiologists. In this connection, he uses the term "pathological inertness", i.e. the learned set of responses becomes sluggish and is not easily amenable to any alteration. Some aspects of this work and the application of Pavlovian methods have been analysed in detail by O'Connor and Hermelin (1963) whose findings do not exactly coincide with those of Luria, but agree with him in some of his major findings.

Soviet science has developed very rapidly and has undergone radical changes in a brief time. In some directions, its successes are manifest. In some respects, however, it would appear that harm has been done by undue dogmatism, as in the case of the Lysenko controversy. It seems possible that psychiatry may also benefit from the present encouragement of diversity of approach and concreteness of appraisal. Because of the general appreciation in the Soviet Union of the value of Pavlov's contribution to neurophysiology, and because of the fact that Pavlov had provided a rationale for sleep therapy in terms of protective inhibition, there was a tendency a few years ago almost to prescribe sleep therapy as a panacea for psychiatric ills. There are signs now that this enthusiasm is tempered by caution. If there is one aspect of Soviet society which deserves to be singled out for special mention, it is the emphasis on and belief in the value of education. Against this background, it is only logical to expect that in the treatment of psychiatric problems, psychotherapy, which may be looked upon as remedial education, should receive special emphasis. Beilin (1954), in his popular (and somewhat uncritical) exposition of the value of sleep therapy, quotes Mayakovsky—"The spoken word is the commander of human forces", and adds—"Why do doctors make so little use of it in medicine?"

References

BEILIN, P. (1954) *A Story About One Big Family*. Moscow, p. 98.

Bolshaya Sovietskaya Entsiklopediya (1955) Vol. 35. Moscow, p. 246.

BRIDGER, W. H. (1964) *Pavlovian Conditioning and American Psychiatry*. New York, p. 195.

EYSENCK, H. J. (1960) *Behaviour Therapy and the Neuroses*. Oxford.

FROLOV, Y. P. (1938) *Pavlov and his School*. London, p. 214.

KERBIKOV, O. V. (1961) *The Teaching of Psychiatry in the USSR*. In: WHO, Public Health Papers 9, p. 159.

KERBIKOV, O. V. (1964) *Klin. Med. (Mosk)* **5**, 3.

KOROLEV, V. V. (1962) *Zh. Nevropat. Psikhiat.* **62,** 716.

LURIA, A. R. and YUDOVICH, I. A. (1959) *Speech and the Development of Mental Processes in the Child*. London.

LURIA, A. R. (1963) *The Mentally Retarded Child*. Oxford and London, p. 195.

MIASSISCHEV, V. N. In: WINN, R. (1962) *Psychotherapy in the Soviet Union*. London, p. 3.

O'CONNOR, N. and HERMELIN, B. (1963) *Speech and Thought in Severe Subnormality: an Experimental Study*. London.

PAVLOV, I. P. (1941) *Conditioned Reflexes and Psychiatry*. New York, p. 171.

PLATONOV, K. (1959) *The Word as a Physiological and Therapeutic Factor*. Moscow.

Popularnaya Meditsinskaya Entsiklopediya (1961) Moscow, p. 882.

ROKHLIN, L. (1959) *Soviet Medicine in the Fight Against Mental Diseases*. London.

SLAVINA, L. S. (1957) In: SIMON, B. (Ed.), *Psychology in the Soviet Union*. London, p. 205.

WINN, R. (1962) *Psychotherapy in the Soviet Union*. London.

CHAPTER 3

Some Statistical and Cybernetic Models
in Recent Russian Psychology

P. M. A. Rabbitt

M.R.C. Applied Psychology Unit, Cambridge

THE achievements of Soviet technologists in engineering, in the cybernetics of electronic guidance systems, and in the physical sciences generally, are very remarkable and extremely well publicized. It might be expected that engineering psychology would also be a flourishing discipline in the U.S.S.R., basking in the prestige of these successes, and borrowing models for human behaviour from the theoretical systems on which they are based. This is not yet the case. The purpose of this review is to suggest some reasons for the disparity between the development of engineering psychology in Russia and in the West, and to document some vigorous attempts by Soviet investigators to close this gap during the last five years.

Fortunately, it is unnecessary to attempt to give an adequate account of the present state of engineering psychology in Russia. Periodical issues of conference abstracts (e.g. Lomov, 1964) and of volumes of collected papers (e.g. Smirnov, 1962; Anan'ev and Lomov, 1963) are comprehensive guides to the range and directions of this work. An excellent hand book on *Engineering Psychology* (eds. A. N. Leont'ev, V. P. Zinchenko and D. Iu. Panov, 1964) has chapters by most of the leading Soviet investigators, and will provide an orientation point for the literature for some time to come. This article was undertaken with a much more modest hope: by drawing the attention of British and American readers to easily available references bearing on current theoretical problems, to arouse their interest in a literature they cannot any longer afford to neglect.

Reviewing the state of Soviet psychology for 1953–5 Professor Smirnov (1957) particularly regretted the relatively weak development of engineering psychology in view of the increasing number of human engineering problems associated with designing control systems and training operators to use them. These economic arguments are further pressed by Soviet reviewers in the early 1960's. K. L. Leont'ev, A. Ya. Lerner and D. A. Oshanin (1960) stress the practical importance to the increase of national productivity of the study of the tasks required of human operators of automatic control systems, and comment that Soviet psychology is less developed in this area than in others. They also make the point that the study of control problems tends to bring about confrontations between psychologists, engineers, mathematicians and physiologists, and so may prove important in changing the direction of thinking in Soviet psychology. Investigation of the Soviet literature of this period reveals a great unanimity on the practical benefits to be derived from the study of engineering psychology, but also a feeling that there are theoretical objections which must be taken seriously before models based on cybernetics are adopted. These objections are of two kinds: Firstly, authors such as Leont'ev and Panov (1962) find it necessary repeatedly to affirm that the adoption of cybernetic models is completely consistent with the materialistic basis of Soviet science. In other words, that this is not an attempt to smuggle a Western ghost into the Marxist machine. A second, more pervasive and important source of diffidence is that the use of cybernetic models marks a movement away from the principles of Pavlovian psycho-physiology which have provided the theoretical basis for so many striking achievements, and which have been so thoroughly incorporated into the canon of Marxist-materialistic behaviourism. The beginnings of a drift away from pure Pavlovian principles in Soviet psychology were detected by O'Connor (1961) some time ago. Before considering experimental work it may be useful to briefly review some recent theoretical papers expressing dissatisfaction with the Pavlovian theoretical context, and suggesting alternatives drawn from probability theory, cybernetics and communications engineering.

The Replacement of Pavlovian Theory

As developed in Soviet Russia, Pavlovian theory is a powerful and subtle attempt to relate the enormous diversity of observed behaviour to a few atomistic hypothetical physiological constructs, principally to the reflex arc and to localized excitation and inhibition in the C.N.S. Precisely because the theory attempts to interrelate behavioural and psychological evidence in such detail, and on such a scale, it is vulnerable to objections at many different levels. For some time there have been signs that the shortcomings of classical Pavlovian theory were being patched out by the introduction of concepts such as positive and negative feedback (Anokhin, 1961) and other analogies drawn from cybernetics (Luria, 1962). Critical emendations to classical Pavlovian theory have been undertaken with great conceptual rigour, and include classical models of how the task of theoretical reconstruction should be undertaken (Konorski, 1948). However, there are signs that many physiologists and psychologists now prefer to move towards entirely new theoretical positions rather than to accept the conceptual restrictions implicit in attempts at modification. Recent discoveries in neurophysiology (Letvin *et al.*, 1959; Hubel and Wiesel, 1962; Rosenblith and Vidale, 1962) resulting from techniques of recording from single cells in the brains of living animals, point to systems for the analysis of perceptual data which are far too complex to be dealt with adequately in terms of these simple constructs. This has been repeatedly stressed by Nebilitsin, whose discussions of neuro-physiological systems have been very influential in drawing the attention of Soviet workers to cybernetic concepts (e.g. Nebilitsin, 1964). This type of material has also recently been commented on in a Soviet psychological journal by B. F. Anan'ev (1963). A second line of criticism of Pavlovian theory is that it has ceased to provide a descriptive system into which the observed complexities of behaviour can be integrated. N. A. Bernstein has been a persistent critic from this standpoint. Over the last 20 years Bernstein has studied the skilled movements made by human beings in walking, running and athletics by means of "kinocyclograms"—successive photographic exposures on a single plate—and by cinephotography. He has been able to record, in great detail, the ontogeny of walking from the first, awkward, energy-wasting movements of infancy to the complex integrated skills observed in adults who dynamically adapt their movements to complex changes in stresses to adjust to different types of surface and gradient, and to prosthetic devices such as artificial limbs. Bernstein points out that in order to make skilled movements adjusted to rapidly changing conditions human beings must operate on the basis of continuous sensory information ("feedback") from receptors in the muscles of their limbs. Bernstein insists that the processes of dynamic adaptation to rapidly changing conditions are too complex to be described in terms of any simple scheme of reflexes. Two recent theoretical papers (Bernstein 1961, 1962) review these criticisms in terms of alternative models provided by cybernetic theory. Bernstein remarks that it is conventional, in Western human engineering, to speak of the human operator of a control system as an enigmatic "black-box" which cannot be opened for direct investigation. The contents of the "box" must be deduced from correlations between the input (signals) fed into it and the output (responses) which emerge. Bernstein suggests that this analogy implies a misleading view of the organism as a "passive" link in a communications system. In fact, he says, human beings obtain their information by actively operating on their environments. A skilled movement implies the existence of a "plan" of an unrealized event somewhere in the brain. Such a "plan" is a prediction by the organism of a state of affairs which it is necessary for it to bring about. The control of skilled movements must involve a constant monitoring of the predicted or planned outcome against the actual state of affairs. In carrying out this process the organism is actively seeking certain types of information and ignoring others—in fact is "interrogating" its environment.†

It is perhaps true that problems of perceptual and motor set have received less than due attention in recent Western experiments, and readers will recall quite similar criticisms put forward by Bartlett in lectures during the 1940's, and more recently by Miller *et al.* (1960).

Pavlovian "reflex-arc" theory also fails to fit the complexity of behaviour observed in the direction and distribution of attention. I. M. Feigenberg (1963) points out that physiological phenomena associated with subjects' responses to sudden changes in their environments have been described, in the terminology of classical Pavlovian conditioning theory, as "orientating reflexes". Feigenberg considers a number of objections to regarding these attentional responses as conditioned-reflex systems. For example, unlike all other reflexes, orienting reflexes may occur to the *absence* of a signal. That is, orienting responses to sounds presented at regular intervals will gradually extinguish, but will reappear if the sequence is broken and an expected sound does *not* occur. Again, unlike other reflex responses, the strength of the orienting reflex is not directly related to the strength of the signal which triggers it. Subjects habituated to repeated presentations of a loud sound will show an increase in intensity of orientating responses if a softer sound is substituted. Feigenberg argues that in these and other cases the organism responds to a discrepancy between its prediction, or expectation, and the actual event. Feigenberg suggests that the brain may be regarded as a system continually forming, testing and modifying probabilistic models of

† In passing it should be mentioned that this represents a line of argument frequently encountered in Russian philosophico–psychological discussions. For example, it is one of the main arguments in favour of the adaption of cybernetic (feedback) analogies put forward by Oshanin and Panov (1961). The concept that learning takes place through the interaction of the human subject with his environment, and especially through his active operation upon it, seems to be a direct link with Marxist political philosophy (e.g. V. I. Lenin in *Materialism and Empirio-criticism*, a point for which the writer is indebted to Dr. N. O'Connor).

the environment. Theoretical systems modelling brain function are therefore more appropriately sought in probability theory and in the principles of analogue computer theory, than in systems of the Pavlovian type.

Another line of criticism based on the inadequacy of simple forms of Pavlovian "stimulus-response" connectionism as explanatory models for complex observed behaviour, will also be familiar to Western readers. Russian investigators working with animals have tended to study sophisticated elaborations of the classical conditioning situation rather than to investigate more complex, sequentially organized types of behaviour. A. V. Napalkov (1962) uses the concepts of "linear" and "tracking" programmes to describe chains of operant responses developed by rabbits and pigeons to meet environmental constraints introduced by the experimenter. Napalkov makes the interesting point that all learned behaviour cannot possibly be stored in terms of separate chains of stimulus-response connections, since this would demand a fantastically large memory capacity. He suggests, instead, that animals learn interchangeable programmes of behaviour to meet certain contingencies, and branch from one programme to another as appropriate environmental cues occur. Napalkov also points out that an animal is responsive to selected cues in his environment only at some times (e.g. when under the influence of specific types of deprivation) and not at others. When under appropriate deprivation the animal will engage in active search for cues incorporated in learned chains of behaviour. None of this is novel, or surprising, to readers familiar with ethological theory, or indeed with any part of the main body of Western animal experimentation. However, it is interesting that Napalkov selects as a model a system bearing strong resemblances to that proposed by Deutsch (1960). His transition from reflex-arc to cybernetic analogies thus short-circuits an entire series of intervening models which have occupied Western workers during the first half of this century.

Arguments in favour of the adoption of cybernetic analogies ancilliary to those mentioned above also follow lines familiar to

Western workers. The study of engineering psychology is advocated because the development of new control systems demands precise knowledge about the limitations of the human operator as an information-processing system. A possible technique is to consider the human operator as a link in a man–machine system, and to assess his performance in terms of metrics developed for the study of the communications and control systems of which he is a part. The most frequently used metric for describing the load placed on human operators in these situations is the theory of information transmission, which assesses performance in terms of the degree of correlation of the input states (signals, etc.) between which an operator has to discriminate, with the output states (responses) into which he must translate the information he obtains. The following section reviews some recent Soviet work on the application of this theoretical framework to the study of human psycho-motor function.

Applications of Information Theory
to Perceptual-motor Skills

Humans operate machines as various as cranes, typewriters and jet aircraft. The description of an operator as a link in a "man–machine system" is an unproductive analogy unless a common metric can be established to compare the demands made by such disparate tasks. The usefulness of information theory as a descriptive metric of performance in a wide variety of situations is now widely accepted by Western workers (Garner, 1962). Leont'ev and Krinchik (1961) review the development of information theory in the context of Western experimental psychology, and make some important criticisms derived from the standpoint of Pavlovian S-R connectionism. They point out that information theory has been legitimately used as a metric for describing the variance in a set of signals presented to subjects, and for assessing the degree of correlation between the signals which subjects receive and the responses which they make in reply. They argue, however, that this is only appropriate where all signals have equal "importance" (as distinct from frequency). They consider that the concept of signal "importance", for instance, cannot be quantified in informational terms.

In a subsequent paper Leont'ev and Krinchik (1962) describe a series of experiments in which subjects were given two-choice response tasks in which information-load was varied by adjusting the probability of occurrence of each signal. It was found that, in general, Reaction time $= a + bH$, where H was the average information of a signal. Leont'ev and Krinchik make the important point that reaction-time (RT) does not vary with the signal probabilities imposed by the experimenter, but rather with a subject's hypothesis as to what these probabilities are (i.e. what is the statistical structure of the sequence). They make the further interesting suggestion that responses to an infrequent signal are slowed because of an "orientational reflex" to a rare event. To demonstrate that RT is affected by factors other than signal information load they undertook an experiment in which subjects were instructed to respond particularly fast to the infrequent signal, being penalized by having to repeat a run when they exceeded a previously-determined "fast mean" RT. Subjects responded faster to this "emergency" signal than in previous (non-emergency) runs, and the mean RT for all responses fell below that obtained when "emergency" instructions were not given.

Leont'ev and Krinchik's (1961, 1962) studies raise the fundamental question as to *why* choice response-time increases with stimulus information load. Their discussion suggests the operation of a different set of factors than those assumed by simple information-theory models such as that offered by Hick (1952), who suggested that subjects might identify signals as the result of a series of successive binary decisions (i.e. by successive dichotomization of the set of possible signals). While Leont'ev and Krinchik's data certainly show a variation in response-time independent of information-load, it is not clear how this result is to be interpreted. For example, their subjects were more practised in the "emergency signal" runs than when they experienced the earlier conditions against which their "emergency" performance is compared. Further, the motivating effects of a penalty for slow responses (repeating conditions) might be expected to improve performance independently of any change in subjects' information-processing strategy.

Arguments similar to Leont'ev and Krinchik's (1961, 1962) are used by Ushatova (1964) in a direct attack on information processing models of the type suggested by Hick (1952). Ushatova's experiment incorporated the interesting variation that subjects made the same response to all members of a variable set of equiprobable signals. Other similar signals occurred, to which they did not respond. Again, responses to a verbally designated "emergency" signal were faster than to other members of the set. It is interesting that Ushatova's data suggest that while response-times to the "emergency" signal are lowered, response times to the other signals in the set are increased. This leaves her findings open to interpretation in terms of the "successive dichotomization model" which, among others, she would wish to reject. For instance, a subject in her experiment might begin his dichotomization by making the decision "is it the emergency signal or one of the others?" If it is *not* the emergency signal he would then go on to decide whether it was a member of the set to which he had to respond, or one of the set of signals to which no response was required. This strategy would imply that responses to signals other than the "emergency" signal would be delayed. This simple form of the "successive dichotomization" hypothesis is open to experimental verification, since the amount by which "non-emergency" signals are delayed should be independent of the number of signals between which the subject has to choose. However large the set of "non-emergency" signals may be, the delay should always be the time required for the decision "is it the emergency signal or one of the others?" To the knowledge of the writer no such experimental test has been made.

A model for choice-response processes proposed by Ushatova (1964) shows a similar preference for an explanatory system related to the balance between excitation and inhibition, and so also to the Pavlovian context. In the experiment described above, subjects faced a display of 12 signal lamps, any one of which might be switched on. During different conditions of the experiment the subject was instructed to respond if any lamp, in verbally designated sets of 2, 4, 6, 8 or 10 lamps, was switched on. The subject made the same response to any lamp in the designated (relevant) set, but did not respond if any of the other lamps came on. Ushatova found that reaction time increased with the number of signals in the relevant set. This increase was monotonic if plotted against the binary logarithm of the number of relevant signals for 2 to 8 alternatives (that is, it was directly proportional to the "information value" of the decision which the subject had to make, expressed in terms of binary numbers). However, when the number of relevant signals was increased to 10 alternatives, a further, disproportionately sharp, increase in response-time occurred. Ushatova interprets her results in terms of an assumption that response-time (RT) is a function of the intensity of the subject's expectancy, and that neural excitatory processes, corresponding to the strength of expectancy, weaken in logarithmic ratio as the number of possible signals over which this expectancy must be "spread" is increased from 2 to 6 or 8 alternatives. Ushatova cites evidence reviewed by Miller (1956) to the effect that the "span of apprehension" or "span of absolute judgement" is limited to a range of from 5 to 9 different signals along any single perceptual dimension. She regards the discontinuity in her data at the transition from 8 to 10 signal alternatives as evidence that different processing techniques must be used by the subject when the number of signal alternatives exceeds the critical range of the "span of apprehension" or "absolute judgement".

Ushatova's results on the times required to classify signals into either of two response categories (relevant/irrelevant) conflict with data recently obtained by Western investigators (Broadbent and Gregory, 1962; Pollack, 1963; Rabbitt, 1959). It is not possible to comment on these differences in view of the lack of information in Ushatova's paper on such points as the relative disposition of the relevant and irrelevant signal lights on the display panel in her various conditions, and the relative frequency of positive and negative *responses* and signals (e.g. if all *signals* were equiprobable all *responses* were not, and vice versa). In spite of these difficulties Ushatova's paper is of great interest for an acute review of the use of informational models in contemporary Western psychology, and for the ingenious model she discusses.

Another objection to the use of information theory as a metric embracing all aspects of the S-R relationship is based on the Pavlovian concept of "the law of force" (i.e. that the strength of a conditioned response is proportional to the intensity of the stimulus which triggers it). A. E. Ol'shannikova (1962) comments that relatively little attention has been paid to the effects of variations in signal strength, or discriminability, upon choice-response time. She describes an experiment in which subjects make choice responses to signal lights of different colours and intensities. The inverse relationship noted between response time and signal strength in simple reaction-time tasks (Pieron, 1919) is also found to apply in a choice-reaction task. Once again ambiguities in the experimental situation preclude comment, but Ol'shannikova's point is well taken in that although the discriminability of signals is known to interact with their information-load (Crossman, 1955) no attention has been paid to cases where subjects must discriminate between signals some of which are easily identified, while others are not. In particular, there is little evidence to predict how RT's to signals within a sub-set maintained at constant relative intensity (discriminability) may be affected by variations in the intensity (discriminability) of other signals, outside this sub-set, to which subjects have also to respond. However, it is likely that Western investigators will favour explanatory models based on recent advances in signal-detection theory (Swets *et al.*, 1961) rather than Pavlovian models for the description of data from such situations.

The concepts of information-theory have proved both useful and disappointing in providing a basis for valid comparison between the demands made on the operator by different types of real-life control situation. For example, the concept that the human operator has a "limited channel capacity" which restricts the speed with which he can make decisions, has surface validity in control situations where it is obvious that there are limits to his efficiency. However, it is extremely difficult, and probably misleading, to attempt to express the complex choices demanded of, say, a jet-pilot in terms of information load (that is, in terms of the number of bits of information which he has to transmit per second). Even in controlled laboratory situations channel capacity (i.e. maximum amount of information which can be transmitted in unit time) has been shown to vary with the precision with which control movements must be made (Fitts, 1954; Annett *et al.*, 1958), with the "compatibility" of stimuli on a display with the responses made to them (Fitts *et al.*, 1953) and with the discriminability of the signals to which they are required to attend (Crossman, 1955). Mowbray and Rhoades (1959) have also made the point that the nature of the relationship between choice-response time and the number of stimulus alternatives is altered considerably by practice.

V. A. Egorov (1965) takes Mowbray and Rhoades' experiment as a starting point for a demonstration that the rate at which human operators transmit information in a complex control task (operating a T.L.I. pilot-trainer) increases with practice. Egorov estimated the information-load for three different types of manœuvre (that is, he calculated how many bits of information must be processed per second in order for the tasks to be correctly completed). Timing of the trainee's performance allowed estimates of rate-of-gain of information to be made for each of these control tasks. Egorov found that early in training information transmission rates were maximal for the simplest manœuvres but that after practice differences in transmission rates for simple and complex control functions were greatly reduced. These results are consistent with recent demonstrations that improvement with practice is greater for incompatible than for compatible S-R situations. Egorov's main interest, however, is to use estimates of trainees' channel capacity as an index of the level of training to which they have advanced, and of their further potential in the training situation. It is interesting to compare this direct approach to the definition of the limits of channel capacity in complex control tasks, with more indirect techniques of measurement pioneered by Brown and Poulton (1961). These investigators have worked on the assumption that variations in the complexity of the demands made on the operator by a main control task (driving a car) are reflected in changes in the efficiency with which operators perform simultaneously-administered subsidiary tasks. This approach has the advantage that it does not beg the question as to how complex control functions varying in terms of S-R compatibility, levels of discriminability of signals, etc., can be accurately quantified and compared in terms of bits of transmitted information.

Application of Communications Theory to Memory

As Zinchenko and Repkina (1964) point out, operators performing complex control functions are seldom in the simple situation of making appropriate responses, in turn, to each of a series of successively presented stimuli. More usually decisions involve responses to connected series of events. In such cases the operator may have to transform information, and store it in his memory for a longer or shorter period, assembling his recollections of series of past signals in order to respond appropriately. Thus in the calculation of channel-capacity for any complex control function we must consider not only the information implicit in the responses which an operator makes and in the signals presented to him, but also the data which he must store. Performance in a variety of situations is known to be severely limited both by the amount of information which a subject can store in immediate memory, and by the time for which he can store it.

This complicates the calculation of information transmission-load, since there is considerable doubt as to whether limitations to short-term memory capacity can be adequately described in terms of information-theory (Miller, 1956; Conrad and Hull, 1964). Discussing this problem Miller pointed out that subjects were able to report back from six to fourteen different items previously presented to them, and that the number of items correctly recalled seemed to be relatively little affected by the size of the vocabulary from which they were drawn (i.e. by their "information value"). Miller suggested that the operational units of memory might not be the "items" presented to the subject by the experimenter, or the "bits" in which their information-value might be expressed, but rather subjectively determined "chunks" into which the subject codes the material. Zinchenko and Repkina (1964) emphasize the importance of investigations of the techniques of coding and grouping practised by operators, and their relative efficiency for material of different kinds. An important experimental investigation of the problem of coding is reported by N. A. Rokotova (1964) who investigated the extent to which subjects learning elementary sequences of operations (switching sequences), which were slightly too long for immediate-memory storage, used natural principals of segmentation of the sequence in order to help their learning.

Rokotova required her subjects to learn 2 programmes of operations on a console of 8 switches. The first programme involved a sequence of 24 operations which could be conceptually divided into 8 groups of 3 operations. The 3 operations within each group were related on the principle that they were made on adjacent switches. A second sequence of 20 operations could be conceptually divided into 4 groups of 5 operations. The 5 operations within each group were related in that their sequence over the console followed the outline of simple geometrical figures. Subjects learnt these sequences, always in the same order, by trial and error. It was never suggested to them that there were any systematic relationships within sequences which might aid their learning. Rokotova observed during the course of the experiment that subjects showed an immediate-memory span for about 2 groups of 3 operations in the first sequence, or for 1 group of 5 operations in the second. Within each conceptual group of operations the incidence of errors during training was highest for the first operation and lower for subsequent operations. The conditional probabilities for making correct responses were analysed at different stages of practice. It emerged that subjects tended to successfully complete groups which they had begun correctly very early in practice. At this stage in practice the conditional probabilities for successfully completing runs of 3 (sequence 1) or 5 (sequence 2) operations, calculated at points other than the beginnings of "natural" groups, were relatively low. Rokotova's data thus demonstrate that subjects recognized these grouping principles early in practice and used them to "organize" their learning.

Rokotova makes another interesting point by comparing the error-incidence in these two experiments with that theoretically predicted by a mathematical model for the serial position effect put forward by Feigenbaum and Simon (1962). For both Rokotova's sequences the congruence between predicted and empirical error-distribution curves is excellent while the *groups* of 3 or 5 operations are considered as the units to be learnt. Rokotova shows that in the second sequence of 20 operations a serial-position error-distribution curve based on single *operations* appears as a sequence of 4 successive bow-shaped curves, each corresponding to 1 of the 4 successive groups of 5 operations. In this case the theoretical predictions from Feigenbaum and Simon's model for the serial position curve based on single *operations* bears no resemblance to the observed results.

Rokotova's results are thus more than a striking demonstration that subjects organize their learning by detecting and using logical principles of coding. Her data emphasize that mathematical models for memory processes can only be successfully applied where the experimenter is confident that he knows the conceptual strategy which the subject employs to organize the material presented to him. Naturally there can be no guarantee that all subjects will use the same conceptual strategy, or that any one conceptual strategy will be used for different types of material. It would be even more interesting to know the relative efficiencies which different strategies permit, and hopefully also to determine what aspects of the material presented lead to the selection of one or other conceptual strategy.

Models for Perceptual Discrimination

Since the publication of Hebb's *Organization of Behaviour* in 1949 a number of probabalistic models for perceptual processes have been put forward. Such models predict both for relatively simple situations, in which subjects are required to discriminate the presence or absence of a signal in noise (Swets *et al.*, 1961), and also for cases where subjects identify complex stimuli, unseen details of which may be extrapolated from perceived cues (Fitts *et al.*, 1956). In identifications of complex stimuli much attention has been paid to the problem of redundancy, and it is recognized (Attneave, 1955, 1959) that subjects discriminate between complex stimuli most efficiently when they learn to recognize and use a small number of cues, which represent critical points of difference, and to ignore others which are misleading or irrelevant to the discriminations required of them.

E. N. Sokolov (1960) follows a similar line of reasoning in stressing that perceptual discrimination is an active process in which subjects may deliberately form and test successive hypotheses until they optimize their performance by discovering, and using, the irreducible minimum of cues. Sokolov demonstrated this by an ingenious experiment in which blindfolded subjects palpated the surface of a 5×5 matrix. Some of the twenty-five cells in the matrix were filled with counters. The patterns of filled cells corresponded to letters of the Russian alphabet between which subjects had to discriminate by touch. Photographic records made during learning allowed Sokolov to observe four stages in the development of this skill: In the first stages of learning all the cells in the matrix were rapidly scanned in some more-or-less ordered sequence. Later the letter represented by filled cells was rapidly located, and its outline briefly traced with the fingers. Sokolov found that this process of outline scanning became progressively more economical until the letter was recognized before its entire outline was traced. Finally, the subject might learn to tactually "test" only the crucial three or four cells which represented the irreducible minimum of cues necessary to discriminate between the letters of the set on which he was practised.

This interesting technique has been extensively applied by Sokolov and Arana, who report their findings in a series of papers in *Dokladi Akademia Pedagogicheski Nauk* for 1961 and 1962. One of Sokolov and Arana's most important findings was that the cue-systems used in tactual and visual discrimination of letters are very similar, demonstrating the generality of the concepts of cue-selection and the elimination of redundancy on which so much recent work has been based.

The study of tactual perception is an area of research uniquely developed in Soviet psychology in contrast to its relative neglect in the West. The reason for Soviet interest in this field is not simply that a subject's activity may be easily recorded in such situations, but rather that the process of tactual search is a concrete demonstration of the theoretical position that a subject "interrogates" his environment by forming and testing successive hypotheses about it (Sokolov, 1960; Bernstein, 1961, 1962). More recent treatments of tactual perception in the Soviet literature tend to employ models drawn from the theory of linear programming to describe the flow of theoretical "optimum" search-programmes. These theoretical programmes may then be compared with the activity actually observed. A. V. Parachev (1963) discusses a sophisticated and complex breakdown of tactual search in programme form; he suggests techniques by means of which subjects may reduce the amount of information which they have to store by using selected features of the test object as reference points, and by relating them to a coordinate system for the hand. It is a natural extension of this line of thinking to examine the search-techniques reflected by eye movements made during the inspection of complex objects. A. L. Yabus (1961) discusses techniques of eye-movement recording, and compares the visual scanning techniques which he has observed with the scanning of objects in tactual search. This parallel between visual and tactual scanning strategies is supported by some important developmental evidence: for example, V. P. Zinchenko (1960) has shown that techniques of visual and tactual search are gradually built up during ontogeny from the random scanning procedures adopted by children aged from 3 to 5 years, to systematic and efficient search programmes observed in adults.

The recording of eye movements during perceptual-motor skills is of particular interest in revealing some of the details of the learning process underlying improvement with practice. V. P. Zinchenko and B. F. Lomov (1960) discuss the development of visual scanning techniques by subjects learning a four-alternative choice-response task in which signal lamps were mounted behind a frosted-glass screen, so that some experience was necessary before their exact positions could be learnt. These signal lamps were switched on in an invariant time-sequence, and Zinchenko and Lomov observed that the subject's initial random scanning of the screen developed, with practice, into a series of accurate fixations anticipating the appearance of each lamp in turn. While this result is not unexpected, the implications of the study of active visual scanning during performance of skilled tasks are far from trite. Western workers will regret that these techniques have not yet been adapted to obtain data on eye movements made during the performance of choice-response tasks in which the order of appearance of stimuli is not constant. For example, it would be particularly nice to know the relationship between the time taken by a subject to respond to a signal, and his direction of regard when the signal occurs. This information would be especially interesting in situations where signals appear with unequal frequency, and where it might accordingly be useful for the subject to modify his scanning strategy according to his estimate of the relative probability of occurrence of the signals presented to him.

Another possible relationship between tactual and visual search strategies is discussed by R. M. Granovskaya and V. A. Ganzen (1964), who consider whether subjects may not only obtain information about perceived objects from their retinal representations, but may also use feedback from the eye-muscle movements which they must make in order to follow the contours of large objects. These authors offer a model for this process in the form of a programme for the recognition of two-dimensional figures by a hypothetical computing system which obtains feedback from two sets of (muscle) receptors monitoring systems controlling ocular tracking along horizontal and vertical axes. Granovskaya and Ganzen also consider in detail systems of code-compression and information-filtering which might allow such a system to discriminate amongst the letters of the Russian alphabet with maximum efficiency. Recent work on visuo-perceptual models (e.g. Selfridge and Neisser, 1957; Green, 1963) has convinced many Western investigators that the formulation of such hypothetical programmes is not only an essential stage in the development of electronic "perceptual" systems, but may also serve to draw attention to constraints on human perceptual coding.

The optimistic goal of all perceptual models is the achievement of some integration between the increasing amount of neurophysiological data now available and the observed phenomena of perceptual behaviour. An attempt to do this on a restricted scale is described by I. M. Tonkonoghu and I. I. Zuckerman (1965) who offer some information-processing models to account for symptoms observed in patients suffering from auditory and visual agnosia related to known brain damage. Two different types of disability are considered. First the authors describe patients who show relatively little impairment when allowed to inspect test objects for an unlimited time, but who show marked deterioration in performance when required to recognize complex stimuli briefly presented to them in a tachistoscope. These authors suggest that this defect may be described as a restriction in the rate-of-gain of information in the visuo-perceptual system. While issue may be taken with the suggestion that the effects of reduction in stimulus exposure duration in tachistoscopic perception are best described in terms of stress on the channel-capacity of the visuo-perceptual system, the marked differences in performance between normals and patients under these conditions are extremely interesting, and reminiscent of similar effects (Wallace, 1956) observed in subjects aged over 60 years (who, of course, also may suffer from some degree of brain-damage).

D

Tonkonoghu and Zuckerman consider a second interesting disability in other agnosic patients who fail to recognize photographs of common objects on which visual "noise" from a television system is imposed. They consider this defect to be a demonstration of a decrement in the patients' ability to integrate information from the component details of a picture presented in this way. They point out that this failure, which they term filtration agnosia, cannot be related to the efficiency of the eye and peripheral visual system since isolated details of the picture may be adequately perceived and reported. They suggest that the ability to integrate information is dependent on some form of short-term store. When this store does not function the subject can grasp isolated details one at a time but cannot build up an integrated percept from many, successively perceived details. Tonkonoghu and Zuckerman found that these visual phenomena are paralleled in cases of auditory agnosia apparently related to temporal damage. For example, they observed that some patients' detection thresholds for pure tones remained unaffected in quiet, but were disproportionately increased, relative to the thresholds of normal subjects, when tones were presented to them against a background of noise. Tonkonoghu and Zuckerman also describe two patients with auditory agnosias who were unable to understand or to repeat back sequences of words, but were nevertheless able to correctly repeat phonemes. They point out that if the basis of the perceptual process is the matching of input against traces of stored information it would, of course, be impossible for subjects to keep in long-term storage an almost infinite range of traces corresponding to all possible combinations of perceptual input. Consequently it must be necessary for perceptual input to be stored briefly in a way which allows selective analysis for critical cues. Damage to such a system would prevent subjects from integrating the wide range of cues which must be considered in order to identify complex stimuli. Tonkonoghu and Zuckerman make the interesting suggestion that short-term storage of this type may be specific to the particular perceptual analyser system involved, since patients suffering from agnosias in one modality (hearing or vision) may attempt to compensate by re-coding information in terms of imagery appropriate to the unaffected modality. These data thus provide a most interesting example of the way in which models drawn from communication theory can be applied to explain changes in performance resulting from known neurological damage.

Speech Perception

The perception of speech implies the use of an extremely elaborate and highly practiced system of coding auditory signals, and is therefore in many senses a paradigm for all psychomotor skills. The work of L. A. Chistovitch and her colleagues at the Pavlov Institute of Physiology at Leningrad is becoming increasingly well known in the West. Interested readers will find a complete account, with a bibliography, in the text edited by V. A. Kozhevnikova and L. A. Chistovitch (1965). The following brief description of some of Chistovitch's recent experiments which bear on the interpretation of recent British work must suffice for the present review.

Subjects are usually considered to have "recognized" speech when they can reproduce the meaningful content of sequences of words which they hear, either in their own words or verbatim. L. A. Chistovitch, A. A. Aliakriuski and V. A. Abul'an (1960) describe an attempt to determine the time-lag between the presentation and verbatim repetition (shadowing) of continuous speech. Eight subjects with normal hearing were required to shadow continuous discourse (newspaper text, etc.) presented to them through headphones. The speech presented to them was also fed through one channel of an ink oscillograph, which recorded a trace corresponding to the sound "envelope". The subject's speech (shadowing) was simultaneously recorded on a second channel of the same oscillograph. Thus the lag between presented and shadowed speech could be determined by comparison of the two oscillograph traces. Errors in shadowing were detected from tape recordings of the subject's output.

Chistovitch *et al.* found that their subjects responded in one of two characteristic ways. Five subjects repeated the text with considerable time-delay $(0 \cdot 5-1 \cdot 5$ sec) and with very few errors. The remaining three subjects shadowed speech with a very brief delay (150–250 msec). In many cases these subjects actually anticipated the sounds presented to them. However, while words were not omitted from continuous discourse, the three fast subjects reproduced the speech sounds presented to them less accurately than the subjects in the first group. When these subjects were subsequently questioned about their performance they stated that they had been repeating the speech "without understanding it" (i.e. simply imitating the noises they heard). The authors point out that the response latencies recorded for this group (150–250 msec) fall well within the limits of simple response time, whereas the degree of congruence of their responses with the complex input they shadowed suggests that they were transmitting information at a rate as high as in many choice-response tasks. This question was further examined by requiring two subjects from the fast group to shadow isolated speech sounds (vowels, consonants and vowel-consonant pairs). In separate conditions these two subjects were instructed either to simply "imitate" the noises they heard, or to repeat them "with understanding". In spite of these rather subjective instructions differences in latency similar to those observed in the first experiment were again obtained. It emerged that subjects made $13 \cdot 1\%$ and $11 \cdot 0\%$ errors when "imitating" sounds presented to them, but that they considerably improved on this when "repeating with understanding" $(4 \cdot 1\%$ errors over both subjects).

In further series of experiments (Chistovitch, 1960; Chistovitch and Klass, 1962) it was shown that the latency for verbal imitation is significantly shorter than for other types of reaction (for example, beginning to write the presented words on a plate wired to record the first contact of a stylus, etc.). It further emerged that subjects "imitating" speech remembered what had been said to them very poorly indeed, while subjects "repeating with understanding" did quite as well as would be expected from results obtained from other immediate memory experiments.

Chistovitch's data may be compared with results obtained by
Davis, Moray and Triesman (1961), who found that subjects
required to imitate nonsense syllables presented to them one at a
time showed no increase in response time when the vocabulary of
nonsense syllables was greatly increased. Chistovitch prefers to
present her results as support for the motor theory of perception
(Liberman, A. M., et al., 1962) according to which processes employed in the articulation of speech sounds are also involved in its
perception, and some form of covert "imitation" is assumed to
provide the basis for decoding of the phonemic content of speech.
A more conservative viewpoint would be that her data reaffirm
the necessity for regarding the perceptual analysis of speech as a
multi-stage process, which the subject can carry to any limit con-
venient to him. Cherry (1953) and Triesman (1964) have separately
shown that subjects required to ignore one of two simultaneously-
presented monologues manage to shadow the other very efficiently if languages differing in phonemic characteristics are simultaneously presented. In other words the subjects do not require to
carry analysis of the rejected voice further than an identification
of its phonemic characteristics. If allowed to do this they can discriminate between the voices quickly enough for their "shadowing" of the relevant voice to be unimpaired.

The important suggestion that latency of imitation may be relatively independent of rate of gain of information cannot be assessed
until further evidence is available. For example, Chistovitch (in
Kozhevnikova and Chistovitch, 1965) makes the points that subjects imitating continuous speech often anticipate sounds which
the speaker has yet to emit, and that errors are more frequent in
"imitated" speech than in speech shadowed "with understanding".
It thus seems probable that subjects use their acquired knowledge
of the transitional probabilities implicit in the phonemic structure
of a language in order to reduce the number of cues which they
need to consider in the material presented to them. Similarly
results of Davis et al. (1961) cannot be fully assessed, since it is not
clear whether their subjects withheld their responses only long
enough to identify the first phoneme of the nonsense syllable

presented to them, and whether actual increases in response time with variations in the vocabulary of presented nonsense-syllables might not have been concealed by overlapping of the processes necessary to decode the syllable and to produce a response to it.

Another experiment reviewed by Chistovitch *et al.* (in Kozhevnikova and Chistovitch, 1965) can also be used as support for the idea that speech-perception is a multi-stage process in which subjects can adjust the coding strategies which they employ in order the better to resolve ambiguities in the presented material. In this study short phrases from three to twelve words long were read to subjects through an attenuating device which filtered out frequencies below 906 and above 1141 cycles. Subjects naturally made errors in reporting back these phrases, and in many cases the errors were found to involve the entire phrase, so that the subject would offer a meaningful sequences of words different to that which was read to him. Examination of such errors showed that for 79 short phrases the erroneously reported equivalents contained the same number of words in 68 cases and contained the same number of syllables in 57 cases. This effect was also clearly apparent for longer sentences. Russian is a highly accented language, and the investigators found that the words which were misreported by the subject seemed to have been selected with the constraint that their stresses fell in the same positions as the stresses in the presented words. In many cases stresses in erroneously reported words were misplaced to correspond with the stress positions in the presented material. As the authors remark, this must mean that although the reported phrases are incorrect, they represent attempts by subjects to synthesize phrases within constraints operating at least at the level of single words, and probably at the level of entire phrases.

As might be expected Chistovitch's data illustrate that the syntactic constraints upon a word increase with its rank-order within a phrase; also, words more recently heard are better remembered. Chistovitch's data also nicely illustrate the importance of immediate memory span in the decoding of ambiguous sequences, since she finds that the probability of correct report for individual words within a phrase slightly rises as phrase-length increases from three to seven items, and thereafter sharply declines. As Chistovitch *et al.* point out, the use of longer time-samples for decoding may be expected to improve the accuracy of reports, since the number of constraints within which reports must be fitted are accordingly narrowed. However, when the sample-size is greater than short-term memory capacity this advantage no longer applies, and information may be lost through forgetting.

Conclusion

The main purpose of this review has been to present evidence for a change in the direction of Soviet work in applied experimental psychology. A detailed comparison of Soviet achievements with Western work would be a pointless exercise in scientific chauvinism. The application of models drawn from control and communications systems to psychological processes was begun, in the West, more than 20 years ago in an intellectual climate perhaps more sympathetic to their rapid adoption. Reviews in Soviet journals leave no doubt as to the comprehensiveness with which the Western experience has been assimilated, nor as to the vigour and acuity of Soviet critics. A great deal of valuable experimentation is sure to follow during the next few years.

Obviously it is an excellent thing that Soviet and Western workers should begin to consider the same problems in the same terminology. Some optimistic predictions of benefits to both scientific cultures may be considered. In adopting mathematical models for the descriptions of psychological processes Soviet workers are likely to become more aware of the possibility of increasing the value of the data yielded by their experiments by using appropriate statistical techniques. This, in turn, may improve the care with which experiments are designed and described. The striking ingenuity of the conceptions motivating much Soviet experimental work is often negated for the reader by his frustration in failing to discover what was actually done. As Soviet workers increasingly enter the field of applied experimental psychology they are also sure to become sensitive to the necessity for improving the reliability of their data by the use of precautions such as balanced experimental designs, equivalent degrees of practice for all subjects in all conditions, the use of control groups and so on. An increasing discipline in Soviet journals in these respects is already detectable, and is very desirable.

However, all these criticisms are picayune in view of some very positive aspects of Russian work. Specifically, one would hope that Western authors may be increasingly influenced to pay attention to individual differences in performance, to examine the variability of performance under certain conditions as well as its consistency in others, and to take an interest in developmental topics such as the ontogeny of skills. More generally, Russian workers show a critical rigour combined with readiness for broad speculation, a preference for witty over pedantic experiments and a drive to synthesize behavioural with physiological evidence that are certain to prove major contributions to a common scientific culture.

Acknowledgement

The writer is glad to acknowledge considerable help from Dr. N. O'Connor and Dr. J. Brozek in obtaining and selecting amongst the Soviet literature, and from Dr. R. Conrad for patient advice in preparation of the manuscript.

References

Russian

ANAN'EV, B. F. (1963) Bilateral'noye regulirovaniye kak mekhanizm povedeniya. *Vop. Psikhol.* **5**, 83–98.

ANAN'EV, B. G. and LOMOV, B. F. (Eds.) (1963) *Problemi Obshei i Industrial'noi Psikhologii.* Izd. Leningradskovo Univ. 156 pp.

BERNSTEIN, N. A. (1961) Puti i zadachi fiziologii aktivnosti. *Vop. Filosofii* **6**, 77–92.

BERNSTEIN, N. A. (1962) Novie linii razvitiya v fiziologii i ikh sootnoshenie s kibernetikoi. *Vop. Filosofii* **8**, 78–87.

CHISTOVITCH, L. A. (1960) Vospriyatie zvukovoi posledovatel'nosti. *Biofizika* **5**, 671–6.

CHISTOVITCH, L. A. and KLASS, IU. A. (1962) Kanalizy skritovo perioda "proizvol'noi" reaktsii na zvukovor signal. *Fiziologicheskii zhurnal SSSR* **48**, 899–906.

EGOROV, V. A. (1965) O propusknoi sposobnosti operatora kak pokazatele trenirovannosti i slozhnosti vipolnyaemoi raboti. *Vop. Psikhol.* **1**, 3–8.

FEIGENBERG, I. M. (1963) Veroyatnostnoi prognozirovanie v deyatel'nosti mozga *Vop. Psikhol.* **2**, pp. 59–67.

GRANOVSKAYA, R. M. and GANZEN, V. A. (1964) O roli motornovo zvena zritel'noi sistemi pri opoznanii ob'ekta po vneshnomu konturu. *Vop. Psikhol.* **1**, 66–82.

KOZHEVNIKOVA, V. A. and CHISTOVITCH, L. A. (Eds.) (1965) *Rech, Artikulatsia i Vospriyatie*. Moscow, Izdatel'stvo "Nauka". 243 pp.

LEONT'EV, A. N. and KRINCHIK, E. P. (1961) O primenenii teorii informatsii v konksetno—psikholegicheskikh issledovaniyakh. *Vop. Psikhol.* **5**, 25–46.

LEONT'EV, A. N. and KRINCHIK, E. P. (1962) O nekotorikh osobennostyakh protsessa pererabotki informatsii chelovekom. *Vop. Psikhol.* **8**, 14–25.

LEONT'EV, A. N. and PANOV, D. IU. (1962) Psikhologia cheloveka i tekhnicheskii progress. *Vop. Filosopii* **8**, 50–65.

LEONT'EV, A. N., ZINCHENKO, V. P. and PANOV, D. IU. (Eds.) (1964) *Inzhenernaya Psikhologia*. Iz-vo. M.G.U. Moskva, 1964.

LOMOV, B. F. (Ed.) (1964) *Problemi Inzhenernoi Psikhologii Leningradskoe Otd. Obshestva Psikhologov.* Len. Dom Nauchno-tekh. Propagandi. 174 pp.

LURIA, A. R. (1962) *Visshiye Korkoviye Funktsii Cheloveka.* Izd. Moskovskovo Univ. 432 pp.

NEBILITSIN, I. K. (1964) Ch. VI in *Inzhenernaya Psikhologia*, eds. Leont'ev, A. N., Zinchenko, V. P., and Panov, D. Iu, izd.-vo. M.G.U., 1964.

PARACHEV, A. M. (1963) Ob algaritmicheskoi strukture aktivnogo osyazaniya. *Vop. Psikhol.* **1**, 67–79.

OL'SHANNIKOVA, A. E. (1962) Vliyanie prodol'zhitel'nosti raboti na zavisimost' vremeni reaktsii ot intensivnosti zritel'nikh signalov. *Vop. Psikhol.* **6**, 52–61.

OSHANIN, D. A. and PANOV, D. IU. (1961) Chelovek v automaticheskikh sistemakh upravleniya. *Vop. Filosofii* **5**, 47–57.

ROKOTOVA, N. A. (1964) Nekotorie elementi organizatsii posledovatel'nosti deostvii pri reshenii chelovekom zadachi otiskania puti v labirinte *Vop. Psikhol.* **2**, 112–24.

SMIRNOV, A. A. (Ed.) (1962) *Voprosi Psikhologii Obucheniya trudu.* Izd. Akad. Pedag. Nauk R.S.F.S.R. Moskva. 260 pp.

TONKONOGHU, I. M. and ZUCKERMAN, I. I. (1965) An information theory approach to perceptual disturbances. *Vop. Psikhol.* **1**, 83–92.

USHATOVA, T. N. (1964) K ponimaniu "zakona Hicka". *Vop. Psikhol.* **6**, 56–64.

YABUS, A. L. (1961) Drizhenie glaz pri rassmatrivanie slozhnikh ob'ektov. *Biofizika* **6**, 207–12.

ZINCHENKO, V. P. (1960) Sravnitel'novo analiz osyazaniya i zreniya. Soobshchenie II. Osobennost orientirovochoi—isslodovatelhikh dvizhenii glaz v detei doshkol'nikov. Dokladi Akad. Pedag. Nauk R.S.F.S.R. **2**.

ZINCHENKO, P. I. and REPKINA, E. V. (1964) K postanovke problemi operativoi pamyati. *Vop. Psikhol.* **6**, 3–12.

English

ANNETT, J., GOLBY, C. W. and KAY, H. (1958) The measurement of elements in an assembly task—the information output of the human motor system. *Quart. J. Exp. Psychol.* **10**, 1–11.

ANOKHIN, P. K. (1961) A new conception of the physiological architecture of the conditioned reflex, pp. 189–227 in *Brain Mechanisms and Learning*, J. F. Delafresnaye, Ed. Oxford: Blackwell.

ATTNEAVE, F. (1955) Symmetry, information and memory for patterns. *Amer. J. Psychol.* **68**, 209–22.

ATTNEAVE, F. (1959) *Applications of Information-theory to Psychology.* New York: Holt, Rinehart & Winston.

BROADBENT, D. E. and GREGORY, MARGARET (1962) Human responses to classes of stimuli. *Nature* **193**, 1313.

BROWN, I. D. and POULTON, E. C. (1961) Measuring the "spare" capacity of car drivers by a subsidiary task. *Ergonomics* **4**, 35–40.

CHERRY, E. C. (1953) Some experiments on the recognition of speech with one and with two ears. *J. acoust. Soc. Amer.* **25**, 976–7.

CHISTOVITCH, L. A., ALIAKRINSKI, A. A. and ABUL'AN, V. A. (1960) Time delays in speech repetition. *Problems of Psychology* **1** and **2**, 64–70.

CONRAD, R. and HULL, AUDREY (1964) Information, acoustic confusion and memory span. *Brit. J. Psychol.* **55**, 429–32.

CROSSMAN, E. R. F. W. (1955) The measurement of discriminability. *Quart. J. Exp. Psychol.* **7**, 176–95.

DAVIS, R., MORAY, N. and TRIESMAN, ANNE (1961) Imitative responses and the rate of gain of information. *Quart. J. Exp. Psychol.* **13**, 78–89.

DEUTSCH, J. A. (1960) *The Structural Basis of Behaviour.* Cambridge Univ. Press.

FEIGENBAUM, E. H. and SIMON, H. A. (1962) A theory of the serial position effect *Brit. J. Psychol.* **53**, 307–20.

FITTS, P. M. and SEEGER, C. M. (1953) S-R compatibility: spatial characteristics of stimulus and response codes. *J. Exp. Psychol.* **46**, 199–210.

FITTS, P. M. (1954) The information capacity of the human motor-system in controlling the amplitude of movement. *J. Exp. Psychol.* **47**, 381–91.

FITTS, P. M., WEINSTEIN, M., RAPPAPORT, M., ANDERSON, N. and LEONARD, J. A. (1956) Stimulus correlates of visual pattern recognition. *J. Exp. Psychol.* **51**, 1–11.

GARNER, W. R. (1962) *Uncertainty and Structure as Psychological Concepts.* New York: John Wiley.

GREEN, BERT. F. (1963) *Digital Computers in Research.* New York: McGraw-Hill.

HEBB, D. O. (1949) *The Organization of Behaviour.* London: Chapman & Hall Ltd.

HICK, W. E. (1952) On the rate of gain of information. *Quart. J. Exp. Psychol.* **4**, 11–26.

HUBEL, D. H. and WIESEL, T. N. (1962) Receptive fields, Binocular interaction and functional architecture in the cat's visual cortex. *J. Physiol.* **160**, 106.

KONORSKI, J. (1948) *Conditioned Reflexes and Neurone Organization.* Cambridge Univ. Press. 267 pp.

LEONT'EV, K. L., LERNER, A. YA., OSHANIN, D. A. (1960) Some problems involved in studying a "man and automatic machine" system. *Problems of Psychology* **4**, 269–78.

LETVIN, J. Y., MATERANA, H., PITTS, W. H., and McCULLOCK, W. S. (1959). How seen movement appears in the frog's optic nerve. *Federation Proc.* vol. 18, No. 1.

LIBERMAN, A. M., COOPER, F. S., HARRIS, K. S. and MacNEILAGE, P. F. (1962) A motor theory of speed perception. Paper presented at Speed Communication Seminar (Stockholm, 1962).

MILLER, E. A. (1956) The magical number seven plus a minus two. *Psychol. Review* **63**, 881–97.

MILLER, G. A., GALANTER, E. and PRIBRAM, K. H. (1960). *Plans and the Structure of Behaviour*. Henry Holt Inc., N.Y.

MOWBRAY, G. H. and RHOADES, M. V. (1959). On the reduction of choice reaction times with practice. *Quart J. Exp. Psychol.* **11**, 16–23.

NAPALKOV, A. V. (1962) Some principles of brain processes. *Problems of Cybernatics*, IV, 1339–51.

O'CONNOR, N. (1961) Introduction, pp. 9–20 in *Recent Soviet Psychology*, Ed. O'Connor. London: Pergamon Press.

PIERON, H. (1919). *Soc. Biol. Compt. Recd.* **82**, 1116–18, quoted in Woodworth, R. S., *Experimental Psychology*. London: Methuen, 1950.

POLLACK, I. (1963) Speed of classification of words into super-ordinate categories. *J. Verb. Learning Verb. Behaviour*, **2**, 159–65.

RABBITT, P. M. A. (1959) Effects of independent variations in stimulus and response probability. *Nature (London)* **183**, 1212.

ROSENBLITH, W. A. and VIDALE, EDA B. (1962) A quantitative view of neuro-electric events in relation to sensory communication. In: Sigmund Koch (Ed.), *Psychology, a Study of a Science*, vol. 4. *Biologically Oriented Fields: Their Place in Psychology and in Biological Science*. New York: McGraw-Hill.

SELFRIDGE, O. G. and NEISSER, U. (1960) Pattern recognition by machine. *Scientific Amer.*, Aug. 1960.

SMIRNOV, A. A. (1957) Psychological Research, 1953–5, pp. 29–45 in *Psychology in the Soviet Union*, Ed. Brian Simon. London: Routledge & Kegan Paul.

SOKOLOV, E. N. (1960) A probability based model of perception. *Problems of Psychology* **1** and **2**, 102–16.

SWETS, J. A., TANNER, W. P. and BIRDSALL, T. G. (1961) Decision processes in perception. *Psychological Review* **68**, 301–40.

TRIESMAN, A. M. (1964) The effect of irrelevant material on the efficiency of selective listening. *Amer. J. Psychol.* **77**, 533–46.

WALLACE, J. G. (1956) Some studies of perception in relation to age. *Brit. J. Psychol.* **47**, 283–97.

ZINCHENKO, V. P. and LOMOV, B. F. (1960) The functions of hand and eye-movements in the process of perception. *Problems of Psychology* **1–2**, 12–26.

CHAPTER 4

Abnormal Psychology in the U.S.S.R.

R. LYNN

Department of Psychology, Exeter University

As in Russian physiology and psychology, so in abnormal psychology, the impact and influence of Pavlov has been exceedingly powerful. Although a number of Western observers have detected a lessening of this influence from the middle 1950's, Pavlovian theory is still the framework within which problems are viewed and remains "the cornerstone of Soviet psychiatry" (Wayne, 1961). Consequently, some general acquaintance with Pavlovian concepts and theory is vital for an understanding of Russian work in this area.

Pavlov's contributions to abnormal psychology are of two main kinds. Initially, his work was concerned with studying the laws of the formation of conditioned reflexes in dogs and from time to time he noticed that the conditioned reflexes were disrupted by various stresses. He called these disruptions "experimental neurosis". He thought of them as simple analogues of human neuroses and he was concerned with working out the principles governing their occurrence. When he had achieved some understanding of experimental neurosis in dogs, he began to turn his attention to human beings suffering from neurosis and psychosis and attempted to apply the same laws to the psychiatric illnesses of human beings.

The work on experimental neurosis began quite early in the century. The first observations appear to be those of Yerofeeva (1916). She used an electric shock as a conditioned stimulus to

92

elicit salivation and established conditioning successfully. But when the electric shock was applied to another part of the body, the normal generalization effect did not occur. Instead, the animal showed alarm and excitement. Even when the original shock was applied the conditioned reaction could not be obtained. In one dog it could not be restored at all, and in another only after 3 months' further training (Pavlov, 1927). This initial experiment illustrates the essential criterion of Pavlovian experimental neurosis: the disruption of conditioned behaviour patterns.

In further experiments, it became evident that experimental neurosis could be produced in other ways. Eventually, five principal means of obtaining the breakdown were obtained:

1. *Intense stimuli.* Following the work of Yerofeeva, whose results are probably to be explained in terms of the intensity of electric shock as a stimulus, more extensive work using intense stimuli was reported by Rickman (1928). The stimuli he used included loud rattles, explosions, and a platform on which the dog stood which began swinging. At the conclusion of these alarming events it proved impossible to elicit any conditioned responses from the dog for a fortnight. In the Leningrad floods in 1924, the animal house was badly flooded and several of the dogs nearly drowned, and this also disrupted previous conditioned behaviour patterns, in some cases for several years.

2. *Delay.* A second way of obtaining neurotic breakdown was to increase the time interval between the presentation of the signal and of the food. Dogs can typically tolerate delays of the order of 5 seconds, but delays of 2 minutes or more are liable to induce breakdown.

3. *Difficult discriminations.* This method involves conditioning the dog to make a reaction to one signal and not to a somewhat similar one. Intermediate stimuli are then presented and these induce the breakdown. Possibly the most famous of all Pavlovian experiments falls in this group. This is the experiment of Shenger-Krestovnikova (1921), who conditioned a dog to salivate to the presentation of a circle but not to an elipse. The dog was trained to make finer and finer discriminations by making the elipse

progressively more circular, and eventually broke down when the discrimination became impossible.

4. *Alternation of positive and negative stimuli.* The animal is trained in a discrimination task and the positive and negative stimuli are continually alternated.

5. *Physical stress.* The final way of producing breakdown is to subject the dog to physical stresses such as castration. Breakdown also occurred very readily after fever and gastro-intestinal disorders.

Having isolated the conditions which produce the breakdowns, Pavlov began to pay attention to the exact forms which the disruption of the conditioned behaviour took. He made two important contributions here. First, he described three stages in the abnormal reactions which occur as the stresses become more severe. At the beginning of breakdown the dogs display "equivalent" reactions, in which the strength of the response does not correspond to the strength of the stimulus, as is normal. Instead, the dog gives equivalent and weaker reactions to all stimuli. The second stage is the "paradoxical", in which weak stimuli produce strong responses, while strong stimuli produce weak responses or none at all. Finally comes the "ultraparadoxical" phase, in which positive stimuli (to which the animals have been trained to respond) elicit no reaction but negative stimuli (to which the animals have been trained not to respond) elicit a reaction. Sargant (1957) compares the last stage to the reactions of human beings in brainwashing, where a system of beliefs which had previously evoked negative reactions of rejection are suddenly accepted.

Pavlov's second contribution to the details of breakdown lay in his theory of personality types. He noticed that some dogs broke down much more readily than others, and also that when the breakdown came it could take two forms. Some animals became highly excited and over-reacted to a wide variety of stimuli while others became quiet and passive and failed to react. Pavlov thought that his dog breakdowns were simplified versions of human breakdown, at any rate in some cases. There has been some difference of opinion in the rest of the scientific world on this matter. One of the fullest discussions is given by Broadhurst (1960), who examines the dog breakdowns in the light of Hebb's (1947) six criteria for neurosis, namely that the behaviour should be undesirable, emotional, generalized, persistent, statistically uncommon, and with no origin in gross neural lesion. Broadhurst concludes that, taking the experiments as a whole, they fulfil these criteria in so far as the dog's behaviour was undesirable, persistent and not due to a known neural lesion. Broadhurst feels there is doubt about whether the disturbance was emotional, generalized and statistically abnormal. These doubts arise mainly from sheer lack of information in the reporting of the experiments and it may well be that dog breakdowns do in fact fulfil the criteria on these points.

Broadhurst's discussion represents a very balanced judgement between psychoanalytically minded psychologists and psychiatrists, who tend to think Pavlov's work has little relevance to human neurosis, and others who press the similarities very hard. A prominent writer among these is Sargant (1957), who likens the dog breakdowns especially to those which human beings suffer in war (as a result of shell shock, for example) and during brainwashing. He argues that the techniques of brainwashers—among whom he includes psychoanalysts and evangelical religious preachers—involve one or more of the five principles of breakdown that Pavlov discovered. For example, the terrors of hell-fire threatened by evangelicals in England in the nineteenth century and in the United States today make the victim afraid in the same way as intense stimuli do in Pavlov's experimental situation. Further, in human neurosis and brainwashing the previously established habits and beliefs are likely to disappear and be replaced by new ones. Sargant's argument is an extremely interesting one and justice cannot be done to it here. It is mentioned to show that there are prominent Western psychiatrists who think Pavlov's findings have very close relevance to human behaviour and beliefs.

Pavlov's Theory

Now that Pavlov's main factual observations have been discussed, we can turn to his theoretical contributions. His many experiments on conditioning led Pavlov to formulate theories about the way the nervous system worked. These theories and later work on them will only be summarized briefly here. First, he assumed two nervous processes of excitation and internal inhibition, the first responsible for initiating and sustaining activity and the second for damping it down. Many individuals have these two processes in more or less equal strength and are then said to be in "equilibrium". However, some dogs and people can have a predominance of one or the other, a predominance of excitation making the subject quick, alert, irritable, hyperactive, aggressive, etc. These characters are *choleric* in the terminology of Hippocrates' fourfold division of personality types, and in human beings extreme cases suffer from mania, of which the chief symptoms are extreme restlessness, irritability and grandiose ideas. Predominance of internal inhibition produces an opposite type, although Pavlov held that this is less common.

A second important theoretical assumption of Pavlov was the process of protective inhibition, which must be carefully distinguished from the internal inhibition discussed above. Protective inhibition is a process generated by excessive or prolonged stimulation and its function is to protect the nervous system from overstrain. It reduces nervous activity and may act against both excitatory and internal inhibitory processes. Pavlov supposed that some dogs and humans generate protective inhibition more readily than others and he described these as subjects with *weak* nervous systems, as opposed to *strong* nervous systems in which protective inhibition is only generated after considerable stimulation and stress. The effect of protective inhibition is to make the subject unreactive, apathetic or tired. (It should be noted that this is not the same as having an excess of internal inhibition, which allows the subject sufficient energy although of a controlled kind.) Pavlov identified the weak nervous system subject with Hippocrates' *melancholic* type, and in human beings this type of person is predisposed to schizophrenia and the neuroses. This part of the theory is in line with the fact that schizophrenics and neurotics do tend to suffer, at any rate at times, from apathy, tiredness and listlessness. The other three Hippocratic types—sanguines, phlegmatics and cholerics—all have strong nervous systems although they differ among themselves in other ways.

The postulation of protective inhibition which underlies this personality dimension has not found much favour with Western psychologists. It should, however, be noted that some recent

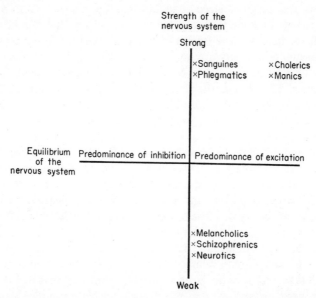

Fig. 2. Pavlov's type theory in two-dimensional form showing positions of the four Hippocratic types and of mania, schizophrenia and neurosis.

progress has been made in Russia towards identifying this hypothetical substance with low phosphorus and ammonia levels in the nervous system (Kreps, 1957; Sytinsky, 1956; Vladimirova, 1953).

Before proceeding to further refinements in Pavlov's theory it may be helpful if the theory thus far is summarized as a two-dimensional system along the lines that have become familiar in the work of Eysenck. The theory as analysed in this way is shown in Fig. 2.

As illustrated in this figure the theory does not differentiate the sanguine and phlegmatic types, nor schizophrenics from neurotics. The sanguines and phlegmatics are distinguished in terms of the *mobility* of the nervous system, i.e. the speed and ease with which a subject can switch from the excitatory processes to the inhibitory ones and vice versa. For example, the speed with which one is able to go to sleep at night (entailing a switch from predominance of excitation to predominance of internal inhibition) might be taken as a reflection of this characteristic. Some people of normal excitability are able to relax and get to sleep quickly. This type of person has good mobility and Pavlov called them *sanguine*. The *phlegmatic*, as the name indicates, has difficulty in shifting from excitation to inhibition and vice versa.

The distinction between schizophrenics and neurotics, and between the different kinds of neurotics, is somewhat more complicated and involves the introduction of a fourth and final personality trait or dimension. This is the relative predominance of the first or second signalling systems. These terms need some explanation. Pavlov noted that the senses of sight and hearing do not themselves convey to us the horrors of pain or the delights of food, drink and sex—the "primary reinforcements" of Western behaviourism. The eye and the ear were evolved because they give us warning that primary reinforcements are in the offing and enable us to take action to avoid or approach them. Pavlov called these warnings "signals", so that when, for example, we notice a tiger the sight or sound of him serves as a signal for us to protect ourselves before we actually feel his bite, the primary (negative) reinforcement. Vision and hearing constitute Pavlov's "first signal system" and have undoubtedly been of great help to animals in their struggle for survival.

However, human beings are unique in having evolved a second signal system, that of language. Pavlov called language the second signal system because words frequently stand for the sights and sounds of the first signal system. It is very useful to man to have a second signal system of this kind. For example, a friend may shout "tiger" before the animal actually gets close enough for us to see or hear him; or we may read "dangerous corner" on a road sign before we actually see the corner itself. In this way Pavlov argued that words act as signals of signals and hence he called language the "second signal system".

Another advantage of the second signal system is that it summarizes a number of experiences derived from the first signal system. For example, the word or shout "danger" summarizes a lot of possible events with one important thing in common. At a more complex level statements like "the free enterprise system is the most efficient way of running an economy" or "nationalization is the most efficient way of running an economy" are also attempts to summarize a lot of actual observations made through the first signal system. But while these verbal summaries of experience are very useful it is also important that once they have been made they can be modified in the light of additional experience. It is here that Pavlov thought there are characteristic personality types. On the one hand there are those who act impulsively and do not check their actions against experience accumulated in the second signal system. These are people in whom the first signal system predominates over the second. They may be simply impulsive people but artists may be of this type. But when a person of this type also has a weak nervous system and is consequently prone to neurosis, the type of neurosis he develops is hysteria with its characteristically impulsive outbursts of emotion. The other extreme is dominated by the second signal system, that is by words and logical systems which are insufficiently checked against experience. This type is the doctrinaire intellectual who clings to his verbal theories in the face of contrary experience. This type, if it occurs in conjunction with a weak nervous system, is likely to develop the form of neurosis called psychasthenia, i.e. obsessional, compulsive and anxiety neurosis. A third type of neurosis is neurasthenia, consisting of excessive feelings of tiredness, and this occurs in people of weak nervous system whose first and second signal systems are well balanced. This type of neurosis does not differ basically from schizophrenia, although Pavlov did suggest nervous mechanisms accounting for the different symptoms of schizophrenia and neurasthenia. Pavlov's theories of neurosis are shown in dimensional form in Fig. 3.

Before we leave Pavlov's theory a note of warning should be sounded. Pavlov wrote a number of essays over a considerable space of years on personality types and mental illness and his hypo-

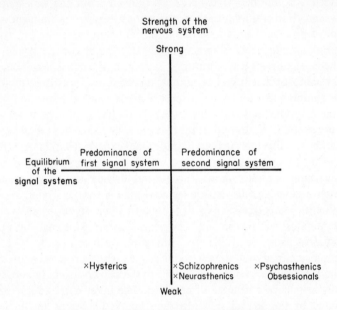

FIG. 3. Pavlov's type theory in two-dimensional forms distinguishing different types of neurosis and schizophrenia.

theses were not always consistent. It is possible to find in some of his works statements which contradict the scheme of his theory presented here. The most important of these is probably another hypothesis that neurasthenics have a predominance of excitation and hysterics of inhibition, a theory which Eysenck has taken up and extended considerably (Eysenck, 1957). However, the form of Pavlov's theory presented here is the one which (in the writer's opinion) occurs most consistently in Pavlov's writings.

Pavlov's Successors

Since Pavlov's death, his successors have followed closely the framework he laid down and have been concerned for the most part with extending his theories and verifying them in detail. There has been a great deal of work on the sympathetic nervous reactions of patients with different types of mental illness. When people are stimulated, for example, by flashes of light, hot and cold pricks, tones, etc., they give a number of physiological reactions which are together called "the orientation reaction" and consist of an increase in heart rate, a pause in breathing, sweating in the palms of the hands, dilation of the pupil of the eye, and constriction of the blood vessels in the hands together with dilation of those in the head. These reactions have been studied a great deal by Russian workers and it has been found that they have a number of peculiarities in mentally ill patients. There are three broad kinds of abnormality. First, the sympathetic reactions may be very large and take a long time to extinguish with repeated stimulation. This type of reaction is found in the early stage of acute schizophrenia and in neurotics. It is also found in patients whose cerebral cortex has suffered some kind of damage or impairment, notably in patients with brain injury, in senility, in idiots and imbeciles, alcoholics and patients with infectious psychoses. The explanation of these large orientation reactions is that the subcortex is released from the inhibiting control of the cortex.

The second type of disorder of the orientation reaction is its weakness or absence. The majority of schizophrenics and depressives show this type of reaction, together with some mental defectives. The explanation is that the protective inhibition which in the first group has only affected the cortex has in this group spread to the subcortex and impaired it too.

The third and final group of mentally ill patients does not give orientation reactions at all but instead gives "defensive reactions". These correspond to a large degree but not entirely to what are called "startle reactions" in the West. The subject reacts with fear instead of interest and there is a different physiological pattern of reactions including vasoconstriction in the head. These defensive reactions have been found in some cases of schizophrenia, usually in patients with paranoid delusions, and also in some cases of infectious psychosis. More detailed discussion of Russian work in this area can be found in the writer's article on Russian experimental studies of schizophrenia (Lynn, 1963).

Where neurosis is concerned, a number of recent writers have moved away from Pavlov's emphasis on nervous types and begun to regard neurosis as the outcome of the faulty learning of social relationships and adjustment (Miasishchev, 1955; Zachepitsky and Yakovleva, 1956). These writers take a fairly similar view to those psychologists in the West who have applied conditioning and reinforcement theory to the problems of neurosis (e.g. Dollard and Miller, 1950; Eysenck, 1960). According to this view, children learn techniques for dealing with others and with the problems of life during the course of their upbringing and these techniques are learned to a considerable extent as a result of the kinds of discipline imposed on them by their parents. Various inadequacies in parental upbringing and especially in the kind of behaviour parents reinforce are likely to lead to neurotic character formation. For example, Miasishchev (1955) takes the view that if the parents are too permissive the child learns that he can behave exactly as he pleases and fails to learn to tolerate boredom and sustained effort and to respect the convenience of other people. In extreme form this type of upbringing may produce the inadequate psychopath. At the other extreme, excessively severe demands are likely to produce over-anxious neurotics.

A similar view is expressed by Zachepitsky and Yakovleva (1955). They consider that the hysterical personality develops as a result of excessive parental attention or from too much frustration; neither of these parental attitudes are conducive to the child's learning to make sustained realistic efforts to deal with its problems. Neurasthenia (feelings of fatigue and weakness) is likely to result where the parents have made excessive demands on the child; the child becomes over-anxious about the standards imposed on him and if he cannot fulfil these demands his anxiety produces the neurasthenic symptoms.

Zachepitsky and Yakovleva discuss five case histories of neurotics in which they attribute the symptoms to faulty upbringing. One case is a hysteric who displayed selfishness, egocentricity and lack of determination. The authors point to his over-indulgent parents who rewarded his temper tantrums and applied inadequate discipline. Another case is that of a pathologically shy girl. Her parents continually denigrated her abilities, restricted her play with other children, gave her no household responsibilities, etc., and thus built up her shy personality. This school of Russian psychiatrists takes an essentially common-sense view of neurosis which is in sharp contrast to the esoteric psychoanalytic approach of many psychiatrists and psychologists in the West, especially in the U.S.A. The recent Western behaviour therapy movement is much more closely in line with the Russian viewpoint.

Treatment

Pavlov viewed treatment as a matter of getting rid of the excessive protective inhibition which disrupts behaviour in schizophrenics and neurotics. His chief contribution here was his use of sleep in treatment. The theory behind this was that the patient has suffered from too much strain and stimulation which have led to the generation of excessive protective inhibition, and that given rest and time the protective inhibition will dissipate by itself. Once a patient has excess protective inhibition, fairly small amounts of stimulation will generate further protective inhibition and keep the illness going. In order to let the patient recover Pavlov recommended extreme quiet, protection from stimulation of all possible kinds, and prolonged sleep. His recommendations have been carried out on an extensive scale in Russia and Russian psychiatrists are pleased with the results although in recent years sleep therapy has been partly replaced by the tranquillizing drugs. At the present time prolonged sleep is induced by drugs, hypnosis, low frequency and intensity electric current delivered to the head, and by a conditioning method in which the patient is made to perform slight rhythmic movements with his arm and at the same time count these or imagine he is swimming and falling asleep. Several psychiatrists have recently reported success with these methods on schizophrenics, neurotics (especially those suffering from exhaustion, depression, anxiety and phobias), and on patients with psychosomatic disorders including hypertension, peptic ulcer and asthma (Andreev, 1960; Lustig, 1963; Davidenkov, 1953; Gorbatsevich, 1955; Sidorova, 1953).

Apart from the use of sleep, Russian psychiatrists also give extensive drug therapy to schizophrenics. The drugs are similar in general type to those used in the West, insulin and chlorpromazine being most commonly used. But the variety of drugs in use is considerably less, because of the absence of competing drug firms in the U.S.S.R. There are advantages and disadvantages to the more limited range of drugs in Russia, psychiatrists gaining in depth of experience with one drug at the expense of a loss of range of experience with many. The most common assumption about the mode of operation of chlorpromazine is that it reduces nervous activity in the reticular formation and thereby reduces reticular stimulation of the cerebral cortex. In this way, it is thought to have a similar effect to sleep in reducing strain on the cortex.

Although these drug treatments in Russia follow those in use in the West, there are two directions in which treatment takes a somewhat novel form. The first of these is the use of hypnosis and persuasion in the treatment of neurosis (Platonov, 1959). The neurotic symptom is removed by suggestion, persuasion, discovering the cause of the neurosis by going over the patient's history, and by hypnosis. Treatment by hypnosis is more effective if the original frightening event can be discovered and fears of it removed directly by hypnotic suggestion. The patient is simply hypnotized and told that he will no longer suffer from the neurosis after he has come out of the hypnotic trance. Platonov claims successful treatment by this means of many neurotic symptoms, including a case of being hopelessly in love. This disagreeable complaint took some four sessions to remove, but some neurotic symptoms can be cured in one session. Hypnosis is very little used in the West because of the Freudian theory that the unconscious complex remains untouched by it and simply manifests itself in some other symptom if the original symptom is removed by hypnotic suggestion. This theory, however, has in recent years been strongly disputed in the West by the behaviour therapy movement (Eysenck, 1960), which denies the existence of any underlying unconscious complex in neurosis, and applies conditioning methods to the treatment of symptoms. Platonov's success in treating neurosis by hypnotic suggestion is very much in line with the outlook of the behaviour therapy movement. In some 30 years of use of these methods, Platonov has made follow-up studies of from 1 to 20 years and found no cases at all of symptom-substitution. These observations are some of the strongest evidence at present available against the psychoanalytic movement in its dispute with the behaviour therapists. It should be noted that the Russians have no sympathy whatever with the Freudian approach to the treatment of psychiatric illness.

A second direction in which there is some difference between Russian and Western treatment lies in the greater importance attached to occupational therapy in the U.S.S.R. Indeed, it is considered vital and central to treatment and not, as sometimes in the West, an adjunct which is more or less a luxury. An excellent discussion of Russian work in this area has been written by Wortis and Freundlich (1964). Historically, the importance of work and occupation was emphasized by Korsakov towards the end of last century. In his view the indolence and apathy of many patients was exacerbated by the lack of work facilities at that time, and he considered work therapy beneficial both as a stimulant for chronic patients and as a source of distraction for acute ones. Korsakov's ideas were extensively taken up after the 1917 revolution when work therapy was introduced into all mental hospitals, and with certain vicissitudes it has continued to play an important role up to the present day. In the last decade about 50% of hospitalized psychiatric patients have been engaged in occupational therapy.

In the view of Russian psychiatrists, occupational therapy serves a number of functions. The most important are as follows: it keeps up the patient's level of arousal and alertness; it maintains his normal daily role and routine and prevents chronic deterioration; it distracts him from his disturbing thoughts; it gives him status; it obliges him to work in co-operation with others; it gives him an income; and it maintains or increases his working skills. Occupational therapy is given concurrently with general supportive therapy, i.e. the psychiatrist discusses the patient's problems with him in a kindly way, makes helpful suggestions and encourages him to adjust to the conditions of normal living.

There are a number of different types of work provided in the occupational therapy programme. Arts and crafts facilities are sometimes available but to a much lesser extent than is common in Western hospitals. The most common types of work are routine hospital duties, agricultural work in country districts, and factory work in production shops set up in the hospital grounds or in sheltered workshops. These work programmes have proved extremely valuable in raising the morale of patients.

Summary

Abnormal psychology in the U.S.S.R. remains firmly entrenched in the Pavlovian tradition. Pavlov's own work was concerned with analysing the conditions of nervous breakdown, which he came to regard as resulting from various kinds of overstrain of the nervous system. He went on to formulate theories about individual differences in nervous activity and to explain in terms of them the four Hippocratic personality types and the different kinds of mental disorder. He also made contributions to the treatment of mental illness based on therapy with prolonged sleep.

Pavlov's successors have concentrated on the testing of his theories of the physiological disturbances in mental illness, for the most part confirming them with a wealth of interesting experimental detail. In the treatment of neurotics there have been developments in the use of hypnosis and an increased emphasis on faulty character training during childhood. The treatment of psychotics is now based mainly on the tranquillizers and there is a strong emphasis on occupational therapy involving work.

References

ANDREEV, B. V. (1960) *Sleep Therapy in the Neuroses*. Consultant's Bureau, New York.

BROADHURST, P. L. (1960) Abnormal Animal Behaviour. In: *Handbook of Abnormal Psychology*, Ed. H. J. Eysenck. London: Pitman Medical Publishing Co.

DAVIDENKOV, S. N. (1953) Lechenie neurozom v suete ucheniya Pavlova [Neurosis therapy in the light of Pavlov's teachings]. *Klin. Med.* **31,** 16–25.

DOLLARD, J. and MILLER, N. E. (1950) *Personality and Psychotherapy*. London: McGraw-Hill.

EYSENCK, H. J. (1957) *The Dynamics of Anxiety and Hysteria*. London: Routledge and Kegan Paul.

EYSENCK, H. J. (1960) *Behaviour Therapy and the Neuroses*. London: Pergamon Press.

GORBATSEVICH, A. B. (1955) Uslovno-Reflektornyi metod vyzvaniya normal' nova i gipnotichesckovo sna [The conditioned reflex method of inducing normal and hypnotic sleep]. *Klin. Med.* **33,** 64–65.

HEBB, D. O. (1947) Spontaneous neurosis in chimpanzees: theoretical relations with clinical and experimental phenomena. *Psychosom. Med.* **4,** 3–16.

KREPS, Y. M. (1957) Biokhimicheskie kharacteristiki deyatel'nosti kory bol'shikh polushavii mozga [Biochemical characteristics of activity of the cortex of the larger hemispheres of the brain]. *Zh. Vyssh. Nerv. Deyat. Pavlov.* **7,** 75–80.

LUSTIG, B. (1963) *Therapeutic Methods in Soviet Medicine*. Monographs of Soviet Medical Science, Fordham Univ., New York.

LYNN, R. (1963) Russian theory and research on schizophrenia. *Psychol. Bull.* **60,** 486–98.

MIASISHCHEV, V. N. (1955) *In Materialy Soveshchania po Psikhologii*. 1–6 July 1955. Moscow, Akad. Pedag. Nauk, R.S.F.S.R.

MIASISHCHEV, V. N. (1956) *In Doklady na Soveshchanie po Voprosam Psikhologii Lichnosti*. Moscow, Akad. Pedag. Nauk, R.S.F.S.R.

PLATONOV, K. (1959) *The Word as a Physiological and Therapeutic Factor*. Moscow: Foreign Languages Publishing House.

RICKMAN, V. V. (1928) Narushenie normal'noi nervno'i deyatel'nosti sobaki, vyzv-annoe sil'nikh postoronnikh razdrazhitelei [Disturbance of the normal nervous activity in the dog, effected by powerful extraneous stimuli]. *Coll. Papers Physiol. Lab., I. P. Pavlov*, **3,** 19–34.

SARGANT, W. (1957) *Battle for the Mind. A physiology of conversion and brainwashing*. London: Heinemann.

SHENGER-KRESTOVNIKOVA, N. R. (1921) Voprosy differentsiatsii zritel'nikh razdrazhitelei i predelov differentsiatsii zritel'nym analizatorom [Contributions to the question of differentiation of visual stimuli and the limits of differentiation by the visual analyser of the dog]. *Bull. Lesgaft Inst. Petrograd.* **3,** 1–43.

SIDOROVA, E. V. (1953) Klinicheskoe i patogennoe lechenie v bronkhial'noi astme [Clinical and pathogenic therapy in bronchial asthma]. *Terap. arkh.* **25,** 63–67.

SYTINSKY, I. A. (1956) Izmeneniya adenozintrifosfatn-ou sistemy v Tkanyakh mozga v nazlichnikh funktsional'nikh sostoyatnyakh tsentral'noi nervnoi sistemy (Variations of the adenosine triphosphate system in brain tissues in different functional states of the C.N.S.). *Biokhioniya* **21,** 361–70.

VLADIMIROVA, G. E. (1953) Functsional'naya Bioxhimiya mozga [Functional biochemistry of the brain]. *Fiziol. Zh. S.S.S.R. Sechenov* **3,** 39–43.

WAYNE, G. I. (1961) Work therapy in the Soviet Union. *Ment. Hosp.* **12,** 21–23.

WORTIS, J. and FREUNDLICH, D. (1964) Psychiatric work therapy in the Soviet Union. *Amer. J. Psychiat.* **121,** 123–8.

YEROFEEVA, M. N. (1916) Contribution à l'êtude des réflexes conditionnels distructifs. *C.R. Soc. Biol.* **79,** 239–40.

ZACHEPITSKY, R. A. and YAKOVLEVA, E. K. (1955) *In Materialy Soveshchania po Psikhologii.* 1–6 July 1955. Moscow, Akad. Pedag. Nauk R.S.F.S.R.

ZACHEPITSKY, R. A. and YAKOVLEVA, E. K. (1956) *In Doklady na Soveshchanie po Voprosam Psikhologii Lichnosti.* Moscow, Akad. Pedag. Nauk R.S.F.S.R.

CHAPTER 5

Soviet Psycholinguistics

DAN I. SLOBIN

Department of Psychology, University of California, Berkeley

PSYCHOLINGUISTICS is a relatively recent label for a long-standing concern of psychology—the relations between language and other forms of human behavior. In the years since World War II, American and British psychologists have been stimulated by new developments in linguistics and communications engineering to take a fresh look at the acquisition and use of language and speech. A similar growth of interest in matters psycholinguistic has taken place in the U.S.S.R. To quote the Soviet psycholinguist Zhinkin: ". . . all that has been achieved by objective methods in physiology, acoustics, linguistics, and other sciences studying language and speech in one way or another, should and must become the heritage of psychology, to the extent to which this is necessary for the posing of the properly psychological problem of the mechanism of the communication of human beings" (1959, pp. 647–8*).

History and Theory

Soviet psycholinguistics† is based on deep practical and theo-retical commitment to the study of human communication and

* Page numbers followed by asterisks refer to pages in the English trans-lation of the work cited. (Many of the works cited are available in English translation, as indicated in the References.)

† Although Akhmanova used the Russian translation equivalent, *psikholing-vistika,* in her 1957 summary of American work, this term never caught on in

linguistically-mediated cognition. The practical concerns are (1) technological (machine translation, design of communication equipment, etc.), (2) medical (psychotherapy, treatment of aphasia and other speech and language disturbances, etc.) and, above all, (3) pedagogical. The pedagogical interest stems not only from problems of foreign-language instruction and school curriculum, but, most interestingly, from the practical task of raising infants and very young children in state nurseries. Zhinkin lists fourteen research institutes concerned with problems of psycholinguistics (1959, p. 655*), each of them clearly connected with at least one of these practical concerns. The strong practical bent of Soviet psychology has frequently been noted; the principal of "the unity of theory and practice" is clearly stated in the current handbook of Soviet psychology: "The results of investigations are directed towards life, towards practice; in practice they find their application. Practice is the criterion of the truth of the results of scientific research" (*Psikhologicheskaya nauka v SSSR*, 1959, p. 6).

Deep theoretical concerns, however, also underlie Soviet psycholinguistics. These concerns are reflected in the general history of Soviet psychology. In the twenties, according to Bauer's historical sketch of Soviet psychology (1959), a great deal of emphasis in psychological research in the U.S.S.R. was based on the principles of *mechanical materialism*. Man's behavior was seen to be determined largely by external material forces, and whatever deficiencies were found in his behavior could be blamed on the remnants of bourgeois forces in the environment. The organism was not self-directed, but tried to return to a state of equilibrium when disturbed by forces coming from without. In the middle thirties, however, with the proclamation that socialism had been achieved and social classes abolished, a fundamental change came about in Soviet psychological theory. Defects in behavior were no longer to be referred to defects in the environment. In a period of rapid

the Soviet literature. The cognate area to our psycholinguistics is generally referred to as *psikhologiya rechi*, "the psychology of speech", the Russian word *rech'* generally referring to the production and comprehension of both spoken and written language (cf. Raevskiĭ, 1958).

industrialization, Bauer argues, the society needed an image of an active, self-directed man, who could be held responsible for his own successes and failures.

Consequently, *dialectical*, as opposed to *mechanical* materialism was introduced as the working principle of psychological science, and has remained so to this day. The dialectical aspect of this principle emphasizes that man does not adjust to equilibrium with the environment, but disturbs equilibrium through his own self-generated, or *autogenic* movement. The materialist aspect emphasizes two factors, the physiological, and the socio-historical. First, mental behavior is based on the brain: mental processes are based upon matter which is organized in a certain way. Second, mental processes and their development are ultimately determined by the material conditions of life in a given society in a given historical stage of development.

Soviet philosophical principles of dialectical materialism are tied together in the "Leninist Theory of Reflection", which states that man perceives the universe by acting purposively upon it, thereby reflecting (cf. "reflex") objectively existing external reality in human consciousness. Consciousness is thus introduced as one of the cornerstones of modern Soviet psychology, and language enters as the inalienable material form of consciousness. "The fundamental position of the Marxist theory of cognition is the doctrine of the unity of thought and language. Thought is not 'linked' with language, but is expressed in language. . . . The study of thought outside the bounds of speech, in isolation from speech, is completely impossible" (Lyublinskaya, 1959, p. 354).

Conscious understanding works through human language to free man from a rigid determinism of the material stimuli present in the immediate environment and makes it possible for him to direct his actions towards goals beyond the present situation. There is, accordingly, a large body of psychological research on pragmatic aspects of language behavior—on regulatory, planning, and directive functions of speech.

For Soviet psychological theory the unity of consciousness and activity is best seen in the development of language, both phylo-

and ontogenetically. Frequent reference is made to the proposal of Marx and Engels that language developed as a result of human activity—namely, the need for cooperation in labor. Engel's theory of human evolution was that: "At first labor, and then, together with it, articulate speech, were the two chief stimuli under the influence of which the brain of the ape gradually changed into the human brain . . ." (Kasatkin, 1958, p. 47). This formulation has helped to motivate extensive research on the development of language in the child as a result of social intercourse and practical needs for communication. The basic problem in this area was early formulated by the great Russian psychologist Vygotsky as "the investigation of how a function, arising in communication and at first divided between two people, can re-structure all of the activity of the child and gradually change into the complicated mediated functional system which characterizes the structure of his mental processes" (Luria, 1959b, p. 524).

Soviet psycholinguistic writing is usually cast in physiological, or quasi-physiological terms by referring to Pavlov's formulation of the "second signal system", a formulation which entered psychology under the influence of the important 1950 "Joint Session of the U.S.S.R. Academy of Sciences and the U.S.S.R. Academy of Medical Sciences Dedicated to the Problems of the Physiological Teachings of Academician I. P. Pavlov" (*Nauchnaya sessiya* . . ., 1950). Late in his life, Pavlov came to the conclusion that, although the underlying reflex principles apply to the behavior of all species, the presence of a complex and organized system of linguistic signals in man makes for a new dimension of behavior. In his words: "The word created a second system of signals of reality which is peculiarly ours, being the signal of signals. On the one hand, numerous speech stimuli have removed us from reality. . . . On the other, it is precisely speech which has made us human" (1927, p. 357). "First signals" are all the individual physical stimuli to which animals and humans alike can respond; "second signals" are, primarily, words. They are signals which can stand for all of the separate stimuli of the first signal system. For example, if a human being is conditioned to make a given response to the sounding of a bell, that response can later be elicited, to some degree, by the word "bell", a signal for bells in general, which was not physically present in the original conditioning situation. It is this phenomenon of "semantic conditioning", or "semantic generalization", which first brought the attention of Soviet scientists to the role of language in human conditioning behavior. While second-order conditioning is, of course, possible in other animals, in man the second signal system is vast and organized—it is a *system*. In distinction to stimuli of the first signal system, a word functions not simply as a physical auditory stimulus with certain physical features, but functions as well on the basis of its semantic content, on the basis of its role as an abstracted and generalized stimulus. It is a special sort of stimulus, which is meaningfully connected with other words, and with other material conditions.

The underlying ontogenetic notion here is that the acquisition of language qualitatively changes the nature of the child's behavior in almost all spheres of activity, rendering human behavior *sui generis* in the Animal Kingdom. Quoting Pavlov again: "Of course a word is for man as much a real conditioned stimulus as are other stimuli common to men and animals, yet at the same time it is so all-comprehending that it allows of no quantitative or qualitative comparisons with conditioned stimuli in animals" (1927, p. 407).

Since man can *speak* language, it follows that he can also signal *himself* with words, and thus he is capable of freeing himself from the domination of immediate environmental stimulation. The role of language in directing and mediating other behavior is phrased in terms of "the interaction of the two signal systems". "According to Pavlov, the second signal system, inseparably linked with the first, and developing on its foundation, significantly changes the functioning of the first system. 'Man first of all perceives reality through the first signal system, then he becomes master of reality by means of the second signal system (language, speech, scientific thought . . .)' " (Raevskiĭ, 1958, p. 27).

It should be emphasized that Pavlov and his followers found it necessary to formulate the notion of the second-signal system *just*

E

because they found man to behave differently from other animals in conditioning experiments. Soviet psychologists argue that, because of language, none of the laws of animal conditioning are applicable to human behavior in simple fashion. In particular, they make the following assertions, all of which derive from the sorts of experiments summarized below. In animal learning it is very difficult to transfer responses to stimuli varying along other dimensions than the original conditioning stimuli; conditioned responses are built up gradually; it takes an animal a long time to differentiate the effective stimulus; and responses extinguish (and extinguish slowly) when reinforcement is removed. In man, on the other hand, responses can generalize to a variety of stimuli on the basis of semantic conditioning. What is more, responses can be established immediately and extinguished immediately on the basis of verbal instructions: conditioning in man is *abrupt*. A man can continue responding long after reinforcement has been removed, on the basis of the formulation of a rule, or self-instructions; or a human subject can be brought to change his response to any sort of stimulus simply by being told to do so. Finally, since man can speak, he can set up learning situations for himself. These points are elaborated below.

Semantic Conditioning

"Semantic conditioning" refers to the establishment of conditioned responses to the meanings of verbal stimuli, rather than to their physical attributes (i.e. how they sound). Soviet work in this area goes back to the laboratories of Ivanov-Smolenskiĭ and Krasnogorskiĭ in the late twenties and early thirties, where it was found that a response conditioned to an object could also be called forth by the name of that object, and, conversely, a conditioned response to a word would generalize to its referent. An early example is the work of Kapustnik (1930), in which a response conditioned to a bell generalized to the word "bell", and vice versa.

The same kind of generalization was found between response to a word and a picture of its referent. A typical experiment of this sort is reported by Ivanov-Smolenskiĭ (1956, p. 10*). A child is conditioned to give a motor reaction when the picture of a cat appears in the apparatus, and to inhibit reaction to the picture of a dog. Immediately thereafter the identical reactions can be obtained to the words "cat" and "dog", although these were not uttered in the original training. This is a pure case of mediation by the second signal system, or by what the Soviet psychologists call "the previously established system of selective connections in the cortex". The term "elective (or selective) irradiation" (*izbiratel'naya irradiatsiya*) was introduced by Ivanov-Smolenskiĭ to refer to this phenomenon of transfer of responses between the two signal systems. Such "irradiation" makes it possible to respond to stimuli not present in the original conditioning situation, but related to that situation on the basis of the previous life experience of the individual.

In much of this work the word is looked upon as a mediator, which, because of its past connection with referents, is called up in the cortex when they are visually presented. For example, Faddeeva (1956) presented children between the ages of 11 and 13 with a series of pictures of flowers and fruits. The subject held a rubber bulb in his hand and, each time a picture of a flower appeared, was told to squeeze it; each time a picture of a fruit appeared he was told not to squeeze it. After this training session, the subject was presented with the word "flower", with the names of various flowers, and pictures of flowers not used before. All of these led to the squeezing response. The word "fruit", the names of various fruits, and pictures of other fruits did not lead to the conditioned response. None of these stimuli—the words and the other pictures—were present in the original conditioning experience; but Faddeeva argues, they were all connected semantically. The point is that the response generalized to stimuli which were not originally present, on the basis of their connections in the past experience of the subject.

Such mediated generalization studies presuppose covert or implicit responding linking the experimental stimuli and the observed responses. Volkova has demonstrated (1953) that it is possible to reveal the action of such mediating responses by conditioning a reaction to them. For example, a subject was conditioned to salivate to the word *desyat'* (ten), and to refrain from salivating to the word *vosem'* (eight), and was then given a series of arithmetical problems, the solutions of which were either eight or ten. He salivated profusely in response to the problems whose correct answer was ten, but hardly at all to those whose answer was eight, even in those cases where problems answered by ten contained the number eight (e.g. $8 + 2$, $80 \div 8$). Presumably, the total problem evoked the covert response "ten", to which the salivary response had been conditioned.

The above examples show that semantic generalization holds for the conditioning of both voluntary and involuntary responses. A variety of involuntary responses have been used in this research. Shvarts, for example, has done work with a photochemical response—reduction in the sensitivity of peripheral vision in response to a flash of light (1960). With a word as conditioned stimulus, response will generalize to words of closely related meaning. But words of similar sound only at first produce the conditioned response, and then become differentiated and cease to do so. Thus a response conditioned to the word *doktor* (doctor) will be evoked by a word like *vrach* (physician), but not by a word of similar sound but unrelated meaning, like *diktor* (announcer). This is strikingly different from conditioning in animals. If an animal is conditioned to give a response to a certain tone, for example, he will generalize his response to sounds related to the original tone on some physical continuum. Generalization in human beings, in experiments such as the above, is not along physical, but semantic continua. Very young children, however, respond to words of similar sound rather than those of similar meaning, as do adults when they are fatigued, ill, or under the influence of drugs which suppress activity of higher cortical centers. Feeble-minded individuals ("oligophrenics") also show response generalization on the basis of the sounds of words, rather than their meanings (Luria and Vinogradova, 1959). Shvarts considers synonyms, such as "doctor" and "physician", as identical stimuli, since each of them, though with different sounds, calls into play the same connections in the cerebral cortex which were built up in previous experience.

The work of Luria and Vinogradova (1959) is especially interesting in that it seems to reveal levels of relatedness of meaning in semantic fields. Subjects were given electric shock upon the presentation of a given word in a series, and the generalization of vasomotor responses to other words was tested. It was found that subjects made an involuntary *defense* response (vasoconstriction of the blood vessels of both the finger and the forehead) to words close in meaning to the word on which they received shock, and that they made an involuntary *orienting* response (vasoconstriction in the finger and vasodilation in the forehead) to words more distantly related to the critical word. For example, if a subject was given a shock to the word "violin", he made a similar defense reaction to such words as "violinist", "bow", "string", "mandolin", and others. He made an orienting response to names of stringless musical instruments, such as "accordion" and "drum", and to other words connected with music, such as "sonata" and "concert". In addition, of course, there were neutral words to which the subject made no autonomic response.

This experiment revealed not only the existence of complex semantic structures, but also the fact that the subjects themselves were largely unconscious of such structures in the experiment. While they responded consistently on an involuntary response basis, when interviewed after the experiment they were usually not aware of obvious semantic clusters of words to which they had responded.

Such research is, of course, of great scientific interest to psychologists throughout the world, regardless of their ideological preferences.† In addition, these findings are compatible with the ideology and psychological theorizing outlined above. Leontiev and Luria make clear the theoretical importance of such empirically determined semantic structures in the following extract.

† The reader is referred to Razran's excellent review (1961) for more examples, insightful interpretation of both Soviet and American investigations of semantic conditioning, and a useful bibliography.

The meaning of a word is never exhausted by pointing to an individual object; . . . it is an ideal, mental, crystallized form of social experience, of the practical social life of man. . . . The human being, who develops within the conditions of society, makes himself familiar with already available meanings; thereby his individual consciousness is by its very nature social . . . he is tied to the ideas and concepts of his epoch and his class. . . .

. . . As many investigations have shown, meaning is not appreciated as such; the individual does not account to himself for meaning, he does not grasp meaning in and of itself, but only through the immediate object which is designated by the word. Only in exceptional circumstances can the meaning itself come to be an object of his conscious thought (Leont'ev and Luria, 1958, pp. 176–7).

Thus one sees a sort of "Whorfian" determination of thought from the direction of language, the linguistic relativity being based more on historical stage and class membership than on the peculiarities of given language families, as in Western formulations of linguistic relativity and determinism. Referring back to the Pavlovian approach to language as a "higher regulator of behavior", words not only direct the individual's behavior, but they do so in socially determined directions.

Semantic generalization, then, because of its implications, is one of the phenomena which led Soviet psychologists to introduce language behavior as an important facet of their theory of man. On the one hand, these experiments demonstrate an important difference between stimulus generalization phenomena in men and other animals; on the other, they also help to reveal the structure of the semantic fields which make up the second signal system. The other main line of argument for the importance of the interaction between the two signal systems comes from what has been called the "abrupt" nature of human conditioning.

"Abruptness" and Human Conditioning

Conditioned responses are built up gradually in animals, with many pairings of stimulus and response. In human beings they can be established immediately by means of verbal instruction—at least this is true for human *instrumental* conditioning. A human being can be told, for example, to press a lever when he sees a green light, and the conditioned response is established "on the spot".

Although the Russians do not make the classical-instrumental or respondent-operant conditioning distinction which we do, they have developed an interesting way of formulating another sort of human verbal conditioning which seems to follow the classical or respondent conditioning paradigm. This is the Ivanov-Smolenskiĭ "speech-motor method". Suppose one wants to develop a lever-press response to a light, but does not want to simply tell the subject what to do in advance. The verbal command—"Press!"—will automatically (at least in the conditions of a psychological experiment) lead to the required pressing response, and can thus be conceptualized in terms of an unconditioned stimulus in that standard paradigm. The method is outlined by Kurshev as follows:

> ... the stimulus was presented for 2–3 sec., the verbal reinforcement, "Press!", being given in the first second, or sometimes the third second of its action. Development of a conditioned reaction before the order "Press!" was regarded as indicating the moment of the formation of a conditioned reflex. The reflex was considered stable when it was constantly present 20–25 times in succession (1959, p. 469).

Soviet psychologists hoped that by using this method they could slow down the conditioning process in man—do away with the "abrupt" or immediate conditioning effect—and examine the gradual process of conditioning, as in animal experiments. Using this sort of "higher-order conditioning" situation, they imagined that eventually it would be possible to stop saying "Press", and observe continued response to the conditioned stimulus, as in classical conditioning. Although the method sometimes did work in this fashion, especially with young subjects, it was bedevilled by an expectable difficulty: adult subjects generally learned to respond only to the verbal command, and, when it was eliminated, either ceased responding, or turned to the experimenter with a question, asking if they were still to keep on pressing.

This problem was brought to Pavlov in 1934, and he said (at one of his famous Wednesday seminars):

I can tell you, for example, about the general law of conditioned reflexes in dogs. Once these two stimuli coincide, they must be related, but the human being does not permit this to occur . . . and the real canine connection is something that he inhibits in human fashion. [He says to himself,] "When they tell me to do so I carry out their order, and when they don't give me any such order why should I interfere? The doctor is testing me for fulfillment of his order, so why should I add something extra?" (Dmitriev, 1962, pp. 9–10*).

Pavlov continued by saying that of course a connection between the light and the response must have been established, but that such first signal system connections are subject to second signal system control in man. He said:

Of course, a connection has to take place on the basis of the general physiological law of coincidence of two stimuli in time, but this is subordinate to a higher control: in one individual this will go in one direction, and in another, in another. . . . The verbal system, the second system, is dominant and particularly valuable in the higher division of the central nervous system and therefore has to exercise a constantly negative induction upon the first signal system . . . the second signal system constantly keeps the first signal system under its thumb (Dmitriev, 1962, p. 10*).

The psychologist Dmitriev, in discussing this problem, adds:

The more highly developed the second signal system (its development rises with age), the more powerfully this inhibition will be expressed. In adults it is so considerable that the motor reaction does not appear at all on response to the signal, and the response occurs only upon order (1962, p. 13*).

"Abruptness" is also demonstrated in other aspects of human conditioning. Soviet psychologists point out that while it takes much time and effort to train an animal to respond to specific stimulus attributes, differentiation can be established with no difficulty in human subjects simply by verbally describing the stimulus; for example: "Press when you see green triangles". Further, in animal learning, conditioned connections extinguish (and extinguish gradually) with the removal of reinforcement. In human learning, however, responding can be quickly terminated by verbal instruction; or, on the other hand, people can continue to behave in the same way long after having been specifically reinforced for their actions: they formulate rules and expectations which goad them on. One of the salient characteristics of human behavior is its extraordinary perseverance, in the face of obstacles, for illusory goals, or goals only formulated verbally, or expectations, or promises.

Finally, Soviet psychologists point out that a man can change a whole system of responses when he realizes that one is changed. The human subject can discover, or be told, for example, that black squares are no longer the effective stimulus—that he should now respond to white squares, or circles, or whatever. As soon as he discovers this rule, or when he is informed of the change, his response pattern changes appropriately. An animal, it is argued, would need lengthy training and step-by-step reinforcement for any such reversal.

Note that Soviet psychologists do not base their argument on the claim that such behaviors are impossible for animals. Indeed, they insist that the underlying laws of neural reflexes hold across species. Nor are they unaware of the sorts of experimental analogues offered by American psychologists for such phenomena as those discussed above—"sensory preconditioning", "higher-order conditioning", "learning to learn", "learning sets", and the like. Rather, they would argue that it is extremely *difficult* to establish such analogues in other species because no species other than our own comes to the psychological laboratory already equipped with a huge and complicated network of generalized and abstracted secondary signals—indeed, a highly developed second signal *system*. This system—language—serves to mediate between the stimulus situation and the individual's response to it, allowing him to control his own mental processes and responses by giving himself explicit verbal instructions and by relating the situation to his past experience and knowledge.†

† See an article by Goss, "Early behaviorism and verbal mediating responses" (1961a), for a lucid and highly informative review of a similar train of thought in the history of American psychology, from Watson to Dashiell to Hunter to Dollard and Miller, and others. Razran (1965) insightfully reviews and compares Russian and American psychological theory in a comprehensive recent article on Russian contributions to American psychology.

E*

Ontogenetic Development of Speech Functions

This formulation of the directive function of language or speech is most highly developed in Soviet child psychology, one of the chief foci of attention in Soviet psychology being the development of higher mental processes. In fact, in a hundred-page review of Soviet psycholinguistics (Raevskiĭ, 1958), covering the period 1918–58, no less than 48 pages are devoted to child speech. Soviet work on the development of the functions of speech is discussed in this section, and research concerning the learning of language itself in childhood is discussed in the following section.

A landmark in this field is the work of Vygotsky, culminating in his book *Thought and Language* (1934), published shortly after his untimely death in 1934, and recently becoming available in English translation. Vygotsky was concerned with the development of thought and language, pointing out that in both phylogeny and ontogeny there are strains of non-verbal thought (e.g. *Werkzeugdenken*, or "tool thought" involved in the solution of instrumental problems) and non-intellectual speech (e.g. emotional cries), and attempting to trace the interacting development of these two strains until the point in man at which speech can serve thought and thought can be revealed in speech.

The impetus for Vygotsky's work was Piaget's first book, *The Language and Thought of the Child* (1923). In this work Piaget distinguished between "egocentric" and "socialized speech", and portrayed development as a transition from one to the other. In egocentric speech, the child

> does not bother to know to whom he is speaking nor whether he is being listened to. He talks either for himself or for the pleasure of associating anyone who happens to be there with the activity of the moment. This talk is ego-centric . . . chiefly because he does not attempt to place himself at the point of view of his hearer. . . . The child asks for no more than apparent interest, though he has the illusion . . . of being heard and understood (Piaget, 1923, p. 32*).

Egocentric speech, for Piaget, is eventually replaced by socialized speech, which takes account of the point of view of the listener and makes true dialogue possible. Piaget was concerned mainly with the development of thought in the child, and assigned no special functions to egocentric speech, attributing it to early "verbal incontinence".

Vygotsky, on the other hand, stressed that all speech is social in origin, and sought to discover the functions served by early overt speech in the life of the child. He opposed both Paiget's notion of the eventual atrophy of "outer speech" and Watson's position (1919) that this speech, under the pressure not to talk out loud, was simply internalized to become sub-vocal speech, and thus the equivalent of thought. Rather, he attempted to show that early egocentric speech splits off from communicative speech, and is a transition stage between full-fledged speech out loud and silent thought. In the process, egocentric speech becomes more and more abbreviated and idiosyncratic, eventually becoming inner speech, or verbal thought, qualitatively different from outer speech. In a series of ingenious experiments, Vygotsky and his co-workers set out to show that the egocentric speech of the young child serves a useful function in his mental development, and that he does try and in fact wants to communicate with others, though at first he cannot well differentiate "speech for oneself" from "speech for others" (Vygotsky, 1934, 1956, 1960; El'konin, 1960; Luria, 1959b; Raevskiĭ, 1958).

In one series of experiments they sought to demonstrate that the spontaneous speech of children serves a practical function, not only accompanying activity, but serving to orient it. For example, a child whose crayon broke while he was drawing said the word "broken" out loud, and then went on to draw a broken car. They also found that spontaneous speech increased markedly when a child was faced by problem situations, and in situations where frustrations were introduced. In other experiments, spontaneous speech seemed to be used to orient and guide the child's activity. Such findings led Vygotsky to propose that the use of speech in such situations facilitates the understanding of the problem, and that speech, even in early years, serves an adaptive planning function in the life of the child.

In other experiments, Vygotsky demonstrated that the child's speech is communicative in its aim. For example, when a child was placed in a group of deaf-and-dumb children, or children speaking a foreign language, or even in a very noisy environment, his own spontaneous speech dropped to almost nothing.

Finally, Vygotsky found that egocentric speech becomes less and less intelligible from 3 to 7 years of age, finally disappearing on an overt level, thus supporting his notion that egocentric speech is on its way to becoming inner speech.

He concludes:

> We consider that the total development runs as follows: The primary function of speech, in both children and adults, is communication, social contact. The earliest speech of the child is therefore essentially social. . . . At a certain age the social speech of the child is quite sharply divided into egocentric and communicative speech (1934, p. 19*).
>
> Our experimental results indicate that the function of egocentric speech is similar to that of inner speech: It does not merely accompany the child's activity; it serves mental orientation, conscious understanding; it helps in overcoming difficulties; it is speech for oneself, intimately and usefully connected with the child's thinking. . . . In the end, it becomes inner speech (1934, p. 133*).†

This approach to the role of language in cognitive development has been followed up through the years by Vygotsky's close friend and collaborator, Luria. A landmark investigation in this field is a study of twins performed by Luria and Yudovich in 1935–6, but not published in the U.S.S.R. until 1956 (the same year which saw republication of Vygotsky's work, and the beginning of a general efflorescence and resuscitation of Soviet psychology). The study dealt with a pair of 5-year-old identical twin boys whose language was retarded. This defect was due primarily to the "twin situation", which facilitated communication with little use of speech. The boys were removed from the twin situation through placement in separate kindergarten classes, and their speech quickly improved. In addition, one twin was given special speech training. This twin at first improved in general mental activity more quickly

† In a commentary to the 1962 translation of Vygotsky's work, Piaget indicates his essential agreement with these positions (1962).

than his brother, but after 10 months the two were on a roughly equal level. The experimenters report that, with the rapid improvement in speech,

> the whole structure of the mental life of both twins was simultaneously and sharply changed. Once they acquired an objective language system, the children were able to formulate the aims of their activity verbally . . . we observed the beginnings of meaningful play; there arose the process of productive, constructive activity in the light of formulated aims (1956, p. 122*).

The results of the changed situation were striking, although it is not clear to what extent speech was the determining factor, and to what extent a role was played by non-linguistic training with new toys and games, and adaptation to a new social environment. There is some tendency in Soviet work of this kind to consider language the overwhelmingly determining variable among a number of variables in a given situation. As a matter of fact, Western psychologists are sometimes accused of underestimating or ignoring the role of speech and language in cognitive development (e.g. Raevskiĭ, 1958, p. 51). More recent experiments on the influences of language on other behavior make some attempt to spell out the relationships more clearly. Throughout Luria's work, for example, the *Leitmotiv* is that concepts are first formed in the process of verbal communication from adults, and behavior is first controlled by their verbal commands; and that eventually the speech of others is "internalized", allowing the child to become an independent organism, who thinks by means of inner speech, and, by means of this same inner speech, plans and controls his own behavior. Thus, Soviet psychologists conclude, the behavior of man is socially determined, yet he is free to direct—and therefore be responsible—for his own behavior.

Verbal Mediation and Cognitive Development

Much of Soviet developmental psycholinguistics deals with the facilitating effect of verbalization on tasks of stimulus differentiation, memory, and problem solving. This research shares much with American work on "verbally mediated similarity-generalization and dissimilarity-discrimination" (e.g. Goss, 1961), "acquired equivalence and distinctiveness of cues" (e.g. Spiker, 1963), and the like. However, it differs in emphasis from the American approach in that developmental and pedagogical questions are central, and in that the verbal mediation studied is that provided by natural language. The bulk of this research is sponsored by the Academy of Pedagogical Sciences of the R.S.F.S.R., and this orientation is reflected in a large number of studies which are concerned with measuring the child's performance on some cognitive task before and after verbal training. This orientation goes back to Vygotsky's wise suggestion that intelligence tests should measure not the child's performance at a single point in time, but rather his ability to improve this performance with instruction or aid: "The discrepancy between a child's actual mental age and the level he reaches in solving problems with assistance indicates the zone of his proximal development. . . . With assistance, every child can do more than he can by himself—though only within the limits set by the stage of his development" (Vygotsky, 1934, p. 103*). In many pedagogical experiments, however, *verbal* behavior is tested before and after *verbal* training, and it is concluded that language influences and changes cognitive processes, though such processes are often not studied independently of verbal criteria. (In fairness it must be pointed out, however, that in many cases the primary goal of the research is to find means to improve children's verbal behavior alone.)

Luria (1961) reviews much good research in this area. For example, Martsinovskaya set out to demonstrate that the speech of an adult can reshape the child's perception of various aspects of a complex stimulus. She took children aged 3, 4, and 5, and showed them the following stimuli: a red circle on a grey background, and a green circle on a yellow background. The child was told to press with his right hand when he sees the first, with his left hand when he sees the second. This was learned very quickly. He was then tested with a red circle on a yellow background, and a green circle on a grey background, and was found to press according to the color of the circle, since that apparently has the greater attention value, or, in Soviet terms, is "the strong component of the optical complex". The question of interest was whether speech can reinforce the weak component—the color of the background. The child was therefore specifically told to press with his right hand in response to the grey background, and with his left to the yellow background. The 3 and 4 year olds were not able to do this, but 5 year olds and older children succeeded. Apparently verbal commands cannot easily control attention until age 5.

However, Abramyan found that, by making speech commands more meaningful, perception could be reshaped even for 3 year olds. In this experiment colored circles were replaced with colored airplanes on the same grey and yellow grounds, and the child was told to press with his right hand for the figure with a red plane on a yellow background, with the additional instruction that "the plane can fly when the sun is shining and the sky is yellow". He was asked to press with his left hand for the figure with the green plane on the grey background, with the explanation that "when the weather is stormy and it rains the plane can't fly". As soon as such instructions were given to the child, the colored backgrounds, which previously were the weaker aspects of the total configuration, become the most meaningful, and even the youngest children were then able to follow the instruction to respond to the colors of the backgrounds, and not the figures.

A typical study of the effect of verbalization upon recall is an experiment by Kezheradze, a Georgian psychologist (1960). Children of ages 4 to 7 were given three tasks using six lotto cards, which depicted familiar objects: (1) to place the cards on a blank piece of cardboard; (2) to place each card upon its matching picture on a large piece of cardboard; and (3) to place each card on its matching picture, naming the picture out loud while making the placement. The child was then asked to recall the six cards. Memory improved with age and with task condition, being best in the third sort of task, and worst in the first. Furthermore, compulsory verbalization seemed to be most facilitative for the younger subjects. The experimenter also notes that in the second condition (matching without naming), children of 4 and 5 carried each card with them to the six-picture array, making a visual match, while the older children looked away from the card to the array, carrying the name of the pictured object as a mediator.

Nikiforova did a study (1961) in which she demonstrated that verbal description of colored geometric forms aided 7-year-old children in accurately reproducing them later. Requiring the children to describe the forms verbally improved their reproduction considerably, and instructing them in means of careful verbal analysis of the figures even more greatly improved their accuracy of reproduction. (Note the pedagogical orientation.) On the other hand, performance suffered greatly under conditions in which speech was handicapped. Nikiforova says:

> Children of this age have an adequate command of outer speech, but inner speech is still weakly developed in them, and therefore . . . even the clamping of the tongue between the teeth constitutes an obstacle to the function of inner speech. Under normal conditions, they tend to solve problems orally (1961, p. 133).

However, it is unfortunate that here, as in most such experiments, there is no control comparing verbally-directed attention with other means of stimulus differentiation and analysis.

Nikiforova and Kezheradze also quote experiments which demonstrate effects of codability (familiarity of name, complexity of verbal description) upon reproduction and recall, in children and adults. It is found that not only are more codable stimuli more easily and better recalled, but that memory for stimuli may be distorted to better conform to their verbal labels or descriptions.

Gan'kova (1960) discusses "the interrelationship of action, image, and speech in the thinking of preschool children", and concludes that, although different tasks require different strategies, there is also an ontogenetic sequence from reliance on active manipulation, to solutions based on verbal manipulation of visual images, to purely verbal-conceptual solutions. In the course of this development, the role of language in problem solving also changes:

For example, children of the lowest age-group used a great deal of what we called "play-talk" (reminiscences, fantasies connected with the objects perceived, various random remarks not connected with the problem). Sometimes there was also "question-talk" [which] shows the direction the child is following in trying to solve the problem. . . . The absence of "planning-talk" (verbal planning of what the child will do in order to solve the problem) can be explained by the fact that young children are incapable of solving a problem on the conceptual plane without having recourse to action (1960, p. 30).

As children grow older, play-talk decreases, question-talk becomes more directed, and planning-talk increases markedly. Older children can move between active manipulation and verbal-visual conceptualization, using manipulation as a means of formulating and testing notions, rather than as the sole means of problem solution (cf. Piaget, Bruner, and other Western psychologists).

Development of the Directive Function of Speech

Since the early fifties, Luria and his co-workers have done extensive work on the development of the role of speech in direction the motor behavior of children (Luria, 1956, 1957, 1958, 1959, 1961). This work is directed at the problem raised by Vygotsky concerning the functions of speech as it passes from overt to covert forms in ontogenesis. Soviet investigators of the directive or regulatory role of speech are interested both in the ways in which the speech of adults can direct the behavior of children (cf. Martsinovskaya and Abramyan, above), and in the ways in which children can influence their own behavior by speaking. The work begins with very young infants. Fradkina, for example, in conditioning infants to respond to auditory stimuli, reports that at the very earliest ages—up until about 7 or 8 months—children do not differentiate vocal from other auditory stimuli. However, by about 10 months of age, conditioning to words occurs four times faster than to other sound stimuli (Fradkina, 1955, as reported in El'konin, 1958, pp. 86–7). Thus it is argued that children become sensitive to verbal commands very early in life.

Luria found that children younger than 2, when asked to give the experimenter one of a number of objects lying on a table, will not necessarily give the one requested. As soon as the experimenter starts to say "Give me . . ." the child already reaches out and hands him the nearest or brightest thing that strikes his eye. The word stimulates him to act—it can direct his gaze and grasp—but then other stimuli take over. Similarly, in a longitudinal study of children from the ages of 1 year and 2 months to $2\frac{1}{2}$ years, Lyamina (1960) concludes that looking at, pointing to, and manipulating a named object are three separable components of responding to names at this age. For example, in response to an instruction such as, "Give me the drum", the child may look at the correct object, and even point to it, and then give the experimenter a different object.

These results seem to indicate that once a child begins to respond, instructions cannot alter his behavior very much, if at all. The same sort of conclusion is suggested by other studies from Luria's laboratory. For example, if a child of this age is given a peg and a collection of rings, one can easily get him to put a ring on the peg with a verbal command. However, if this command is repeated several times, the child gets going "under his own steam", and it is impossible to get him to stop by telling him to stop putting rings on the peg, or to start taking them off: instructions to stop just increase his activity. The same phenomenon is revealed in other experiments, in which the child is given a rubber bulb to hold and instructed to squeeze it whenever a light goes on. Once the child begins to squeeze, he ignores the light, and it is extremely difficult to get him to terminate this behavior, and respond only to the light. Again, the instruction, "Don't squeeze", given when the light is off, simply stimulates the child to squeeze all the harder.

After about 3, according to Luria, the child can control his own motor behavior by producing his own verbal cues. It is apparently easier for him to learn to say "Squeeze!" each time he sees the light—or even to say a nonsense syllable—than it is for him to control his squeezing response. Accordingly, he can be taught to respond verbally to the light, and then the verbal response can serve to integrate the squeezing response. Speech seems to demarcate the short time duration in which squeezing is to occur, and the child can control his squeezing by saying a sound at the same time. Apparently, the meaningful aspect of speech is irrelevant here—he can say "squeeze", or he can say "here", or "go", or a nonsense syllable; this is what Luria calls the "impulsive aspect" of speech, as opposed to its "semantic aspect". It is easier for the child to regulate his speech behavior than his hand behavior, and the speech responses are able to regulate the hand responses. This is the very simplest example of the directive function of speech which is uttered by the child himself.

The situation is more interesting—and more complicated—when the effect of speech in regulating *differentiated* motor tasks is studied. Again, the child is seated before light stimuli with a rubber bulb in his hand. In one case, for example, he is told to squeeze to a red light and not to a green one. Although it is extremely difficult to get a child to refrain from responding, by about age 3 he can perform appropriately if the experimenter gives instructions each time—"Squeeze!" and "Don't squeeze!" If the 3-year-old child gives these instructions himself, however, he squeezes in response to both instructions; again, the act of speaking itself excites him to squeeze. But children of this age *can* be taught to say "Squeeze!" to one of the lights, and remain silent to the other, and, in this way, even 3 year olds can control their own motor behavior verbally. By the time they are 4, children can direct their behavior by saying both "Squeeze!" and "Don't squeeze!"—it seems that by now speech is not just an impulsive director, but also a semantic one. And by 5, initial instructions alone are sufficient to set the child off, and he can perform appropriately even if he is silent. Luria argues that he has internalized the speech of the experimenter, so to speak, and that he now directs himself by his own inner speech, by the rule he has formulated. And to shore up his interpretation, he finds that 5 and 6 year olds will give themselves verbal commands out loud if the task is speeded up—if it gets very difficult—and that such commands improve their performance.

Similar conclusions are drawn in regard to a task where the child must press once to one stimulus and twice to another: the youngest children cannot perform this task silently, and speech at first simply confuses them. Then speech functions only as an impulsive director—that is, if the child is instructed to say "one" to one light, and "two" to the other, he is not aided: he says one word each time, and, accordingly, he presses once each time. However, if he learns to say a syllable once in response to one light, and twice in response to the other ("tu" and "tu–tu"), then he is able to better control these differentiated responses; and, if he learns to say "one" and "one–two", thus combining both the impulsive and semantic aspects, then his performance is best of all.

Such, at least, are the conclusions drawn from Luria's summaries of this work. Looking in detail at the work itself, however, one could perhaps more easily conclude that up to a certain age the child has difficulty with motor co-ordination generally, and adding his own speech to the task makes it all the more difficult; that by 4 or 5 the child may be able to handle both speaking and squeezing at once (many of the detailed data show that the addition of speech neither improves nor hinders performance at this age); and that by 5 or 6, when the child can handle the task without speaking out loud, it may simply be that his general motor co-ordination has developed sufficiently to enable him to do so. In fact, Jarvis, in attempting to replicate part of Luria's findings in a recent doctoral dissertation at the University of Rochester (1963), was not able to demonstrate any special effect of verbal self-instructions on motor performance between the ages of 3 and 7, and concludes that only a general improvement with age in performance on a simple sensory-motor task could be shown.

Jarvis's finding is instructive, because it points up some of the difficulties involved in interpreting and replicating Soviet research; it would be well to pause to discuss them at this point. Since Luria has made so many important contributions to world psychology through the years, the writer hopes he will not mind the work of his laboratory being used as an example in this case. Jarvis offers a warning to those interested in Soviet psychology:

> In attempting to understand this failure to confirm Luria's hypothesis, this failure of replication, two factors seem significant. The first is the fact

that Luria used only one order of presentation of the experimental conditions while we used an experimental design incorporating all possible
orders. Furthermore, considering the order used by Luria alone, we
found an insignificant trend in the direction he reports. We can suggest,
then, without a great deal of supporting evidence, that his results may be
partly an artifact of an inadequate experimental design. . . .

What, then, are the implications of this experience for other psychologists who may be tempted to pursue questions stimulated by the work
of Soviet psychologists ? . . . I think you should be prepared to find some
novel and stimulating ideas presented with something of a vagueness
about the details of the evidence supporting them. The ideas and the
evidence for them are often presented in a rather anecdotal manner . . .
which can be rather disarming. I would suggest . . . that you ask yourself
what kind of experimental design seems to have been used, what experimental variables have been left uncontrolled, what subject variables have
been ignored ? . . . You might well consider personality variables in
particular. . . . You may find it valuable to correspond directly with
Soviet psychologists whose work you are interested in. In our correspond-
ence with Luria, we found him to be a charming and generous corres-
pondent. . . . In conclusion, the very nature of some of these difficulties
that American psychologists are likely to encounter in attempting to
utilize and adapt the work of our Soviet colleagues suggests that a
successful coping with them, a successful application of some of our tools
to the unusual Soviet approaches to some problems may pay substantial
dividends (1964, pp. 10–11).

It should be pointed out that Soviet psychologists have also been
aware of the need for methodological care, although statistical
treatment of data is just beginning to be used in a few recent
studies. But a decade ago, reviewing Soviet psychological research
of the period 1953–5, Smirnov pointed out to his colleagues that:
"The scientific level of research is not always satisfactory. . . .
Sometimes, instead of a fundamental analysis of assembled material, an author gives an assortment of examples illustrating his
theory; in such writings it is impossible to judge whether the theory
has been upheld" (1955, p. 44*).

Ontogenetic Development of Language

Much careful work has been done in the U.S.S.R. on the acquisition of Russian and other Soviet languages in childhood, on
problems of childhood bilingualism (e.g. Imedadze, 1960), and on

problems of first- and second-language instruction in the schools. A chief impetus to Soviet developmental psycholinguistics has been the practical task of raising infants and very young children in state nurseries. Lyamina pointed out in 1958 that "insufficiencies of group upbringing have an especially unfavorable influence on the development of the speech of children" (p. 119), and much effort has therefore been devoted to the improvement of early speech stimulation and training (see reports in Bauer, 1962).

Perhaps because the morphological system of the Russian language facilitates neologisms—which are a marked and delightful aspect of Russian child language—Soviet psychologists have not been attracted by mechanistic and imitation-based, passive models of language acquisition. They see first-language learning as a highly active, creative process, rivalling the productions of the poet and artist in subtlety and originality. Gvozdev, whose diary study of his son's language development is probably the most careful and intensive of such studies ever published anywhere, emphasized that: "The keenness of the child's observations and the artistic clarity of many childish words are common knowledge; they are truly very close to the linguistic creativity of literary artists. We are therefore dealing here with authentic creativity, attesting to the linguistic endowment of children" (1949, Part 2, p. 187). And El'konin, one of the Soviet Union's leading developmental psychologists, says: "It is perfectly clear that [language acquisition] is not a mechanical process in which the child acquires each separate linguistic form by means of simple repetition" (1958).

Although American developmental psycholinguistics has made great strides in recent years, the overwhelming majority of this work has dealt with English as a first language. Unfortunately, extensive data on child speech in non-Indo-European languages are not yet available; but the sizeable Soviet body of literature is definitely worthy of the attention of Western psycholinguists. Although Russian is also an Indo-European language, it is sufficiently different from English—most clearly in its highly inflectional grammatical structure—to serve as a useful contrast case to sharpen notions of universal aspects of language acquisition and linguistic competence.

Grammatical Development

The diary study of Gvozdev (1961), taken together with a number of studies of preschool and young school children, reveal many similarities in the first stages of language acquisition of English- and Russian-speaking children (see Slobin, 1966; Ervin and Miller, 1963). The grammatical structure of early two-word sentences is strikingly similar. Likewise, word order is quite inflexible at each of the early stages of syntactic development, although one might have predicted that Russian children, being exposed to a great variety of word orders, would first learn the morphological markers for such classes as subject, object, and verb, and combine them in any order. However, in both English- and Russian-speaking children grammar begins with unmarked forms, arrayed in a fixed order.

An experiment performed by El'kin (1957) seems to indicate that the reliance upon ordering as a linguistic device may continue well after Russian children have mastered the language. He conditioned an eyeblink response to sentences as stimuli in subjects aged 10 to 14. In children in the 12–14-year-old range, reversing the word order in the stimulus sentence had no decremental effect on the conditioned reflex activity. Because Russian is an inflected language, the reversed sentences were grammatical and synonymous with the original sentences, and apparently were treated by these older subjects as very similar or identical stimuli. This was not the case, however, for the younger children. Admittedly this experiment is difficult to interpret—perhaps, however, for children even as old as 10 or 11 the reversed sentences were somehow not quite the same stimuli as the original sentences.

The basic learning of grammatical classes is accomplished quickly by Russian children, although the learning of specific morphological and morphophonemic details goes on for much longer. It takes until 7 or 8 for the child to sort out all of the proper conjugational and declensional suffixes and categories, stress and sound alternations, and the like. The Russian child does not fully master his total morphological system until he is several years older than the age at which the American child is believed to have essentially completed his primary grammatical learning. In this sense it may be more difficult to learn to speak one language natively than another—though the basic learning is nevertheless accomplished very rapidly in both Russian and English.

Studies of Russian child speech show, as do American studies, that regular patterns and rules are more important than practice and reinforcement in language development, highly practiced correct forms frequently being abandoned when a more general productive pattern can be over-generalized (e.g. Popova, 1958; Zakharova, 1958).

Russian psycholinguists stress the importance of the semantic nature of grammatical concepts in determining their order and rate of acquisition. For example, gender, which is an arbitrary categorization of nouns, is relatively late to be learned; classes based on relational semantic criteria—cases, tenses, and persons of the verb—emerge later in development than those with concrete reference, such as singular-plural, diminuitive, imperative, and prepositions of spatial relations. Likewise, the conditional mood, though its grammatical structure is very simple, is late to be learned, apparently because of its semantic difficulty.

Space does not allow discussion of the many ingenious methods used by Soviet psychologists to investigate child speech. Table 1 summarizes some of the methods, and refers the reader to outstanding examples of their use.

TABLE 1. SOVIET METHODS OF INVESTIGATING CHILD LANGUAGE

PHONOLOGICAL COMPETENCE
1. Conditioned response to words: Fradkina (1955), Shvachkin (1948)
2. Concept formation experiments: Zhurova (1963)
3. Direct questioning of children: Zhurova (1963)
4. Elicited imitation: Lyamina (1958), Lyamina and Gagua (1963)
5. Object naming: Lyamina (1958), Lyamina and Gagua (1963)
6. Recording and noting: Levina (1940)

GRAMMATICAL AND LEXICAL COMPETENCE

Comprehension
1. Ability to follow instructions to manipulate objects: Sokhin (1959)
2. Ability to follow instructions to identify objects named by *E*: Istomina (1960), Lyamina (1958, 1960), Mallitskaya (1960)
3. Interpretation of suffixes attached to new words: Bogoyavlenskiĭ (1957)
4. Conditioned responses to verbal stimuli: Detgyar' (1957), El'kin (1957), El'konin (1955)
5. Direct questioning of children: Patrina (1959), Zhuĭkov (1955)

Production
1. Ability to name presented objects: Istomina (1960), Lyamina (1958)
2. Analysis of picture descriptions and written compositions: Feofanov (1958, 1960), Meerson (1959)
3. Analysis of answers to questions designed to elicit certain forms: Babin (1958), Karpova (1955), Popova (1958), Zakharova (1958)
4. Ability to apply suffixes to new words: Bogoyavlenskiĭ (1957)
5. Recording and noting: Gvozdev (1960), Imedadze (1960), Kasatkin (1958)

Learning of Meaning

A fairly large body of Soviet pedagogical-developmental research deals with the problem of teaching tiny children to understand and use individual new words. The impetus for this work is the problem of collective child-rearing, as noted above. Soviet investigators have a great advantage in investigating a child's original learning of word meanings, in that large numbers of very young children are available for research in the state nurseries. In this research, consistent with Soviet psychological theory, action is seen as a principal component of the learning of word meanings. Language learning is seen as an active process in which the child develops speech in order to communicate with adults and get them to satisfy his needs—both physical and intellectual. Soviet psychologists have found that almost from the beginning of life, words call forth orienting reactions from the child. (Soviet psychologists have long emphasized the importance of the "orienting reflex"— a concept apparently first introduced by Pavlov, and bearing similarity to more recent Western theorizing on exploratory drives, curiosity motivation, and the like.) Soviet investigators claim that reinforcement by means of activity and objects is more important

than by food or the satisfaction of other organic needs. The child
is therefore motivated to explore and manipulate the environment
because novel aspects of stimuli are revealed in this way. In this
process of exploration and manipulation, constant speech from the
surrounding adults is responsible for language learning.

In a typical and careful experiment, Kol'tsova (1958), presented
a doll 1500 times to each of ten 20-month-old children in the course
of several months. None of them knew the word "doll". For five of
the children, the presentation was accompanied by a limited number of sentences which treated the doll simply as an object ("Here
is the doll", "Give me the doll", etc.). The other five children heard
thirty different sentences, bringing the word "doll" into meaningful
connections with a number of other words, denoting doll-specific
actions ("Rock the doll", "Feed the doll", etc.). Finally the
children were presented with an array of dolls and other toys and
asked to "Give doll". (Russian has neither definite nor indefinite
article, thus the command is neutral in relation to the obligatory
English differentiation between "a doll" and "the doll".) The
children of the first group picked only the experimental doll,
while the children of the second group selected other dolls as well.
Kol'tsova explains that in dealing with objects in a variety of
different ways word meanings develop from proper names of
concrete objects to more general names of categories.

Lyamina (1960) studied thirty-two children longitudinally from
the ages of 1 year and 2 months to $2\frac{1}{2}$ years, attempting to teach
them new word meanings. She found it extremely difficult to work
with children younger than a $1\frac{1}{2}$ years—as one might well imagine
—but did succeed in teaching children older than this age to point
to objects whose names they had learned, and to hand named
objects to the experimenter. She found it easiest to teach a child
the name of an object if it was the one new object among a collection of familiar ones. Under such conditions, in Soviet terms, the
new object calls forth an orienting response which facilitates word
learning. In another paper, Lyamina (1958) reports that contrary
to previous opinion and report (such as that of Kol'tsova), her
subjects (between the ages of 1 year 8 months and 2 years 1 month)

were not better at naming familiar, everyday objects than they were at naming objects whose names were taught in an experimental setting without the opportunity to manipulate them: apparently the important variable was the child's attention to the new object. As a matter of fact, Lyamina proposes that motor and verbal responses may often be in competition for children of this age, because: (1) it is more difficult to name objects while playing with them, (2) the output of speech is said to be diminished while the child is learning to walk, and while he is walking, and (3) the form of speech is said to be more primitive while the child is walking. She proposes further that there is a rapid spurt in language development once various motor acts are co-ordinated with each other and with speaking.

Mallitskaya (1960) attempted to work with children even younger than those of Lyamina. Her subjects were ten children between the ages of 9 months and $1\frac{1}{2}$ years. Pictures were attached to four sides of a cube. The experimenter would point to a picture and repeat its name two or three times (e.g. *Vot lisa*, "This is a fox"), and would then turn the cube, removing the designated picture from view, and tell the child to find that picture. It took several weeks to train the children to sit calmly and attend to the experiment, and even longer to train them to perform as required. Once this training was completed, however, the children became very adept at the task, and by 11 or 12 months of age could generally learn a new word after two or three repetitions, and could easily differentiate and find eight different pictures on two cubes. After this stage, the child was presented with three pictures, one of which was new to him. Mallitskaya states that the new picture evoked a strong orienting response, which weakened as soon as the picture was named, and that the children were generally able to learn such names after one presentation. She concludes that:

> even at the age of 12 to 13 months [word-image] connections can be formed under some conditions after a single reinforcement. The most important condition for developing these connections is the presence of an intense orienting reaction to the named image, as is the case when a new image is placed among other images whose names the child already knows (1960, p. 126).

These are but a few examples of an approach to developmental psycholinguistics almost unknown in the West—painstaking, longitudinal experimental investigation of very early stages of native language development, using large numbers of children. Similar careful work is done with groups of children of a given age, studied at a given point of time. For example, Sokhin (1959) found that the understanding of some prepositions by 2 year olds is very much tied to action: while a child could correctly perform the action of "put the block under the table", he could not "put the block under the ring", when the ring was lying on the table. Sokhin argues that "under", in the second case, requires two actions—lifting up the ring and placing the block under it—whereas "under" in the first case requires only one. This notion is supported by the fact that some children held the block under the table, beneath the point where the ring was lying, rather than pick up the ring and place the block under it on the surface of the table. (The experiment included not only blocks and rings, but a variety of objects.) In this very insightful study of the understanding of prepositions by children of various ages, Sokhin points out that the meaning of a word changes with age; in this case, for example, although 2 year olds have a general idea of the spatial relations denoted by the preposition "under", they have yet to separate this notion from specific actions—it is not yet a general concept of spatial relations, though the children seem to understand it correctly when dealing with a variety of everyday situations.

Inner Speech in Thinking and Listening

Consonant with Soviet psycholinguistic theory as discussed above, Soviet psychologists are partial to a speech-motor theory of thought, although Vygotsky warned that inner speech need not have a motor component. This orientation is well rooted in Russian thinking, going back to "the father of Russian physiology", Sechenov, who wrote in 1863: "When a child thinks he invariably talks at the same time. Thought in five-year-olds is mediated through words or whispers, surely through movements of tongue and lips, which is also very frequently (perhaps always, but in different degrees) true of the thinking of adults" (1863, p. 498). Pavlov, too, emphasized the role of speech kinesthesia in thinking: "Speech, especially and, first of all, *its kinesthetic stimuli going from the speech organs to the cortex* [italics added] are second signals, signals of signals, that are in essence abstractions of reality and means of generalization constituting our extra *uniquely human higher thought*" (1932, p. 1154).

A. N. Sokolov (1959) has actively investigated this theory, and concludes: "Generally active forms of thinking, connected with the need for more or less prolonged and developed deliberation, are always accompanied by a strengthening of the speech kinesthesiae, whereas repeated thought actions are accompanied by their reduction" (1959, p. 684*). He has used three main methods to test his theory: (1) mechanical impeding of articulation (e.g. clamping the tongue and lips between the teeth, holding the mouth open wide), (2) obligatory pronouncing out loud of material either relevant or irrelevant to the task at hand, and (3) electromyographic investigations (acknowledging pre-war American work as the source of Soviet work of this type, and stressing its importance). The results of experiments using the first two methods are difficult to accommodate to the theory, in that subjects get used to articulatory impediments and to repetition of words. Results of electromyographic investigations, however, are frequently of interest. (Sokolov, however, does not hold that all inner speech is peripherally reflected; in some cases it may be totally central.)

For example, Sokolov begins a study of inner speech in the study of foreign languages (1960) with the observation that people tend to pronounce words subvocally when they face difficulty in understanding something spoken or read, or when the meaning must be remembered exactly. He postulates that such inner silent speech plays an important role in both first and second language learning. He recorded electrical potentials from the tongue and lips while subjects performed various linguistic tasks in their native language (Russian) and in a foreign language (usually English), discovering greater muscular movement when subjects were

F

reading a foreign language than when they were reading Russian, and, further, that the amount of muscular movement increased with the difficulty of the text, or with the limitations of the subject's foreign-language ability. As a control, he found that subjects with a good command of English showed no difference in subvocal speech for reading either language. Further, Sokolov was also able to record tension in the articulatory system while his subjects were listening to linguistic material—both in the native language, if the material listened to is to be remembered or worked with later, and in the foreign language, especially if the material is difficult for the subject to understand. He concludes that kinesthetic feedback is necessary for comprehension of difficult linguistic material, and, accordingly, stresses the importance of conversation practice in the early years of foreign language study. Apparently it is easier for the student to grasp new linguistic material if he can "mouth it".

From here it is a short step to a motor theory of speech perception, which, indeed, seems to be embraced by most Soviet psycholinguists. Raevskiĭ states, for example: ". . . comprehension of vocal speech presupposes its internal uttering on the part of the listener . . ." (1958, p. 39). An empirical example is an experiment of Chistovich, Klaas and Alekin (1961), in which it was found that a rapid series of vowels was better discriminated by listeners than a similar series of tones, presumably because it is easier to discriminate sounds which can be imitated.†

Investigations of speech perception emphasize the role of linguistic habits and expectations. An experiment by Selezneva (1957) exemplifies this approach. If subjects are asked to compare a string

† As Pick (1964) has pointed out, a motor theory of speech perception is congenial to the Soviet "copy theory" of perception. He reviews a number of experiments carried out in the laboratories of Leont'ev and Chistovich, showing that pitch discrimination is improved with vocal practice of various sorts. Pick summarizes the Soviet position "as suggesting that, on the basis of reinforcement, an association is established between the pitch of the sound and a particular activity of the vocal chords. The activity then serves as an indicator of the pitch. Such an interpretation implies a two-level theory of perception . . . in which an apparently lower-level reflex response occurs which forms the basis of the conscious discrimination of pitch" (p. 29). In support of the

of four equally-stressed sounds with a similar string in which the
intensity of the second sound is reduced, they report that the first
sound in the latter string sounds as if it were stressed. If, however,
the four sounds are syllables of a Russian word, it is the linguistic-
ally-stressed syllable which seems to stand out in such a comparison. For example, if the word *nalomala* (pronounced *nalamála*)
is presented (1) with all four syllables stressed equally, and (2) with
the intensity of the second syllable decreased, subjects hear the
second presentation as a normal Russian word, with stress on the
third syllable—even though the first syllable should be, according
to the results with the non-linguistic string of sounds, the strongest
on a physiological basis. Selezneva presents a number of such
findings which demonstrate that language habits introduce a new
factor in auditory perception. (See also Artemov [1960] for a
review of such research.)

Other Areas

Space allows for only a brief mention of other areas of concern
in Soviet psycholinguistics. Much work is carried out in the
Georgian Republic on questions of phonetic symbolism, the basis
of naming, and bilingualism. Unfortunately, much of this work
appears only in Georgian. The reader is referred to a review by
Natadze (1957), and an interesting study by Ramishvili (1954).

Soviet psychologists are actively concerned with speech disorders and their treatment. Luria's pioneering work on traumatic
aphasia is a landmark (1947), and his laboratory has also been

---

approach is the finding of Leont'ev and Gippenreïter (1959) that while pitch
discrimination was impaired for Russian subjects when pure tones were
replaced by sounds varying in both pitch and timbre, Vietnamese subjects
were much less affected by pitch-timbre pairings, their differential pitch thres-
hold either not changing at all, or changing very little relative to the Russian
subjects. The authors argue that, in Vietnamese-speaking children, both
timbre and pitch discrimination are built up on the basis of language practice,
while the Russian-speaking child must learn to ignore pitch differences as not
being linguistically relevant. See also pp. 83–7.

concerned with the directive function of speech in feeble-minded ("oligophrenic") and brain-damaged children and patients, and its role in compensating for defects caused by illnesses such as Parkinson's disease (reviewed in Luria, 1959b).

Interesting work is also being done in many places in the U.S.S.R. on problems of educating deaf and deaf–blind children (see Shif, 1954). Much of this work is of definite relevance to psycholinguistics.

The interaction between the two signal systems is of special interest to psychiatrists, who see speech in therapy as a way of getting at and changing cortical processes. Hypnotic suggestion and other suggestion is seen as an example of the effect of the second signal system upon the first—an effect which can produce physiological changes of a wide variety. There is some interest, for example, in studying how mentally-assumed emotional states are reflected in such autonomic measures as the GSR and others (e.g. Korotkin, 1964; Simonov et al., 1964).

Interest in the effects of individual differences on language behavior is generally limited to Pavlov's famous fourfold typology of higher nervous system temperaments—"mobile, sluggish, excitable, and weak"—with some further refinements (e.g. Meleshko, 1960).

Recent work in American linguistics and psycholinguistics is beginning to enter Soviet laboratories, and interest has been aroused in information theory, and, most recently, in generative and transformational grammar. For example, Lushchikhina has very recently reported an experiment (1965) in which subjects listen to sentences of varying grammatical structure through white noise, with the finding that, holding sentence length constant, immediate memory for sentences is a function of their syntactic complexity (as defined by the "depth" measure proposed by the American linguist Yngve).

Undoubtedly there are more areas of investigation, and significant experiments, which have escaped this reviewer's attention. (For valuable first-hand accounts of many areas of Soviet psycholinguistics—and Soviet psychology generally—see Bauer's recent anthology, published by the American Psychological Association [1962].) Suffice it to say that much of value can be found—and will be found—in Soviet work, and one can only hope that fruitful contacts between the Eastern and Western components of the scientific study of the nature of man will continue to flourish.

References

AKHMANOVA, O. S. (1957) *O Psikholingvistike* [*On Psycholinguistics*]. Moscow: Moscow Univ. Press. [Translation in *General Systems: Yearbook Soc. Gen. Syst. Res.*, 1960, **5**, 181–207.]

ARTEMOV, V. A. (1960) O vzaimootnoshenii fizicheskikh svoĭstv, vosprinimaemykh kachestv, yazykovykh znacheniĭ i smyslovogo soderzhaniya rechi [On the interaction of physical attributes, perceived qualities, linguistic meanings, and the semantic content of speech]. *Vop. Psikhol.* **3**, 98–105.

BABIN, V. N. (1958) Ponimanie protivorechiĭ shkol'nikami II-VII klassov [Understanding of contradictions by pupils in grades 2 to 7]. *Vop. Psikhol.* **3**, 99–105.

BAUER, R. A. (1959) *The New Man in Soviet Psychology*. Cambridge, Mass.: Harvard Univ. Press.

BAUER, R. A. (Ed.) (1962) *Some Views on Soviet Psychology*. Washington, D.C.: Amer. Psychol. Assoc.

BOGOYAVLENSKIĬ, D. N. (1957) *Psikhologiya usvoeniya orfografii* [The psychology of learning orthography]. Moscow: Akad. Pedag. Nauk R.S.F.S.R.

CHISTOVICH, L. A., KLAAS, YU. A. and ALEKIN, R. O. (1961) O znachenii imitatsii dlya raspoznavaniya zvukovykh posledovatel'nosteĭ [The role of imitation in discrimination of sound series]. *Vop. Psikhol.* **5**, 173–82. [Translation in *Sov. Psychol. Psychiat.* 1963, **2** (1), 38–45.]

DETGYAR', E. N. (1957) Slovo kak uslovnyĭ tormoz u deteĭ pervykh trekh let zhizni [The word as a conditioned inhibitor in infants during the first three years of life]. *Trudy Inst-a. im. I. P. Pavlova*, **6**, 212–16. [Translation in *Sov. Psychol. Psychiat.* 1963, **1** (3), 14–17.]

DMITRIEV, A. S. (1961) O dvigatel'noĭ metodike na rechevom podkreplenii [On a motor technique with verbal reinforcement]. *Vop. Psikhol.* **3**, 70–79. [Translation in *Sov. Psychol. Psychiat.* 1962, **1** (1), 8–15.]

EL'KIN, D. G. (1957) Ob uslovnykh refleksakh na slozhnye slovesnye razdrazhiteli u shkol'nikov [On conditioned reflexes to complex verbal stimuli in children of school age]. In: *Materialy soveshchaniya po psikholgii*. Moscow: Akad. Pedag. Nauk R.S.F.S.R., pp. 371–9.

EL'KONIN, D. B. (1955) Osobennosti vzaimodeĭstviya pervoĭ i vitoroĭ signal' nykh sistem u deteĭ doshkol'nogo vozrasta [The interaction of the first and second signal systems in children of preschool age]. *Izvestiya Akad. Pedag. Nauk RSFSR*, **64**, 27–47.

EL'KONIN, D. B. (1958) *Razvitie rechi v doshkol'nom vozraste* [*The development of speech at preschool age*]. Moscow: Akad. Pedag. Nauk R.S.F.S.R.

EL'KONIN, D. B. (1960) *Detskaya psikhologiya* [*Child psychology*]. Moscow: Uchpedgiz.

ERVIN, SUSAN M., and MILLER, W. R. (1963) Language development. In: Natl. Soc. Study Educ. Yearbook; *Child Psychology*, 1963. Chicago: Natl. Soc. Study Educ., pp. 108–43.

FADDEEVA, V. K. (1956) O roli izbiratel'noĭ irradiatsii i induktsii v nekotorykh slozhnykh formakh sovmestnoĭ deyatel'nosti dvukh signal'nykh sistem [On the role of elective irradiation and induction in certain complex forms of joint activity of the two signal systems]. *Trudy Inst. Vyssh. Nervn. Deyat., Seriya patofiziologicheskaya*, Vol. II. [Translation in *Works Inst. High. Nerv. Act., Pathophysiological Series*, Vol. II. Washington, D.C.: Natl. Sci. Found., 1960, pp. 163–76.]

FEOFANOV, M. P. (1958) Ob upotreblenii predlogov v detskoĭ rechi [On the use of prepositions in child speech]. *Vop. Psikhol.* 3, 118–24.

FEOFANOV, M. P. (1960) Oshibki v postroenii predlozheniĭ kak pokazatel' stepeni usvoeniya grammaticheskogo stroya yazyka [Mistakes in sentence structure as an indicator of the level of mastery of the grammatical structure of the language]. *Dok. Akad. Pedag. Nauk RSFSR*, 1, 37–38.

FRADKINA, F. I. (1955) Vozniknovenie rechi u deteĭ [The origin of speech in children]. *Uch. zap. LGPI*, Vol. 12.

GAN'KOVA, Z. A. (1960) K voprosu o sootnoshenii deĭstviya, obraza i rechi v myshlenii deteĭ doshkol'nogo vozrasta [The interrelation of action, image, and speech in the thinking of children of preschool age]. *Vop. Psikhol.* 1, 69–77. [Translation in *Problems of Psychol.* 1960, 1, 26–35.]

GOSS, A. E. (1961a) Early behaviorism and verbal mediating responses. *Amer. Psychologist*, 16, 285–98.

GOSS, A. E. (1961b) Verbal mediating responses and concept formation. *Psychol. Rev.* 68, 248–74.

GVOZDEV, A. N. (1949) *Formirovanie u rebenka grammaticheskogo stroya russkogo yazyka* [*Formation in the child of the grammatical structure of the Russian language*], Parts I and II. Moscow: Akad. Pedag. Nauk R.S.F.S.R.

GVOZDEV, A. N. (1961) *Voprosy izucheniya detskoĭ rechi* [*Questions of the study of child speech*]. Moscow: Akad. Pedag. Nauk R.S.F.S.R.

IMEDADZE, N. V. (1960) K psikhologicheskoĭ prirode rannego dvuyazychiya [On the psychological nature of early bilingualism]. *Vop. Psikhol.* 1, 60–68.

ISTOMINA, Z. M. (1960) Vospriyatie i nazyvanie tsveta v rannem vozraste [Perception and color naming in early childhood]. *Izvestiya Akad. Pedag. Nauk RSFSR*, 113, 102–13. [Translation in *Sov. Psychol. Psychiat.* 1963, 1 (2), 37–45.]

IVANOV-SMOLENSKIĬ, A. G. (1956) Puti razvitiya eksperimental'nogo issledovaniya raboty vzaimodeĭstviya pervoĭ i vtoroĭ signal'nykh sistem [Developmental paths of experimental research into the work and interaction of the first and second signal systems]. *Trudy Inst. Vyssh. Nervn. Deyat., Seriya patofiziologicheskaya*, Vol. II. [Translation in *Works Inst. High. Nerv. Act., Pathophysiological Series*, Vol. II. Washington, D.C.: Natl. Sci. Found., 1960, pp. 1–31.]

JARVIS, P. E. (1963) The effect of self-administered verbal instructions on simple sensory-motor performance in children. Unpub. doct. dissert., Univer. of Rochester.

JARVIS, P. E. A failure to replicate some Soviet research and some implications for American psychologists. Paper read at meeting of Colorado Psychol. Assoc., 29 May 1964.

KAPUSTNIK, O. P. (1930) Vzaimodeĭstvie mezhdu neposredstvennymi uslovnymi razdrazhitelysmi i slovesnymi ikh simvolami [Interaction between direct conditioned stimuli and their verbal symbols]. In: *Osnovnye mekhanizmy uslovnoreflektornoĭ deyatel'nosti rebenka*. Moscow.

KARPOVA, S. N. (1955) Osoznanie slovesnogo sostava rechi rebenkom doshkol'nogo vozrasta [Awareness of the word content of speech in pre-school children]. *Vop. Psikhol.* **4**, 43–55.

KASATKIN, N. V. (1958) Gruppovaya rech' kak osobyĭ vid rechi [Group speech as a special form of speech]. *Vop. Psikhol.* **2**, 47–59.

KEZHERADZE, E. D. (1960) Rol' slova v zapominanii i nekotorye osobennosti pamyati rebenka [The role of words in memorization, and some features of the memory of the child]. *Vop. Psikhol.* **1**, 78–85.

KOL'TSOVA, M. M. (1958) *Formirovanie vyssheĭ nervnoĭ deyatel'nosti rebenka* [*The formation of the higher nervous activity of the child*]. Moscow: Medgiz.

KOROTKIN, I. I. (1964) Izmeneniya vyssheĭ nervnoĭ deyatel'nosti, vyzvannye predstavleniem zadannogo obraza [Changes in higher nervous activity evoked by imagining a given image]. *Zhurn. vyssh. nervn. deyat.* **14**, 937–46. [Translation in *Sov. Psychol. Psychiat.* 1965, **3**, 4.]

KURSHEV, V. A. (1959) Patterns of external inhibition (negative induction) in the joint activity of the signal systems and their clinical significance in patients with aphasia. *Pavlov. J. high. nerv. Act.*, **9**, 468–74.

LEONT'EV, A. N. and GIPPENREĬTER, YU. B. (1959) Analiz sistemnogo stroeniya vospriyatiya: Soobshchenie VIII. Vliyanie rodnogo yazyka na formirovanie slukha [Analysis of the systemic structure of perception: Communication VIII. Influence of native language on the formation of hearing]. *Dokl. Akad. Pedag. Nauk RSFSR*, **3** (2), 59–62.

LEONT'EV, A. N. and LURIA, A. R. (1958) Die psychologischen Anschauungen L. S. Wygotskis. *Z. für Psychol.*, **162**, 3–4, 165–205.

LEVINA, R. E. (1940) *Nedostatki chteniya i pis'ma u deteĭ* [*Reading and Writing Defects in Children*]. Moscow: Uchpedgiz.

LURIA, A. R. (1947) *Travmaticheskaya afaziya* [*Traumatic aphasia*]. Moscow: Akad. Med. Nauk.

LURIA, A. R. (Ed.) (1956–8) *Problemy vyssheĭ nervnoĭ deyatel'nosti normal'nogo i anomal'nogo rebenka* [*Problems of higher nervous activity of the normal and abnormal child*]. Moscow: Akad. Pedag. Nauk R.S.F.S.R.; Vol. I, 1956; Vol. II, 1958.

LURIA, A. R. (1957) The role of language in the formation of temporary connections. In: B. Simon (Ed.), *Psychology in the Soviet Union*. Stanford, Calif.: Stanford Univ. Press, pp. 115–29.

LURIA, A. R. (1959a) Experimental analysis of the development of voluntary action in children. The role of speech in child development. In: *The Central Nervous System and Behavior: Selected Translations from the Russian*

Medical Literature. Bethesda, Md.: U.S. Dept. Health Educ. Welfare, pp. 529–35/556–74.

LURIA, A. R. (1959b) Razvitie rechi v formirovanie psikhicheskikh protsessov [Speech development in the formation of mental processes]. In: *Psikhologicheskaya nauka v SSSR*, Vol. I. Moscow: Akad. Pedag. Nauk R.S.F.S.R., pp. 516–77. [Translation in *Psychological Science in the USSR*, Vol. I. Washington, D.C.: U.S. Joint Publication Res. Serv. No. 11466, 1961, pp. 704–87.]

LURIA, A. R. (1959c) The directive function of speech; I: Its development in early childhood; II: Its dissolution in pathological states of the brain. *Word*, 15, 341–52, 453–64.

LURIA, A. R. (1961) *The Role of Speech in the Regulation of Normal and Abnormal Behavior.* Oxford: Pergamon.

LURIA, A. R. and VINOGRADOVA, O. S. (1959) An objective investigation of the dynamics of semantic systems. *Brit. J. Psychol.* 50, 89–105.

LURIA, A. R. and YUDOVICH, F. YA. (1956) *Rech' i razvitie psikhicheskikh protsessov u rebenka.* Moscow: Akad. Pedag. Nauk R.S.F.S.R. [Translation: *Speech and the Development of Mental Processes in the Child.* London: Staples Press, 1959.]

LUSHCHIKHINA, I. M. (1965) Ispol'zovanie gipotezy Ingve o strukture frazy pri izuchenii vospriyatiya rechi [Application of Yngve's hypothesis of sentence structure to the study of speech perception]. *Vop. Psikhol.* 2, 56–66.

LYAMINA, G. M. (1958) K voprosu o mekhanizme ovladeniya proiznosheniem slov u deteĭ vtorogo i tret'ego goda zhizni [On the mechanism of mastery of pronunciation of words by children in the second and third years of life]. *Vop. Psikhol.* 6, 119–30.

LYAMINA, G. M. (1960) Razvitie ponimaniya rechi u deteĭ vtorogo goda zhizni [Development of speech comprehension in children in the second year of life]. *Vop. Psikhol.* 3, 106–21.

LYAMINA, G. M. and GAGUA, N. I. (1963) O formirovanii pravil'nogo proiznosheniya slov u deteĭ ot polutora do trekh let [On the formation of correct pronunciation of words in children from one and a half to three years of age]. *Vop. Psikhol.* 6, 93–105. [Translation in *Sov. Psychol. Psychiat.* 1964, 2 (4), 15–27.]

LYUBLINSKAYA, A. A. (1959) *Ocherki psikhicheskogo razvitiya rebenka (ranniĭ i doshkol'nyĭ vozrast)* [*Outlines of the Mental Development of the Child (early and pre-school age)*]. Moscow: Akad. Pedag. Nauk R.S.F.S.R.

MALLITSKAYA, M. K. (1960) K metodike ispol'zovaniya kartinok dlya razvitiya ponimaniya rechi u deteĭ v kontse pervogo i na vtorom godu zhizni [A method for using pictures to develop speech comprehension in children at the end of the first and in the second year of life]. *Vop. Psikhol.* 3, 122–6.

MEERSON, YA. YA. (1959) Ob osobennostyakh vzaimodeĭstviya signal'nykh sistem u deteĭ s raznym urovnem razvitiya rechi [Features of the interaction of the signal systems in children at various levels of speech development]. *Doklady Akad. Pedag. Nauk RSFSR*, 3, 85–88.

MELESHKO, S. D. (1960) Typological features in the speech activity of junior school children. *Pavlov. J. high nerv. Act.* 10, 574–80.

SOVIET PSYCHOLINGUISTICS 149

NATADZE, R. G. (1957) Voprosy myshleniya i rechi v trudakh psikhologov gruzinskoĭ SSR [Questions of thought and speech in the work of Georgian psychologists]. *Vop. Psikhol.* **5**, 91–107.

Nauchnaya sessiya, posvyashchennaya problemam fiziologicheskogo ucheniya akademika I. P. Pavlova [*Scientific Session dedicated to the Problems of the Physiological Teachings of Academician I. P. Pavlov*]. Moscow: Akad. Nauk S.S.S.R., 1950.

NIKIFOROVA, O. I. (1961) Znachenie rechi dlya tochnosti vosproizvedeniya zritel'nogo obraza [The role of speech in the accuracy of reproduction of visual images]. *Vop. Psikhol.* **1**, 133–40. [Translation in *Sov. Psychol. Psychiat.* 1963–4, **2** (2), 11–17.]

PATRINA, D. T. (1959) O ponimanii znacheniya slov doshkol'nikami [On the understanding of the meanings of words by preschoolers]. *Vop. Psikhol.* **4**, 59–63.

PAVLOV, I. P. (1927) *Conditioned Reflexes: An investigation of the physiological activity of the cerebral cortex.* London: Oxford Univ. Press.

PAVLOV, I. P. (1932) Fiziologiya vyssheĭ nervnoĭ deyatel'nosti [The physiology of higher nervous activity]. *Priroda*, 1139–54.

PIAGET, J. (1923) *Le Langage et la pensée chez l'enfant.* Neuchâtel–Paris: Delachaux & Niestle. [Translation: *The Language and Thought of the Child.* New York: Meridian, 1955.]

PIAGET, J. (1962) *Comments on Vygotsky's critical remarks concerning "The Language and Thought of the Child" and "Judgment and Reasoning in the Child".* Cambridge, Mass.: M.I.T. Press.

PICK, H. L., Jr. (1964) Perception in Soviet psychology. *Psychol. Bull.* **62**, 21–35.

POPOVA, M. I. (1958) Grammaticheskie elementy yazyka v rechi deteĭ preddoshkol'nogo vozrasta [Grammatical elements of language in the speech of pre-school children]. *Vop. Psikhol.* **3**, 106–17.

Psikhologicheskaya nauka v SSSR, Vol. I. Moscow: Akad. Pedag. Nauk R.S.F.S.R., 1959. [Translation: *Psychological Science in the USSR*, Vol. I. Washington, D.C.: U.S. Joint Publications Res. Serv. No. 11466, 1961.]

RAEVSKIĬ, A. N. (1958) *Psikhologiya rechi v sovetskoĭ psikhologicheskoĭ nauke za 40 let* [The *Psychology of Speech in Soviet Psychological Science for 40 years*]. Kiev: Kiev Univ. Press.

RAMISHVILĬ, D. I. (1954) O psikhologicheskoĭ prirode donauchnykh ponyatiĭ [On the psychological nature of prescientific concepts]. In: *Doklady na soveshchanii po voprosam psikhologii.* Moscow: Akad. Pedag. Nauk R.S.F.S.R., pp. 100–8. [Translation in *General Systems: Yearbook Soc. Gen. Syst. Res.* 1960, Vol. 5, pp. 231–5.]

RAZRAN, G. (1961) The observable unconscious and the inferable conscious in current Soviet psychophysiology: Interoceptive conditioning, semantic conditioning, and the orienting reflex. *Psychol. Rev.* **68**, 81–147.

RAZRAN, G. (1965) Russian physiologists' psychology and American experimental psychology: A historical and a systematic collation and a look into the future. *Psychol. Bull.* **63**, 42–64.

SECHENOV, I. M. (1863) Refleksy golovnogo mozga [Reflexes of the brain]. *Meditsinskiĭ Vestnik*, **3**, 461–4, 493–512.

SELEZNEVA, I. S. (1957) Nekotorye osobennosti vospriyatiya udareniya v slovakh russkogo yazyka [Some features of the perception of stress in words of the Russian language]. *Vop. Psikhol.* **4**, 70–79.

SHIF, ZH. I. (1954) *Ocherki psikhologii usvoeniya russkogo yazyka gluk-honemymi shkol'nikami* [*Outlines of the Psychology of Acquisition of the Russian Language by Deaf-and-Dumb Pupils*]. Moscow: Uchpedgiz.

SHVACHKIN, N. Kh. (1948) Razvitie fonematicheskogo vospriyatiya rechi v rannem detstve [Development of phonematic perception of speech in early childhood]. *Izvestiya Akad. Pedag. Nauk RSFSR*, 13.

SHVARTS, L. A. (1960) Uslovnye refleksy na slovesnye razdrazhiteli [Conditioned responses to verbal stimuli]. *Vop. Psikhol.* **1**, 86–98. [Translation in *Sov. Psychol. Psychiat.* 1964, **2** (4), 3–14.]

SIMONOV, P. V., BALUEVA, M. N., and ERSHOV, P. M. (1964) Proizvol'naya regulyatsiya kozhno-gal'vanicheskogo refleksa [Voluntary regulation of the galvanic skin response]. *Vop. Psikhol.*, **6**, 45–50. [Translation in *Sov. Psychol. Psychiat.* 1965, **3** (4), 22–5]

SLOBIN, D. I. (1966) The acquisition of Russian as a native language. In: F. Smith and G. Miller (Eds.), *The Genesis of Language: A Psycholinguistic Approach.* Cambridge, Mass.: M.I.T. Press, 1966.

SMIRNOV, A. A. (1955) O sostoyanii nauchno-issledovatel'skoĭ raboty v oblasti psikhologii [On the state of empirical scientific work in the area of psychology]. *Vop. Psikhol.* **5**, 38–53. [Translation in B. Simon (Ed.), *Psychology in the Soviet Union.* Stanford, Calif.: Stanford Univ. Press, 1957, pp. 29–45.]

SOKHIN, F. A. (1959) O formirovanii yazykovykh obobshcheniĭ v protsesse rechevogo razvitiya [On the formation of linguistic generalizations in the process of speech development]. *Vop. Psikhol.* **5**, 112–23.

SOKOLOV, A. N. (1959) Issledovaniya po probleme rechevykh meckanizmov myshleniya [Studies on the problem of the speech mechanisms of thinking]. In *Psikhologicheskaya nauka v SSSR*, Vol. I. Moscow: Akad. Pedag. Nauk R.S.F.S.R., pp. 488–515. [Translation in *Psychological Science in the USSR*, Vol. I. Washington, D.C.: U.S. Joint Publications Res. Serv. No. 11466, 1961, pp. 669–703.]

SOKOLOV, A. N. (1960) Vnutrenyaya rech' pri izucheniya inostrannykh yazykov [Inner speech in the study of foreign languages]. *Vop. Psikhol.* **5**, 57–61. [Translation in *Sov. Educ.* 1961, **3**, 7, 10–14.]

SPIKER, C. C. (1960) Verbal factors in the discrimination learning of children. In: J. C. Wright and J. Kagan (Eds.), *Basic Cognitive Processes in Children. Monogr. Soc. Res. Child Develpm.*, Vol. 28, 2, 53–69.

VOLKOVA, V. D. (1953) O nekotorykh osobennostyakh formirovanie uslovnykh refleksov na rechevye razdrazhiteli u deteĭ [On certain characteristics of the formation of conditioned reflexes to speech stimuli in children]. *Fiziol. zhurn. SSSR* **39**, 540–8.

VYGOTSKY, L. S. (1934) *Myshlenie i rech'*. Moscow: Sotsekgiz. [Translation: *Thought and Language.* Cambridge, Mass., and New York: M.I.T. Press and Wiley, 1962.]

VYGOTSKY, L. S. (1956) *Izbrannye psychologicheskie issledovaniya* [*Selected Psychological Investigations*]. Moscow: Akad. Pedag. Nauk R.S.F.S.R.

VYGOTSKY, L. S. (1960) *Razvitie vysshykh psikhicheskikh funktsiĭ* [*Development of Higher Mental Functions*]. Moscow: Akad. Pedag. Nauk R.S.F.S.R.

WATSON, J. B. (1919) *Psychology from the Standpoint of a Behaviorist.* Philadelphia: G. B. Lippincott.

ZAKHAROVA, A. V. (1958) Usvoenie doshkol'nikami padezhnykh form [Mastery by pre-schoolers of forms of grammatical case]. *Doklady Akad. Pedag. Nauk RSFSR,* **2** (3), 81–84.

ZHINKIN, N. I. (1959) Na putyakh k izucheniyu mekhanizma rechi [On ways of studying the speech mechanism]. In: *Psikhologicheskaya nauka v SSSR,* Vol. I. Moscow: Akad. Pedag. Nauk R.S.F.S.R., pp. 470–87. [Translation in *Psychological Science in the USSR,* Vol. I. Washington, D.C.: U.S. Joint Publication Res. Serv. No. 11466, 1961, pp. 645–68.]

ZHUĬKOV, S. F. (1955) Pervonachal'nye obobshcheniya yazykovogo materiala u mladshikh shkol'nikov [Initial generalization of linguistic material in the youngest school pupils]. *Vop. Psikhol.* **2,** 54–64.

ZHUROVA, L. E. (1963) Razvitie zvukovogo analiza slov u deteĭ doshkol'nogo vozrasta [The development of sound analysis of words in preschool children]. *Vop. Psikhol.* **3,** 20–32. [Translation in *Sov. Psychol. Psychiat.* 1963–4, **2** (2), 17–27.]

CHAPTER 6

Studies on the Mental Development of the Child

LEVY RAHMANI

Kfar Schaul Work Village, Government Mental Hospital, Jerusalem

THERE are two sources of Soviet psychologists' interest in the mental growth of the child. The first is that this field—together with the psychology of sense organs and the comparative psychology—is seen as one which can provide evidence for the materialistic-evolutionist theory of the mind. Secondly, the Russians' deep concern with educational matters has led them to an intensive study of child development. It is apparent, at least in recent years, that the second source has become predominant and a good part of the studies on child psychology are closely related to paedagogy (Levitov, 1960). Psychologists at the Academy of Paedagogical Sciences have been studying problems of instruction by themselves teaching in special experimental classes and various procedures and didactics have been elaborated by psychologists like Menchinskaya (1958, 1961) for mathematics, Kabanova-Meller (1962) for geography, Bogoyavlenskii (1957) for grammar, and others.

Underlying these studies are a number of propositions, some of which were advanced by Rubinshtein (1946), 30 years ago. At about the same time, Vygotskii (1956, 1960) formulated his ideas on the social nature of the child's mind and the paramount role of instruction and communication with the adult for his mental growth. These studies, which have been developed by Leont'ev (1959a and b), Luria and Yudovich (1959), Luria and Polyakova

152

(1959a) and their many co-workers, have oriented later researches and represent a major school of thought in modern Russian psychology. One encounters this line of reasoning in studies on the development of perception, memory, thought and voluntary action and even among the works of scholars who have developed entirely different theories. Some of the main propositions and experimental investigations into child psychology are presented below.

Development and Education

Divergent ideas about the relation between mental development and education have been put forward. Menchinskaya and Bogo-yavlenskii stated that one cannot speak of an intrinsic autogenetic evolution of the child's mind, although they agreed that the efficiency of education is contingent with the developmental level already reached. On the other hand, Leont'ev (1957) held that there is an inner evolution of the mind, independent of the individual process of learning. This spontaneous evolution is not an abso-lutely autonomous process; it is a product of learning that has taken place during the course of the evolution of human society.

Despite these differences, all Soviet authors agree that instruc-tion and education are of supreme importance in the child's mental growth. Certainly, the role of the biological factor is not denied, but there is a strong tendency to bring the environmental-educational factor to the fore. Thus, Anan'ev (1957, 1965) is of the opinion that the child's transition from one kind of activity to another most be prepared for by educators. Consequently, not only should instruction be begun in the play period, but also preparation for future work. Thus self-care and simple actions should be introduced in the kindergarten. Leont'ev has been much concerned with the theoretical foundation of the above approach. Here is the core of the argument.

The individual development of mental functions and abilities follows a process of assimilation of social experience. The mental processes take shape on the basis of certain morphological pro-perties of the brain and the latter are absolutely necessary if the former are to develop. Yet mental processes have a specific content and fill certain functions in man's life. It is precisely to this content that one refers, when one talks of the human mind. This is produced by the child's adjustment to, and assimilation of, the surrounding world of things, words and ideas. Any mental process, even if considered somewhat elementary, e.g. the sensory processes, are developed through experience. The mere imprinting of impressions—a capacity of the brain to retain stimulation—turns into logical memory; the involuntary orienting reaction to any stimulus becomes voluntary attention, etc. Thus the environment does not represent a mere condition, but the source itself of the child's development. Leont'ev points out that the world of objects which embodies the human abilities is not understood by the child from the very beginning. In order to realize the human nature of surrounding objects, the child has to act upon them in a human manner, i.e. not by natural movements. This is why his communication with the adult plays a leading role. So the child's activity and his communication are the two major factors of his mental growth (Leont'ev, 1959b).

The above view of the relationship between the biological and social aspects is fairly well illustrated in an investigation conducted by Luria. This was carried out many years ago, but it has only recently been published (Luria, 1962).

Luria compared the development of elementary visual memory, of the remembering of words, with and without the aid of corresponding pictures, in two groups of mono- and bizygotic twins. The pairs of twins were presented with nine geometrical figures, which they were subsequently asked to recognize among twenty-five figures. It was noted that the differences between bizygotic twins of pre-school age were $3 \cdot 3$ times greater than the differences between unizygotic twins, at the same age. A significant difference was also obtained at the school age, although the coefficient fell to $2 \cdot 5$. Luria assumed that these results indicated the relevancy to this function of the hereditary factor.

In a second series of experiments, subjects had to recall fifteen heard words. This time the difference within the bizygotic pairs of twins of the pre-school age was only $2 \cdot 5$ times that of the other group of twins. The coefficient decreases to $1 \cdot 75$ at the school level. Luria supposed that this was due to the increased environmental influence in this function as compared with the former one and to the reduced role of genotypical factors. This assumption found further support in a third series of experiments.

The subjects were again asked to remember fifteen words, but this time accompanied by pictures. While the results at the pre-school age were not significantly different from those at the same age in the previous experiment—$2 \cdot 3$ times—a considerably decreased coefficient—$0 \cdot 8$—was registered among schoolchildren. This was taken to mean that there was no relevant difference between the pairs of mono- and bizygotic twins with regard to so-called mediated memory. Luria concluded that "with age, new and complex mental processes develop. Old tasks begin to be accomplished in new ways, and there is an essential change in the relationship between the mental processes and the genotype. The variability of complex forms of mental activity (which are social in their genesis and mediated in their structure) may even lose any relations to the genotype" (Luria, 1962; Leont'ev and Rozanova, 1951).

Two Methods of Study

Soviet authors do not deny the value of diaries compiled by trained psychologists, and some of them have published such works (Menchinskaya, 1957). However, they object to the tendency to interpret the child's behaviour by analogy with adult mental life and to ascribe to the child feelings and thoughts that do not belong to him (El'konin, 1960a). They are also very critical of tests. Among other objections, these are said to disregard the paramount influence of the environment on the child's upbringing. Furthermore, underlying testology is the claim that tests are capable of measuring constant personality traits, and that these are not at all influenced by external factors (Luria, 1962).

Leont'ev took it for granted that the study of both age- and individual-differences is to be carried out with experimental-diagnostic instruments. One has to guarantee well-controlled conditions and, as far as possible, to avoid the variety of factors which intervene in test situations and lead to ambiguous results. In this way, one is able to pursue the formation of mental processes, the relation between certain abilities and the variance of activity with various conditions of life. Such a study is likely to be of high practical value: one passes from registration of the child's level of development to an explanation of the sources of the activity and then to the future effect of educational action.

In Russian psychology two experimental methods of studying the child have appeared: the cross-sectional and the longitudinal study (El'konin, 1960b). In the first method, a comparative study of a specific mental process in various age groups is used. This was the way chosen by Leont'ev (1951) and Zinchenko (1961) in their studies on memory development. In El'konin's view one cannot get to the sources of development by using this method. It only enables the pursuit of successive changes. The longitudinal study, that he advocates, consists of the investigation of the same child, or the same group of children, over a certain period. El'konin felt that such a study permits better acquaintance with the formation of mental processes and personality traits. In addition, age and individual differences can be studied together by this method. El'konin's investigations were carried out in experimental classes which were conceived of as a sort of "clinic of normal development" (El'konin, 1960b).

On the other hand, Bozhovich pointed out the limitations of the paedagogical experiment. It is said to be useful only in the final stage of a research on the psychology of personality. The "educational" experiment should not replace other experimental methods aimed at disclosing the laws of development (Bozhovich and Blagonadezhina, 1961). In fact, El'konin himself realized that the method proposed by him had some shortcomings. He noted that it was time-consuming and limited to small groups. This led him to draw the conclusion that it should be combined with the cross-sectional method. The latter would be used to reveal the line of development of a certain mental process, and the former to disclose more exact data, such as the crucial points of the development.

Types of Activity

One of the basic propositions of Soviet child psychology is that the developing child goes through a number of major types of activity. These have been described as the principal ways in which the child reacts to the surrounding reality, above all the human world. There are three main types of relationship to the external world and three corresponding types of activity: play, study and work. Certainly, the pre-school age is the age of play, while the school age is for study. This should not be interpreted as meaning that these are the only activities of the respective ages, but as the predominant types which determined the mental growth at these two stages. Each is seen as contingent with the most significant changes in the child's personality.

The most scientifically fruitful work has been done in the pre-school age—3–7 years—with the vast majority of studies being concerned with the 3–5 range. This age is considered the time when some basic aspects of the personality take shape. As Leont'ev stated: "the pre-school period is that period when the child discovers the surrounding human reality. In his activity, and above all in his play, which now goes beyond the narrow limits of manipulation of objects, the child enters the wide world, which he masters in an active way" (Leont'ev, 1959b). At this time the first hierarchy of motives is discernible and the child acquires something approaching adult motivation (El'konin, 1960b).

The main activity of the pre-school age is the game with roles and rules. The major activity of the child under 3 years of age is manipulation, which develops his ability to discern properties of objects. The transition to play with roles requires an important change in the child's mental make up. He is able, now, not only to perceive objects but also to imagine certain situations. This is also linked to another factor, strongly emphasized by Soviet authors: the child's tendency to independent play. He plays without the participation of adults; although their actions and reciprocal relations are taken as a model. The child of 3–4 already rejects the suggestion that he should play at being himself; he perceives the game merely as the imitation of adult actions. In other words, his play has a social content. The evolution of this content, between the ages of 3 to 7, illustrates the "socialization" of play. Roles are performed in an ever more correct fashion, and actions are more and more subordinated to the attainment of goals. The child realizes the main aspects of the activities he is reproducing.

El'konin asked children to play the role of educators. He noticed that while the youngest "educators" fed the children and dressed them, etc., the elder ones paid attention above all to the children's behaviour and to the relations between them. The evolution of play is described by El'konin, and other authors, as passing from games in which adult actions upon objects held the main role, to games which reproduce the relations between adults and, finally, to games consisting of the submission to certain rules.

Soviet students have raised the question of whether the child's phantasy is entirely unconstrained by reality, as some investigators have supposed. There is a strong tendency in Russian psychology to admit that strong elements of realism can be found in children's drawings, in their play and in the way that they understand stories. The child's phantasy is considered to be closely linked to his life experience; the richer the experience, the greater the ability to discern real from unreal. Observational and experimental evidence has been provided to support these propositions. El'konin asked 3–4 year olds to change the order of their meal, i.e. to start with the second or third course. The children accepted the suggestion without protesting. However, when he suggested to 5 year olds, who were playing at giving injections, that they change the order of their actions, they refused to do so. They maintained the logical sequence of events, although they were not able to explain it. Yet 6 and 7 year olds could. Zhukovskaya also noted that the richer the child's knowledge of a certain topic provided to him, the wider and more linked to reality is his phantasy (Zhukovskaya, 1961).

Particular emphasis has been given to the influence of the game-with-roles upon the development of the child's motivation. It has been shown that this gradually corresponds more and more with reality and becomes broader, going beyond strictly personal interests. While playing, children feel attracted to toys belonging to others, but during the course of play with roles, they subordinate these temptations to the aim of the game. A good example of this line of thought is to be found in one of Neverovich's studies (1955). He noticed that pre-school children could get better results when they were asked to make paper serviettes for their mothers than when they had to make them for other children or for themselves. The differences between three age-groups were significant: among the 3–4 year olds, only 28 % worked in accordance with the experimenter's instructions, 50 % of the 5 year olds and 80 % of the 6–7 year olds. Another example of the relation between the child's motivation and the content of the task may demonstrate the point. When children were asked to make small flags for their mothers, the results were poor. Some of them even queried: "What will Mummy do with the flag?" However, when asked to make flags for other children they worked better.

The Growth of Intellectual Operations

Thought and its development is the field in which the desire of Russian authors to combine theoretical studies with practical educational interests can most easily be seen. Many of the experiments carried out on school children belong to the psychology of thought as well as to didactics.

Various theories of the nature of thought have been developed in modern Russian psychology. Each of them has assumed that a different factor is responsible for the process of problem-solving, and, of course, the development of thought has been implicitly supposed to be dependent on the formation of that same factor.

The following survey of these theories is limited to the presentation of four main trends.

The Leont'ev–Gal'perin school is the first and in it the emphasis is placed on the internalization of external acts. Leont'ev's conjectures on this subject are a result of his general conception of the child's mental development. For him, the formation of the intellectual operations that make the assimilation of human knowledge possible require that the child pass through a number of stages. Firstly, the adult must create concrete external actions. These have an advantage in that they can be demonstrated and the child's performance can be corrected. Then the external actions pass to the verbal plane, from whence they can be guided by verbal instructions. The attempt to solve a problem is subsequently seen in the form of speaking aloud, and finally problem-solving becomes a mental act of thinking. Although these stages are not considered as necessary for the development of each specific mental process, they are thought of as a general scheme of the development of mental operations.

Gal'perin elaborated these stages of the development of a mental operation (1959, 1961). For example, the formation of the first arithmetical procedure—an elementary model of a mental operation—is assumed to take place in the following way. The starting point for the child who has to learn to add up to ten, is the concrete addition of one group of objects to another. That is, if the child has to add $4 + 3$, he first makes up two separate groups, and then counts them together. Later, the manual action is replaced by the visual tracking of the objects. Counting gradually loses the characteristics of an external action and turns into an explicit verbal operation, which is no longer dependent on concrete objects. Finally, addition becomes a mental operation. This process of internalization is linked to a continuous narrowing of the action. Initially, the mental operation is a replica of the structure of the corresponding external action in which the child adds unit to unit. Then he adds to the first term, now taken as a whole, the second term, which is still subdivided into units. Only later is the second term also regarded as an entity. The internalization of the action is accompanied by three major changes, the abstraction of the essential conditions of the action, the reduction of the process and its auto-matization, and the consolidation of the action into a stereotype.

Davydov, one of Gal'perin's co-workers, studied the above mentioned stages in the formation of the concept of quantity (Davydov, 1957). The experiments were performed on children between the ages of $4-6\frac{1}{2}$ who knew how to count and could com-bine groups by adding one unit at a time. The research was designed to investigate the transition from concrete to abstract counting. It was observed that this transition was made possible by the transfer of movements used for the counting of seen objects, to the counting of hidden objects and then to imaginary, verbally suggested, quantities. These movements enabled the child to take the real things as the subject of his action and in this way to realize that they represented a quantity expressed in a numeral. Yet the abstract quantity was counted in units, i.e. the imaginary objects were not seen as a whole. This ability was developed in a special series of exercises, in which concrete objects were used initially, only to be subsequently replaced by imaginary objects. The origi-nal movements of separating each object were gradually replaced by a continuous movement of the hand as if it were embracing the whole quantity, which was expressed in a numeral. In Davydov's view, the transition from concrete to imaginary quantities is in-strumental for the abstraction of the quantitative aspect of the things. The quantification itself becomes a particular subject of the mental operations.

The proposition that the development of thought is linked to the transition from external to internal actions is accepted by other authors too, among whom one must mention Kabanova-Meller (1962). She disagrees with Gal'perin as regards the generality of this method which was found useful in only two cases. Kabanova-Meller showed that this is the way schoolchildren reproduce knowledge, i.e. the way they remember something. In such a situa-tion, the activity is merely a matter of reproducing acquired know-ledge and not of developing new mental operations. Furthermore, the transition to mental action may play a leading role in situations where the child is being taught to realize the relation between various aspects of an object. In one experiment, this method was used to form the child's ability to distinguish between the right and left banks of a river. Pupils have been taught to establish a relation between their own position toward a river, its course and the right bank.

As has been mentioned, this is only one of the methods that Kabanova-Meller has recommended and it is included in a system of five methods of developing intellectual activity. She sees the formation of an intellectual approach as including the passing on of the knowledge of how to act, and the fostering of the ability to make use of this knowledge. When it is complete the method can be applied to the solving of a new practical problem, or to the formation of a new concept. Thus, in another experiment she studied the way in which visual material could be used to teach the geographical concept "plain" to pupils in grade 4. The results confirmed the general hypothesis of the author that at least two images are necessary for the formation of a concept with the aid of visual material. The usual textbook illustration of a plain—a single picture of an open, smooth region—is likely to lead pupils to the wrong conclusion that a plain is always an open, smooth region. Experimentally, the concept was formed in two stages. In the first, the children compared two pictures of plains, one of which was an open region and the other was afforested. The pupils were able to compare two different images and in this way to discover the essential common attribute, the flat surface. In the second stage, another comparison was made, but attention was paid to the secondary, changeable characteristics. Thus, the non-essential characteristics were noted, and it was concluded that a plain can be either smooth or undulating, covered by grass or forest, etc. Kabanova-Meller saw in this method a means for the child to get acquainted with the methods of analysis, abstraction, correlation and generalization of attributes of objects, with which they have to deal.

These views are shared by several other authors who are interested in the formation of logical thinking in schoolchildren

(Bogoyavlenskii, 1957, 1962; Bogoyavlenskii and Menchinskaya, 1959; Gurova, 1961; Kal'mykova, 1961). Bogoyavlenskii points out that not all types of instruction lead to mental growth and for that purpose it is necessary to develop corresponding methods of intellectual operations for problem-solving. Menchinskaya and her co-workers are also interested in the development of "intellectual skills" that are manifest in nearly all practical circumstances, i.e. they are neither specific to a certain kind of activity nor to particular knowledge. These are assumed to represent a central aspect of the child's mental growth, and their formation is dependent on three conditions: (a) getting acquainted with the rule that is to be put into practice, (b) the practice of corresponding actions and (c) self control of logical procedures. The development of logical, self-controlled thought is not considered as merely the result of acquiring knowledge and various skills, but as something which can only be developed under special conditions, which are designed to make the child perceive the logical relations of the material that they are handling. A co-worker of Menchinskaya, Gurova, noticed that even pupils in grade 10 were not conscious of the logical operations that they performed in the classification and definition of objects. In other words, the practical application of a logical procedure is not necessarily based on the consciousness of the intellectual operations underlying it. The ability to use certain logical procedures was closely related to the factual content of the concepts and to the habitual way of dealing with them, but was not indicative of the existence of intellectual skills.

This lack of intellectual skills was well illustrated in experiments, in which the majority of the subjects failed to solve practical problems, although they had the necessary theoretical knowledge. For example, in an experiment conducted by Zykova (1958), pupils of the sixth grade had to solve two similar problems, one theoretical and the other practical. The first one consisted of deciding which side of a triangle was the longest, which the shortest, and why, when the size of the angles was known. The second problem is that of a building contractor. He knows that the angle between the rafters of the roof is 80° and that both rafters make angles of 50° with the topmost beam of the house that he is building. He has planks of various lengths at his disposal and his problem is "where must the longer planks go; on the roof (parallel to the rafters) or on the ceiling (parallel to the beam)?" Despite the fact that the second problem was given after the subjects had successfully solved the first one, only a few of them managed to reach the solution. This was explained by the fact that while the pupils were accustomed to working with already abstracted geometrical relations, they had no experience in perceiving them in concrete objects.

This study, as did other similar ones (Kal'mykova, 1961), led Menchinskaya to the conclusion that the development of intellectual operations and the formation of correct concepts should generally be made in two stages. Primarily, emphasis should be placed on the essential elements of the material studied, and the introduction, in abundance, of practical items should be avoided, as it is likely to result in side-associations. It is only in the next stage that the concept should be applied to the complexity of realistic activities.

The reader will have noted the divergence of the above view and that of Gal'perin. Although Kal'mykova (1961) is of the opinion that Gal'perin's method is efficient for the formation of concepts or the acquisition of simple actions, she does not think it useful for developing the skill of applying theoretical knowledge. This line of thinking is influenced by the current trend to introduce polytechnical education into the Soviet school system, and the consequent need to connect the theoretical study of a subject like physics to the technical problems of common practise.

Rubinshtein's school emphasizes the processes of analysis and synthesis in the course of problem-solving. Rubinshtein (1958, 1960) saw thought as a process of analysis of the properties of an object and their interrelations in addition to a process of synthesis of the detached elements. Analysis is dependent on the characteristics of the whole object, and is closely related to the opposite process of synthesis so that it will not lead to disintegration of the whole, but to its reorganization. Synthesis is the establishment of new relationships among the isolated elements. The process of abstraction during the course of conceptual thinking is a particular form of analysis. In solving a problem, the use of acquired knowledge is not a mere act of reproductive memory. Solution requires an analysis of both the problem and the previous knowledge, and their correlation by synthesis. The possibility of transfer on the rational plane—at the level of the "second signalling system"—is due precisely to these processes of analysis and synthesis which form the basis of abstraction.

According to Rubinshtein, the development of thought is intrinsically connected to the formation of these processes. Experiments have shown that, in younger pupils, analysis is confined to the framework of the given mathematical problem and is limited to the coordination of available information and the immediate problem. In older children, the problem was analysed with reference to analogous problems. It was also noticed that, in general, the younger pupils solved problems step by step, while the older ones tried to realize the meaning of the whole problem and afterwards turned their attention to its solution. These differences were assumed to be due to different levels of transfer.

Rubinshtein disagreed with the two contrary theories of the relationship between sensorial-concrete and abstract-verbal material in the course of the development of thinking. He could not accept that, in the first stages of thought, the child handles concrete material better than abstract. Nor could he agree with the opposite view that abstract tasks were easier for the child. Rubinshtein thought that concrete things could be approached in an abstract fashion, if the characteristics that were to be abstracted were made to stand out by the experimenter (or by the teacher). A child counts identical objects easier than different ones because he can disregard the varying sensorial characteristics. That is a child has less difficulty in handling the abstract relations of objects if these are outlined in a concrete sensorial form. He thinks more efficiently on a sensorial plane than on the plane of abstract concepts, provided that the non-essential characteristics have already been excluded.

One of the experiments conducted under Rubinshtein's direction gives a good illustration of the role of the conditions that enable the problem and the acquired knowledge to be included in a single procedure of analysis and synthesis. Slavskaya (1960) asked pupils of the seventh to ninth grades to demonstrate that two of the triangles formed by the diagonals of a trapezium are of equal area. Then a second guiding problem of demonstrating that the diagonals of a rectangle are equal was presented. The subjects were divided into two groups, the first of which was given the auxiliary problem while the subjects were in the initial stages of solving the main problem. The second group received the auxiliary problem at a more advanced stage. It was noticed that after having solved the secondary problem, the pupils of the first group began to connect the two problems. Although no hints were given, they quickly realized that the two problems had something in common, but exactly what, they could not say. ("This is a trapezium . . . the diagonals are not equal, nor are the sides. I don't see how the diagonals can be of any help.") Only later did they discern the relation between the two problems. ("The angles are of no use, nor are the diagonals, but one can use the common base.")

Subjects of the second group, from the beginning, attempted the secondary problem by directly connecting it with the first, as if it were a continuation. They were able to disregard the secondary elements—the equality of the angles and of the triangles—and took note of the common height of the two triangles. In this case, the transfer from one problem to another was almost simultaneous. Slavskaya concluded that immediate and correct transfer is dependent on the degree of analysis already reached.

The final school has approached the growth of thought as the formation of systems of associations. Despite their differences, Shevarev and Samarin, the two main scholars of this school, share the idea that the establishment of an association between two or more elements is the central factor of thought, and that the organization of associative connections should be the purpose of educators.

Shevarev's researches (1959) on the way schoolchildren solve problems in arithmetic, algebra and geometry led him to the conclusion that certain general associations are basic to the process of problem solving. These associations represent the general rules of solving problems of a corresponding category. A generalized association is the major premiss of the judgement needed to solve the problem. Bringing the premiss to the fore, i.e. the inclusion of a given problem to a certain class, enables the process of reasoning to be shortened. When a pupil in grade 7 had to find the logarithm of $3a^3b^2$, he said, "I immediately read 'log 3'. Then I noticed 3 as the coefficient of a, so I read '3 log a'." Thus, Shevarev considered that the ability to solve algebraic problems is a particular aspect of thinking according to rules.

Samarin regards association as a general concept of psychology, and consequently it must be taken as the basis for the study of any mental activity, including the intellectual processes (Samarin, 1962). The development of thought is dependent on the formation of associations from elementary "local" ones to complex systems which include elements from most of the various fields of knowledge. The purpose of education is conceived as being the selection and consolidation of the correct associations, the exclusion of the wrong ones, and the inclusion of limited associations in broader systems.

The Development of Voluntary Movements

There is an old Russian interest in the study of the development of voluntary movements. Its source can be found in Sechenov's works (undated), in which motor development was ascribed a supreme role in the child's mental growth. There is a direct line between this study and the current investigations of Zaporozhets and his co-workers (1960, 1964) with which we will be particularly concerned in this section. The pre-school child's tendency for independent play, the occurrence of his own wishes, his attempt to take part in adult activities, the demands that adults are beginning to make on him—all guided the investigators to search the development of voluntary actions at this age. They emphasize the considerable growth of these actions during this period, and above all the increasing ability to handle tools, to imagine future actions and to control them. The writer calls the reader's attention to the common point between the studies reported in this section and those of Gal'perin. This is particularly clear with regard to the attempt to present the child's mental growth as the internalization of external acts. Zaporozhets, who worked with Leont'ev, may be considered as belonging to the school of thought that bases itself on Vygotsky. Over the last 25 years, one can see three main directions in his studies. They are: (a) the role of imitation; (b) the development of an orienting activity; (c) the role of language.

Imitation is seen as the main way of developing voluntary actions in young children. In play, the child's identification with a certain person or profession, the improvement of his capacity to observe, the refinement of the action taken as a model, all help to develop his ability to imitate. Polyakova (1958) conducted an experiment to clarify the role that imitation plays, by comparing two ways of learning the path of a labyrinth: by imitation and by independent trial and error. The children had to pass through the alleys of a labyrinth to a centrally placed flag, on their own, the first group without any additional information, while for the second group the action was demonstrated but without any verbal account. The results show that the second group needed less trials and also made less errors than the first group. The differences were greatest at the beginning—the first stage of the formation of the skill. In the second group, the movements were better organized from the start and there were few errors in the first part of the path. These results were obtained for all ages, but the older the children in the sample, the more proficient the first group became.

The attention to the so-called orienting activity which precedes the action itself was a consequence of the study of the formation of motor skills, both by imitation and by other methods. In fact—as the reader will have noticed from other chapters of this book— man's orientation preceding a task-directed action is one of the current subjects of Soviet neuropsychology. Zaporozhets' investigations convincingly show that the child's ability to act in a voluntary and efficient manner is dependent upon the development of orientation to the task with which he has to cope. It was noted that even in the learning of a simple motor action orientation to the task was necessary.

Tsvetkova (1958) asked pre-school children to react to three colours projected on to a screen, by pressing on three different buttons. Response patterns could be divided into two categories. The first one consisted of the children who listened to the instructions carefully and were very attentive to the signals. This "intensive" orientation resulted in an initial negative effect on the actual performance. The reaction was inhibited and the children did not press the buttons, although on inquiry it was revealed that the children knew exactly what they had to do. Only after five to six trials did the children react, and even then cautiously. The length of the orienting action decreased after eight or nine trials, the rate of pressing rose, and the children became more confident. There were only a few, and then mainly minor, errors. In the other category, the children behaved in an entirely different fashion. They did not pay attention to the instructions. Some did not even wait for the experimenter to finish before they started to press the buttons, regardless of the signals. Subsequently the responses improved, orienting reactions appeared and the rate of pressing decreased. However, these children made more mistakes than the others, took longer to learn the action and indeed some even failed to do this.

Poddyakov (1959, 1960) has provided some findings about age differences in orienting reactions. Two groups of children, 4–5 and 5–6 years of age, had, by pressing on buttons, to guide the movements of a doll in accordance with directions given by the experimenter. The younger children started pressing without any preliminary orientation. The investigatory actions appeared only after the children had noticed that they did not obtain the desired results. On the other hand, the older children started by orienting to the task.

Three forms of orienting activity were distinguished. The first consisted of concrete, effective actions. In the second, the orienting reactions were reduced to certain imitative movements, and the pressing of the buttons was stimulated. Finally, in the third form, the orientation took place on the mental plane and was limited to the visual examination of the situation.

Poddyakov also delineated two aspects of the relationship between the orienting activity and the actual action. He noticed that the investigatory activity was directly related to the given task. The children endeavoured to find out which buttons had to be used to move the doll in the required direction. In addition, general orienting actions were observed. These were designed to investigate what was going on around the child, without having any connection with the experimental task. This seemed to be a "pure" cognitive activity.

The stages just described corroborate the broader scheme of developmental stages of orienting activity that Zaporozhets formulated. This schema was supported by experimental findings on the changing manual and ocular movements during the formation of an object-image on the retina. Yet the writer feels that the problem of the relation between the stages of the ontogenetical development of orienting activity and the stages of orientation preceding a certain action has not been thoroughly clarified. There has been some inconsistency among the different formulations. The following description—comprising four stages—apparently reflects the view of Zaporozhets' school of thought.

The first stage is one of disorganized reactions which can be produced by any stimulus. In children under the age of 3, the orientation cannot be distinguished from the actual action. After the first stage, there is what might be called a "fixation" of what has been revealed of the required movements. In older children one can see a certain organization of the orientation and some stereotyped investigatory movements that have been formed through previous experience. These have a regulatory function with regard to the task on hand, but as yet, do not form a systematic exploration of the situation.

In the second stage, the orienting reactions begin to form a system; orientation to one stimulus stimulates the next reaction. Children no longer react to peripheral aspects of the situation, and their attention is directed, on the whole, to the principal condition of the task. Systems of tactile-motor reactions develop in younger children. At this stage the so-called "acceptor of effect"—a term introduced by Anokhin—that provides the basis for the imagination of a specific situation, is formed. This image is still limited because of its being linked to the perception of the object and to the current sample orientation. As yet, it is not based on previous sensorial experience.

In the next stage, the third, the role held by visual orientation in accompanying the movements of the hand increases. It gradually replaces investigatory handling of the object. Tactile-kinaesthetic associations begin to be formed with the help of vision. It has been shown that 6–7 year olds were able to follow the paths of a labyrinth with their eyes, and consequently perform the required movements with relatively few errors.

Highly interesting experiments on the development of visual orientation were conducted by Zinchenko (1962), another of Zaporozhets' co-workers, and also by Poddyakov (1965). Zinchenko registered ocular movements during the process of perceiving images of objects. In this way he was able to observe the developmental changes occurring in children of the ages 3 to 5 in the perception of the focal points, particularly the outline of the object.

Furthermore, the development of the sensorial orientation is accompanied by the formation of verbal associations. Children are guided by the given instructions and by a sort of self-direction, i.e. they repeat aloud whatever they have to do. The system of orienting reactions becomes consolidated and is no longer only dependent on observing the situation.

Finally, verbal reactions are substituted by mental orientation on the level of silent speech. At the same time, the orienting movements are reduced to essentials, being appropriate not only to that particular situation, but to a whole class of similar circumstances.

The function of language for orienting activity and for the acquisition of motor skills must be pursued further. In fact, Soviet work on the functions of language in mental development deserves more space than it has been allocated here. This reduction is only warranted by the fact that the English reader has lately had the opportunity to come into direct contact with the works of Luria (1961; Luria and Yudovich, 1959), one of the Russian authorities in this field. Consequently, we will confine ourselves to a small part of Luria's work, while more emphasis will be placed on Zaporozhets' co-workers.

All authors agree that language plays a leading role in the development of the child's voluntary activities. They emphasize the role held by language in the organization of motor responses, its contribution to the child's growing knowledge and to his increased self-control.

In experiments conducted by Luria and Polyakova (1959a and b) and Luria and Rozanova (1959), it was noticed that a child under $1\frac{1}{2}$ years of age was not able to look for a coin hidden in front of him under one of two objects (a glass or a cup). Instead of doing what he was told to, he started fingering the two objects. Obviously, he could not help reacting to the immediate stimuli that reached him. When a child of $2 \cdot 7$ years was told where the coin had been hidden, without having seen the actual process of hiding, he started to look for it, but not in the place he had been told, but rather in places where he had repeatedly looked for it in previous trials. Only 3 year olds were able to search according to the experimenter's instructions, as opposed to the earlier methods of relying on visual control or stereotyped solutions.

In Zaporozhets' laboratories, Endovitskaya (1955) studied the ability of pre-school children to accomplish a simple task. Three cubes, three pyramids and three cylinders of various sizes were placed in front of the children, who were then asked to put each object in a corresponding box. The subjects could be divided into four groups. Members of the first one could not organize their action in accordance with the given instructions. They only kept to the general meaning of the instructions for each action, despite the fact that the order of the movements was dependent on the positions of the figures on the table. They took whatever came to hand regardless of its shape or size. They worked correctly only if they were told what to do before each movement. The second group listened to the experimenter's instructions and acted accordingly, but they were somewhat uncertain and waited for confirmation after each action. The children of the third group were able to organize their actions although some of these were wrong. The final group acted independently and correctly. There was a high positive correlation between the type of behaviour and the child's age; mainly 3–5 year olds formed the majority of the first two groups, while the 5–7 year olds were concentrated in the last two groups. Hence, as the child grows older, language plays an increasingly more important role in his voluntary actions.

On the other hand, experiments conducted by Kislyuk (1956) and Grebenshchikova (reported by Zaporozhets), another group of Zaporozhets's disciples, showed that for all pre-school children direct demonstration of required actions was more efficient than verbal explanations. In Kislyuk's experiments, the subjects were asked to use four different movements in responding to four signals, while Grebenshchikova asked her subjects to perform various gymnastic exercises. To account for these rather contradictory results, Zaporozhets assumed that the nature of the task was an additional intervening factor to age. Thus some of the experiments, e.g. that of Endovitskoya, were concerned with very simple movements, the difficulty being in their serial order. Yet in the other experiments the performance of the movements themselves was difficult and in such cases organization on the verbal plane would be less desirable. Certainly this does not explain everything, and merely points to the need for further investigation.

A Final Comment

The reader will have noticed the significant differences between Soviet and Western approaches to mental development. There has been no need to have recourse to psychoanalytical terminology in

o

this article, and indeed, Russian authors do not use it in their discussions on changes in the motivation of the child's behaviour. They also disagree on principle with some of the major Western conjectures on the relation between biological and environmental factors in the growth of the child. The most obvious example of this is their negative and critical opinions of Gesell's view.

One could find many other points of difference, but common spheres of interest and similarities are abundant. Thus, for example one can take the study of the connection between abstract and concrete in the development of thinking. Russian scholars often remind one of Piaget. Despite the fact that his approach is criticized, the Russians point out the great value of his work. Similarly, the dispute over cross-sectional and longitudinal methods are very reminiscent of analogous arguments in the West.

References

ANAN'EV, B. G. (1957) O razvitii detei v protsesse obucheniya [The development of children in the process of instruction]. *Soviet Paedagogy (Sov. Paed.)* 7.

ANAN'EV, B. G. (1965) Chelovek kak predmet vospitaniya [Man as a subject of education]. *Soviet Paedagogy* 1.

BOGOYAVLENSKII, D. N. (1957) *Psikhologiya Usvoeniya Orfografii [Psychology of Mastering Spelling]*. R.S.F.S.R. Acad. Paed. Sci. Press.

BOGOYAVLENSKII, D. N. (1962) Formirovanie priemov umstvennoi raboty uchashchikhsya kak put' razvitiya myshleniya i aktivizatsii ucheniya [Formation of methods of intellectual work in school children as a way of development of thinking and activation of learning]. *Problems of Psychology (Vop. Psikhol.)* 4.

BOGOYAVLENSKII, D. N. and MENCHINSKAYA, N. A. (1959) *Psikhokogiya Usvoeniya Znanii v Shkole [Psychology of Learning in School]*. R.S.F.S.R. Acad. Paed. Sci. Press.

BOZHOVICH, L. I. and BLAGONADEZHINA, L. V. (Eds.) (1961) *Voprosy Psikhologii Lichnosti Shkolnika [Problems of Psychology of Pupil's Personality]*. R.S.F.S.R. Acad. Paed. Sci. Press.

DAVYDOV, V. V. (1957) Obrazovanie nachalnogo poniatiya o kolichestve [Formation of the concept of quantity in children]. *Problems of Psychology* 2.

EL'KONIN, D. B. (1960a) Opyt psikhologicheskogo issledovaniya v eksperimental'nom classe [A psychological investigation in an experimental class]. *Soviet Paedagogy* 5.

EL'KONIN, D. B. (1960b) *Detskaya Psikhologiya [Child Psychology]*. R.S.F.S.R. Ministry of Education, Paedagogical Press.

ENDOVITSKAYA, T. V. (1955) Rol' slova v vypol'nenii prostykh deistvii det'mi doshkol'nogo vozrasta [Role of language in performance of simple actions by pre-school children]. Bulletin R.S.F.S.R. Acad. Paed. Sci. *Izv. APN R.S.F.S.R.* **64.**

GAL'PERIN, P. YA. (1959) Razvitie issledovanii po formirovaniyu umstvennykh deistvii [Advances in the study on formation of mental operations]. In: B. G. Anan'ev *et al.* (Eds.), *Psikhologichaskaya Nauka v SSSR [Psychological Science in the USSR]*, Vol. I. R.S.F.S.R. Acad. Paed. Sci. Press.

GAL'PERIN, P. YA. and TALYZINA, N. F. (1961) Formation of elementary geometrical concepts and their dependence on directed participation by the pupils. In: N. O'Connor (Ed.), *Recent Soviet Psychology.* Pergamon Press.

GUROVA, L. L. (1961) K voprosy o formirovanii logicheskikh operatsii [Formation of logical operations]. In: N. A. Menchinskaya (Ed.), *Primenenie Znanii v Uchebnoi Praktike Shkol'nikov; Psikhologicheskie Issledovaniya [Application of Knowledge in the Training of School Children; Psychological Investigations].* R.S.F.S.R. Acad. Paed. Sci. Press.

KABANOVA-MELLER, E. N. (1962) *Psikhologiya Formirovaniya Znanii i Navykov u Shkol'nikov; Problema Priemov Umstvennoi Deyatel'sti [Psychology of Development of Knowledge and Skills in School Children; the Problem of Methods of Intellectual Work].* R.S.F.S.R. Acad. Paed. Sci. Press.

KAL'MYKOVA, Z. I. (1961) Effektivnost' primeneniya znanii po fizike v zavisimosti ot razlichnykh uslovii ikh usvoeniya [The relation between the application of knowledge of physics and the conditions of its mastering]. In: N. A. Menchinskaya (Ed.), *Primenenie Znanii v Uchebnoi Rabote Shkol'nikov [Application of Knowledge in Pupils' School Work].* R.S.F.S.R. Acad. Paed. Sci. Press.

KISLYUK, G. I. (1956) K voprosu o formirovanii dvigatel'nykh navykov u detei doshkol'nogo vozrasta [The problem of formation of motor skills in pre-school children]. *Problems of Psychology* **6.**

LEONT'EV, A. N. (1957) Teoreticheskie problemy psikhicheskogo razvitiya rebenka [Theoretical problems of child's mental development]. *Soviet Paedagogy* **6.**

LEONT'EV, A. N. (1959a) *Problemy Razvitiya Psikhiki [Problems of Mental Development].* R.S.F.S.R. Acad. Paed. Sci. Press.

LEONT'EV, A. N. (1959b) Ob istoricheskom podkhode v izuchenii psikhiki cheloveka [The genetic approach to study of human mind]. In: B. G. Anan'ev *et al.* (Eds.), *Psychological Science in the USSR*, Vol. I. R.S.F.S.R. Acad. Paed. Sci. Press.

LEONT'EV, A. N. and ROZANOVA, T. V. (1951) Zavisimost' obrazovaniya assotsiativnykh svyazei ot soderzhaniya deistviya [Dependence of formation of associative connections on the content of actions]. *Soviet Paedagogy* **10.**

LEVITOV, N. D. (1960) *Detskaya i Paedagogicheskaya Psikhologiya [Child and Educational Psychology].* R.S.F.S.R. Ministry of Education Paedagogical Press.

LURIA, A. R. (1961) *The Role of Speech in the Regulation of Normal and Abnormal Behaviour.* Oxford: Pergamon Press.

LURIA, A. R. (1962) Ob izmenchovosti psikhicheskikh funktsii v protsesse razvitiya rebenka [Variability of mental functions in child's development]. *Problems of Psychology* 3.

LURIA, A. R. and POLYAKOVA, A. G. (1959a) Nablyudeniya nad razvitiem proizvol'nogo deistviya v rannem detstve [Observations on the development of voluntary action in early childhood] Vypol'nenie slovesnoi instruktsik na rannykh etapakh razvitiya rebenka [First Report, Fulfilment of verbal instructions in early stages of child's development]. *Reports R.S.F.S.R. Acad. Paed. Sci.* 3.

LURIA, A. R. and POLYAKOVA, A. G. (1959b) O sootnoshenii afferentnykh sistem na posledovatel'nykh etapakh formirovaniya proizvol'nogo deistviya [Observations on the development of voluntary action in early childhood. Second Report, The relations between afferent systems in the successive stages of a voluntary action]. *Reports R.S.F.S.R. Acad. Paed. Sci.* 4.

LURIA, A. R. and ROZANOVA, V. A. (1959) O formirovanii orientiruyushchei roli rechi u detei predoshkol'nogo vozrasta [Observations on the development of voluntary action in early childhood. Third Report, Formation of the orienting role of speech in pre-school children]. *Reports R.S.F.S.R. Acad. Paed. Sci.* 6.

LURIA, A. R. and YUDOVICH, T. YA. (1959) *Speech and the Development of Mental Processes in the Child; an experimental investigation.* London: Staples Press.

MENCHINSKAYA, N. A. (1957) *Razvitie Psikhiki Rebenka; Dnevnik Materi* [Mental Development of a Child; a Mother's Diary]. R.S.F.S.R. Acad. Sci. Press, 2nd ed.

MENCHINSKAYA, N. A. (Ed.) (1958) *Psikhologiya Primeneniya Znanii k Resheniyu Uchebnykh Zadach* [Psychology of Application of Knowledge to Solving School Tasks by Pupils]. R.S.F.S.R. Acad. Sci. Press.

MENCHINSKAYA, N. A. (Ed.) (1961) *Primenenie Znanii v Uchebnoi Praktike Shkol'nikov* [Application of knowledge to practical tasks by pupils]. R.S.F.S.R. Acad. Paed. Sci. Press.

NEVEROVICH, YA. Z. (1955) Motivy trudovoi deyatel'nosti rebenka doshkol'nogo vozrasta [Motivation of pre-school child's work]. *Bull. R.S.F.S.R. Acad. Paed. Sci.* 64.

PODDYAKOV, N. N. (1959) Usloviya preobrazovaniya ispol'nitelonykh deistvii v issledovatel'skie [Conditions of transformation of practical in investigatory actions]. *Reports R.S.F.S.R. Acad. Paed. Sci.* 5.

PODDYAKOV, N. N. (1960) Osobennosti orientirovochnoi deyatel'nosti u doshkol'nikov pri formirovanii i automatizatsii prakticheskikh deistvii [Peculiarities of the orienting activity of pre-school children during the formation and automatization of practical actions] *Problems of Psychology* 2.

PODDYAKOV, N. N. (1965) Razvitie dinamichnosti zritel'nykh predstavlenii u detei doshkol'nogo vozrasta [Development of visual representations in pre-school children]. *Problems of Psychology* 1.

POLYAKOVA, A. G. (1958) Analiz protsessa usvoeniya navykov putem podrazhaniya u detei doshkol'nogo vozrasta [Analysis of the process of mastering skills by imitation in pre-school children]. *Problems of Psychology* 6.

RUBINSHTEIN, S. L. (1946) *Osnovy Obshchei Psikhologii* [*Foundations of General Psychology*]. 2nd ed., U.S.S.R. Acad. Sci. Press.
RUBINSHTEIN, S. L. (1958) *O Myshlenii i Putyakh Ego Issledovaniya* [*Thought and the Ways of Investigating it*]. U.S.S.R. Acad. Sci. Press.
RUBINSHTEIN, S. L. (Ed.) (1960) *Protsess Myshleniya i Zakonomernosti Analiza, Sinteza i Obobschenosti* [*Process of Thought and the Laws of Analysis, Synthesis and Transfer*]. U.S.S.R. Acad. Sci. Press.
SAMARIN, YU. A. (1962) *Ocherki Psikhologiya Uma; osobennosti umstvennoi deyatel'nosti shkol'nikov* [*Studies on Psychology of Intellect; peculiarities of school children's intellectual work*]. R.S.F.S.R. Acad. Paed. Sci. Press.
SECHENOV, I. (undated) *Selected Physiological and Psychological Works.* Foreign Languages Publishing House.
SHEVAREV, P. A. (1959) *Obobshchennye Assotsiatsii v Uchebnoi Rabote Shkol'nikova* [*Generalized Associations in Training of School Child*]. R.S.F.S.R. Acad. Sci. Press.
SLAVSKAYA, K. A. (1960) Protsess myshleniya i ispolzovanie znanii [Process of thought and the use of knowledge]. In: S. L. Rubinshtein (Ed.), *Process of Thought and the Laws of Analysis, Synthesis and Transfer.*
TSVETKOVA, L. S. (1958) Rol' orientirovochn issledovatel'skoi deyatel'nosti i razlichnykh podkreplenii v obrazobvanii dvigatel'nykh navykov [Role of orienting-investigatory activity and reinforcement in the formation of motor skills]. *Reports R.S.F.S.R. Acad. Paed. Sci.* 2.
VYGOTSKII, L. S. (1956) *Izbrannye Psikhologicheskie Issledovaniya* [*Selected Psychological Researches*]. R.S.F.S.R. Acad. Paed. Sci. Press.
VYGOTSKII, S. L. (1960) *Razvitie Vysshikh Psikhicheskikh Funktsii* [*Development of Higher Mental Functions*]. R.S.F.S.R. Acad. Paed. Sci. Press.
ZAPOROZHETS, L. V. (1960) *Razvitie Proizvol'nykh Dvizhenii* [*Development of Voluntary Movements*]. R.S.F.S.R. Acad. Paed. Sci. Press.
ZAPOROZHETS, L. V. and EL'KONIN, D. B. (Eds.) (1964) *Psikhologiya Detei Doshkol'nogo Vozrasta; Razvitie Poznavatel'nykh Protsessov* [*Psychology of Pre-school Children; Development of Cognitive Processes*]. R.S.F.S.R. Acad. Paed. Sci. Press.
ZHUKOVSKAYA, R. I. (1961) Development of the child's imagination. *Soviet Paedagogy* 8.
ZINCHENKO, P. I. (1961) *Neproizvol'noe Zapominanie* [*Involuntary remembering*]. R.S.F.S.R. Acad. Paed. Sci. Press.
ZINCHENKO, V. P., CHZHI-TSIN, VAN and TARAKANOV, V. V. (1962) Stanovlenie i razvitie pertseptivnykh deistvii [Formation and development of perceptive actions]. *Problems of Psychology* 3.
ZYKOVA, V. I. (1958) Psikhologicheskii analiz primeneniya geometricheskikh znanii k resheniyu zadachi s zhizneno-konkretnym soderzhaniem [Psychological analysis of the application of geometrical knowledge to solving practical problems]. In: N. A. Menchinskaya (Ed.), *Psychology of Application of Knowledge to Solving School Tasks by Children.*

CHAPTER 7

Contemporary Soviet Psychology

JOSEF BROŽEK†

Research Professor, Lehigh University, Bethlehem, Pennsylvania

The 1963 Literary Harvest

The lists of recent Soviet publications, published from time to time in *Contemporary Psychology*, are concerned with books and monographs. The most complete listing of recent (1963) Soviet publications in psychology, including journal articles, was published in *Voprosy Psikhologii* (Berezina and Lyubimova, 1964). The specification of the areas and the number of publications in each area provides a useful though gross characterization of the present Soviet psychological scene (see Table 1).

Educational psychology, combined in Table 1 with child psychology, is clearly the dominant area. By contrast, studies on animal behavior represent, numerically, a surprisingly weak category. It is interesting that the majority of the animal studies that were cited refer to investigations on monkeys.

The history of psychology ranks fifth among the twelve categories concerned with technical scientific literature. Other criteria, outside the index of the 1963 publications, would confirm the strong interest of Soviet psychologists in the historical development of their discipline. Actually, the category could be further strengthened by a substantial number of entries placed in the highly heterogeneous category labelled "General Psychology".

† Prepared in the framework of activities supported by National Science Foundation Grant GN-351.

It is in this category that the authors register a new monograph on Pavlov (Rozental', 1963) and a volume of contributions on *The Psychological Heritage of K. D. Ushinskii* (Group of authors, 1963b). More importantly, the centenary of the publication of J. M. Sechenov's *Cerebral Reflexes* led to a flurry of journal articles and to two conferences, held in Kiev and in Odessa (Group of authors, 1963b, 1963c).

TABLE 1. AREAS OF SOVIET PSYCHOLOGY AND THE NUMBER OF PUBLICATIONS IN EACH AREA WHICH APPEARED IN THE SOVIET UNION IN 1963 (COMPILED FROM THE INFORMATION PROVIDED BY BEREZINA AND LYUBIMOVA, 1964)

	N	%
1. General psychology	216	22·6
2. Child and educational psychology	359	37·5
3. Psychology of work, engineering psychology, psychology of sports	72	7·5
4. Abnormal psychology, (defectology), medical psychology, psychopathology	86	9·0
5. History of psychology	42	4·4
6. Animal behavior	9	0·9
7. Experimental methods	24	2·5
8. Teaching of psychology	8	0·8
9. Psychology abroad	17	1·8
10. Critique and bibliography	28	2·9
11. Scientific chronicle	30	3·1
12. Discussions and debates	23	2·4
13. Popular scientific literature	44	4·6
TOTAL	958	100·0

American psychologists, examining Table 1 would probably note with some amazement that, with all the efforts at the "pavlovization" of Soviet psychology exerted in the fifties, the index carries no separate entry on conditioning. This is accounted for, fundamentally, by the fact that research on conditioning is referred to in Pavlovian terminology as "the physiology of higher nervous activity" (H.N.A.). Studies on conditioning had been regarded in the Soviet Union as the province of physiologists, not of psychologists, although there is no absolute unanimity on this issue.

In the section on Experimental Methods, the index makes reference to Gambaryan's (1963) general treatise and the bibliography compiled by Petrovskaya *et al.* (1963). A small number of references are scattered through the other sections of the bibliography. The majority of references to studies on "higher nervous activity" is contained in the first category, labelled "General Psychology", and deal, for the most part, with the major events rather than the much larger work-a-day technical literature published in the journals.

(1) The monograph of Alekseenko on *The Interaction of Simultaneous Conditioned Reactions in Man* (1963), Ivanov-Smolenskii's *Methods* (1963), and two collections of articles (Biryukov, 1963; Group of authors, 1963).

(2) The proceedings of the 1962 conference on the philosophical aspects of the physiology of higher nervous activity and psychology (Fedoseev, 1963), and the proceedings of the conference held in New York in 1960 under the joint sponsorship of the New York Academy of Sciences and the Soviet Academy of Medical Sciences (Anokhin, 1963).

(3) The reports on the 20th conference on the physiology of higher nervous activity, held in Leningrad in April 1963 (Pavlov and Lange, 1963) and the conference on research methods in pathological physiology of man's higher nervous activity and medical psychology, held in Leningrad in October 1962 (Myasischev and Tonkonogii, 1963).

Most of the cited contributions to the study of the "typological characteristics of the nervous system" or, alternately, "of man's higher nervous activity", were published in the third volume of collected papers, edited by Teplov (1963). In spite of the apparent vacillation in the basic concepts and terminology, this phase of the Soviet work is relevant to the psychology of individual differences and should be reviewed, critically and systematically, in English.

Luria, who published in 1963 a major work on *Man's Brain and Mental Processes*, gave his monograph the subtitle "Neuropsychological Investigations". This may have served the purpose of differentiating his approach from the traditional methodology of the "physiology of higher nervous activity", largely centered on the study of conditioned responses.

In addition to a few theoretical and some philosophical, "ideological", and organizational papers, the category of General Psychology covers also the literature dealing with such topics as sensation and perception (cf. Maizcl', 1963), experimental studies on "set" (cf. Prangishvili and Khodzhava, 1963), studies in psychophysiology and physiological psychology (few and far between), and an occasional paper on personality. A number of research articles deal with verbal behavior, frequently in relation to the study of thinking but not neglecting the psychophysiological aspects, such as the electromyographic analysis of the "inner speech". Most of these papers appeared in a volume edited by Zhinkin and Shemyakin (1963).

A half-dozen entries deal with cybernetics, considered in relation to such topics as thinking, orienting reflex, or imagery. Another half-dozen papers are concerned with a relative *novum* in Soviet psychology—social psychology.

In the section on "Psychology Abroad", in addition to the monograph edited by E. V. Shorokhova (1963), the following topics are covered, reflecting some of the current interests of the Soviet psychologists: theory of social action, structure of perceived space, engineering psychology, space flight, psychoanalysis (be it psychoanalysis "in the service of reaction"), psychology of memory and information theory, intelligibility of spoken words, programmed learning, and development of thinking.

Soviet Psychologists meet in Leningrad

The second conference of the Psychological Society, formed and maintained under the aegis of the R.S.F.S.E. Academy of Pedagogical Sciences, was held in sunny Leningrad on 24–29 June 1963 (cf. Razran, 1964a).

In keeping with the common Soviet pattern, the information concerning the Leningrad meetings was provided in the form of three kinds of publications:

(1) The *Program* (Psychological Society, 1963a), containing the titles of the presentations, a minimum of organizational details and the alphabetic index of speakers.

(2) The five volumes of *Abstracts*, better referred to by the term *Theses* (Psychological Society, 1963b) since they are much longer than the abstracts of papers presented at the meetings of the American Psychological Association or the Federated Societies for Experimental Biology. Thus several of the "theses" extend over 6 printed pages. The modal length is about 500 words.

(3) The texts, later published in full in *Voprosy Psikhologii*, of the papers presented at the plenary sessions held on the first day of the congress. I was sorry to miss them because of my late arrival in Leningrad. The addresses dealt with engineering psychology (A. N. Leont'ev and B. F. Lomov), the significance of "the basic properties of the nervous system" for the psychology of individual differences (B. M. Teplov and V. D. Nebylitsyn), various aspects of educational psychology (P. Y. Gal'perin, A. V. Zaporozhets and D. B. El'konin; G. S. Kostyuk, N. A. Menchinskaya and A. A. Smirnov), social psychology (E. V. Shorokhova, N. S. Mansurov and K. K. Platonov), relations between education and psychology (L. V. Zankov), development of personality of the school child (L. I. Bozhovich), and psychology of personality considered in reference to "social practice" (A. G. Kovalev and V. N. Myasishchev).

The fact that the Abstracts (*Theses*) of the 1959 meeting were published in three volumes (a total of 475 pages) while those of the 1963 meeting required five volumes and totalled 991 pages may serve as a gross indication of the growth of research output during the intervening period. But the qualitative changes are more impressive, more relevant, and more significant. Principal among these is the emergence, in force, of engineering psychology and the groping endeavor to establish social psychology as a legitimate sphere of psychological research. In 1959 neither the field of engineering nor of social psychology was even mentioned in the *Abstracts*.

Industrial Psychology

It is true, some papers were presented in 1959 dealing with the psychology of work but they were few in number and highly heterogeneous in subject matter. At the 1963 meeting not one, not two, but six half-day sessions were held under the banner of engineering psychology, with a special symposium added as a topping.

Altogether at Leningrad there were five special symposia and forty-seven sessions of contributed papers (see Tables 2 and 3).

TABLE 2. PROGRAM OF THE SECOND CONGRESS OF THE (SOVIET) PSYCHOLOGICAL SOCIETY: SYMPOSIA

1. Reception and processing of information by man.
2. Properties of the nervous system and problems of individual differences.
3. Psychological aspects of increasing the effectiveness of instruction in schools.
4. Formation of the personality of the child and problems of education (upbringing, *vospitanie*).
5. Problems of social psychology.

TABLE 3. PROGRAM OF THE SECOND CONGRESS OF THE (SOVIET) PSYCHOLOGICAL SOCIETY: HALF-DAY SESSIONS (CONTRIBUTED PAPERS) DEVOTED TO SPECIFIC AREAS. THE NUMBER OF SESSIONS IS GIVEN IN PARENTHESES

1. Educational (pedagogical) psychology (14).
    Academic instruction (6).
    Vocational training (5).
    Education, personality formation (3).
2. General psychology (8).
    Sensation (1).
    Attention, will personality (1).
    Speech and language (1).
    Thinking (2).
    Set (1).
    Esthetics (1).
3. Medical psychology (8).
    Psychopathology (5).
    Defectology (3).
4. Engineering psychology (6).

5. Child psychology (5).
   Pre-school (3).
   School (2).
6. Comparative psychology (2).
7. Psychology of physical education and sports (2).
8. History of psychology and contemporary psychology abroad (2).

Two of the symposia (items 3 and 4) were devoted to educational (pedagogical) psychology. The symposium on "The Study of the Properties of the Nervous System and Problems of Individual Differences in Psychology" would be sure to arrest the attention of an American psychologist. It compensated, in part at least, for the absence of a session or sessions on physiological psychology. More novel for the Soviet psychologists, was the symposium on "The Reception and Processing of Information", a topic in the burgeoning engineering psychology. But perhaps the most intriguing item on the program was the symposium on "The Problems of Social Psychology" (Psychological Society, 1963a, vol. 5, pp. 180–236, 1963).

Social Psychology

The *status nascendi* of social psychology in the U.S.S.R. is clearly documented by the character of the papers that were given. Out of thirteen presentations, the overwhelming majority seeks to clarify the subject matter and the acceptable methods of social psychology. One author considers, in general terms, morale (*obshchestvennoe nastroenie*) as a subject of research; two others discuss the relations between social psychology and the psychology of personality.

Perhaps, in some ways, it would be more appropriate to speak of a *status renascendi*, of a rebirth of social psychology in the Soviet Union. But its roots in the local soil, especially in the work of V. M. Bekhterev reported in the twenties (cf. his *Collective Reflexology*), are deeply buried by years of ideological harangue and neglect. The ideologists, who "liquidated" early Soviet social psychology and the study of man for a long time, are still at hand loudly bewailing, at the same time, the "abstract approach of Soviet psychology to the study of man" (cf. Filatov, 1963) and the fact that social psychology became a "monopoly of bourgois psychologists and sociologists" (*ibid.*, p. 207). It is not so many years ago that S. L. Rubinshtein, then the leading Soviet psychologist, characterized endeavors to defend the scientific status of social psychology as an attempt, "dear to the heart of the reactionaries", to sneak idealism into the study of social phenomena. These were strong words of disapproval and cast a long shadow.

Reports of investigative work at the symposium were conspicuous by their rarity. In his paper on research methods, E. S. Kuz'min cited the application of the sociographic technique of Moreno to the study of personal interrelations in teams of workers. He referred also to the study of A. A. Bodalev in which the method of "polar profiles" (involving, for example, comparisons of one's own view of oneself and the view ascribed to another person, such as a teacher) was used with schoolchildren. Time budget of workers and incentives to work are some other topics that were studied.

Strangely enough, at the symposium the two papers dealing specifically with empirical research—personality of the workers and personal interrelations in workers' collectives—came from the Institute of Philosophy of the U.S.S.R. Academy of Sciences from which once Rubinshtein pontificated against social psychology.

The preamble of the report by Bashilov *et al.* (1963) is still ideological:

> Bourgeois science, in its endeavor to fight marxism, psychologizes social phenomena. Soviet psychologists, having totally rejected the theory of bourgeois social psychology, can accept some of its concrete investigations. It has become essential at present to develop a Marxist social psychology.

Using observational approach and non-standard interviews, the authors studied five groups of industrial workers classified in terms of the complexity of the job. The latter proved to parallel a "progressively more rounded development of personality" and a "tendency toward a progressive, integrated, steadfast, and active philosophy of life" (*mirovozzrenie*). In spite of the serious limitations of the method, we have here a broadly based, empirical investigation or rather a series of investigations concerning factors related to the interest of the workers in their job (heavy work, monotony versus diversity of operations and their rhythmicity, cohesiveness of the worker team, role of the team leader), esthetic and moral attitudes, and creativity.

O. I. Zotova (1963) cites among her methods sociometric analysis. The attempt to use this approach was considered to have been a failure since the choices (to share work, apartment, an outing) were dictated not by personal sympathies or antipathies between the workers but by the criteria of performance on the job. In a large number of groups no negative choices (rejections) were made whatsoever, even though the instructions asked for them: "I can work with anybody" was the pat answer. The author is honest enough to tell us that the questioned workers frequently had caustic comments to make about the whole enterprise. But she does not let us know why and forces the reader to "read between the lines".

Educational Psychology

In contrast to the American scene, Soviet psychology in general and the program of the 1963 Congress in particular is dominated by concern with education. Soviet "pedagogical" psychology is separated, fairly rigorously, into (1) the psychology of instruction (*obuchenie*), concerned with school learning (academic instruction) and vocational training (*trudovoe obuchenie*), and (2) psychology of education, in the narrower sense (*vospitanie*), concerned with the formation of personality.

The dominant position of pedagogical psychology is clearly manifest in Table 3 which indicates the number of half-day sessions devoted to the specific areas.

In addition to the sessions of contributed papers, two of the five symposia held in Leningrad were devoted to pedagogical psychology. These dealt, respectively, with the problem of increasing the effectiveness of school instruction and with the formation of child's personality. In the latter symposium the term "collective" or "collectivism" was mentioned, specifically, in more than half the titles.

Closely related to pedagogical psychology are the studies in child psychology. As we have seen, in the index of the 1963 psychological literature the two categories were combined. The materials presented at the Leningrad congress were about equally divided between papers on the pre-school child and the child of school age.

Miscellaneous Problems

The area of general experimental psychology is well represented but calls for little comment. Research on personality, outside of the educational context, is a weak spot in Soviet psychology. This is reflected in the fact that the program included only one session concerned with personality. Even then, it shared its place on the program with two, terminologically rather old-fashioned, bed fellows, attention and will. Presence of sessions devoted to verbal behavior, esthetics, and to the study of "set" should be noted.

"Set" continues to be a Georgian speciality; of the seven speakers in the session six had names ending in -*dze* or -*shvili*, and lived in Tbilisi. The session on the psychology of art had also a "southern flavor", with most of the speakers coming from the Ukraine (Kiev) and Armenia (Erevan).

The work on "set" was for a long time ideologically suspect, since set refers to non-conscious factors in behavior. It was a dangerous undertaking in a context in which psychology was defined as the study of consciousness and in which the chain of associations went from "subconscious" to "Freud" to "freudism" to "bourgeois" and worse. This was so in spite of repeated statements by the Georgian psychologists that their concepts are radically different from Freud's. Times have changed and we find M. A. Mazmanyan, an Armenian from Erevan to be sure, speaking at the Leningrad congress on "unconscious (*bessoznatel'nye*) components of creative processes".

The area of "medical psychology" was well represented. In the Soviet practice, the term does not correspond exactly to what is denoted by the label "clinical psychology" in America or England. The Soviets divide the field of medical psychology into (a) psycho-pathology (*patopsikhologiya*), dealing with the psychological aspects of nervous and mental diseases and disturbances, and (b) the psychology of "exceptional" children—the deaf, the blind, and the mentally retarded (*defektologiya*).

General Observations on Soviet Psychology

Six sessions were labelled "engineering psychology", without a further specification of the subtopics. The range of topics was broad. A small fraction of the contributed papers was concerned with theoretical issues, such as the replacement of considerations of energy expenditure, as the dominant concern of the physiology of human work, by the cybernetic approach to the regulation of functions. At the same time, the study of control functions in their psychological aspects is viewed as the central task of contemporary industrial psychology.

Among the empirical studies, about one-third was carried out in industrial and other realistic settings, two-thirds in the laboratories. Thus, in regard to the first category, reports were presented on problem solving in the context of industrial operations (such as those involved in the repair and setting of machines, and in the directing of railroad traffic by dispatchers working in important railroad junctions); on the handling of information by airport dispatchers; facilitation of the timing of industrial operations by programmed signals; awareness of deviations from the norm in work at an assembly line of a tractor factory and their correction; and emotional stress associated with airplane flight at supersonic speeds.

No studies were reported on the psychological aspects of space flight but several papers dealt with closely related issues, especially the effects of prolonged isolation (up to 2 weeks) in restricted space on time perception, psychophysiological functions and performance.

The laboratory studies were concerned with the typical topics of engineering psychology, with heavy emphasis on visual perception, but not neglecting decision making and the operation of control panels.

The level of papers on engineering psychology and, even more so, on industrial psychology, was not even. One had the impression that the formulation of some of the problems could have been dated 1923. But, on the whole, the reported work was up to date, a 1963 vintage. The latter qualification applies, in particular, to the papers presented at the symposium on the Reception and Processing of Information.

Two sessions were devoted to comparative psychology. This is a more impressive show of strength than the index of works published in 1963 would have suggested. However, in animal research, which is of interest to psychologists, the dominant position of investigations on monkeys and, in particular, on anthropoid apes, is confirmed. Out of a total of fifteen papers, eight belonged clearly in this category.

More surprising to a psychologist from America or Western Europe would be the fact that an equal number of sessions was concerned with the psychology of physical education and sports, and with the history of psychology.

The Soviet ideologists, at times wearing an historian's hat, contend that the basic theoretical positions in psychology are determined by the materialist and the idealist view on the nature of the psyche: materialists regard the psyche as a property (product) of matter; idealists view the psyche as a separate substance, independent of matter and determining the development of matter. It created consternation in the lecture hall at a session on the history of psychology when I stated that such a polarity and concern are obsolete, that such distinctions do not fit the facts, and that it is altogether hopeless to make them a basis of a viable history of the scientific psychology of the twentieth century.

Conclusion

The present portrait of the contemporary Soviet psychology was drawn on the basis of the analysis of the 1963 literary production and of the presentations made at the congress of the Soviet Psychological Society, held in June 1963.

It is an incomplete portrait, especially as far as the interests of Western psychologists are concerned. The other half (and some might say, "the better half"), referred to in the Soviet parlance as "the physiology of higher nervous activity (H.N.A.)", is largely missing. Representing the continuation of research activities stimulated and long directed by Pavlov, physiology of H.N.A. is a well-established discipline. The fact that the *twentieth* meeting of specialists in the study of H.N.A. preceded the *second* meeting of the Psychological Society is an outward symbol of the difference in status and stability.

Psychology and Physiology

Psychology and the physiology of H.N.A. have been running on parallel rails, with little switching over. Not that it does not occur, especially in recent years. Typically, it is the psychologists who cross the lines. Thus, Anan'ev's paper (1963) on the contemporary significance for psychology of I. M. Sechenov's 1863 volume on *Cerebral Reflexes* appeared in *The Journal of Higher Nervous Activity*.

The two groups were brought together, formally, at the 1962 conference on "The Philosophical Problems of Higher Nervous Activity and Psychology", and on other occasions, such as the symposium on "Structural and Functional Bases of Mental Activity" (Sarkisov and Shorokhova, 1963) at which the introductory presentation was made by the Georgian physiologist, I. S. Beritashvili, well known for his interest in behavior.

In the applied field, educational psychology continues to represent the largest segment. "Medical" psychology is growing but the most remarkable proliferation has taken place in the sector of engineering (and industrial) psychology (cf. Anan'ev and Lomov, 1963; Levitov, 1963; Lomov, 1963). However, some of the "discoveries" are simply rediscoveries of facts, approaches and points of view that were well known not only in the West, all along, but in the Soviet Union itself prior to the 1936 liquidation of educational "testology" and of other branches of applied psychology, "guilty by association". Subsequently, for years, in situations in which the problems of selection of personnel proved to be a vital necessity, primitive methods (*kustarnye metody*; N. I. Maizel', 1963) were used.

The major addresses at the closing session of the Second Congress were delivered by A. A. Smirnov (Moscow), chairman of the Presidium of the Society, and B. G. Anan'ev (Leningrad), chairman of the Organizing Committee of the Congress.

Psychologists in the U.S.S.R.

According to the information provided by the speakers, in 1963 the Soviet Psychological Society had 1240 members and 20 divisions. The number of the participants (speakers and guests) at the congress totalled 3205, making the congress the largest Soviet psychological gathering ever. The congressists averaged 35 years of age, with a range from 18 to 83. The communications presented at the congress numbered 366. In terms of quantitative criteria, the Leningrad congress documented convincingly the rise of psychology in the Soviet Union. In relative terms, 70% of the participants were males, 30% females; 34% were associated with scientific institutes, 63% with higher educational institutions (*vuzy*, of the university rank), and 13% with medical schools, middle schools and other establishments.

In addition to individuals who consider themselves psychologists, there were representatives of twenty-one other specialties. Anan'ev pointed out the complexity of the interrelations between scientific disciplines relevant to the study of man—mathematics, chemistry and physics, philosophy and economics, medicine and engineering—and emphasized the potential role of psychology in making more effective the communication between the sciences. Some of the recent Soviet conferences, such as the conference on literary creativity or on the perception of time and space, were genuinely interdisciplinary in character.

In reviewing the events taking place since 1959, the speakers expressed their satisfaction with the strengthening of the ranks of the Psychological Society with young people. The Psychological Department of the Leningrad State University graduated, between the years 1947–63, 307 students. Soviet advanced degrees are not comparable to the Western system, both the degree of the Candidate of Science and of the Doctor of Science representing a much higher level of accomplishment than the American Master's and Doctor's degrees. Thus, in Leningrad, out of 307 individuals completing "graduate" work, in American terminology, fifty-three earned the degree of Candidate of Science and thirty-four are working on their thesis. Only one person has been awarded the degree of the Doctor of Science while ten individuals are engaged in work on their dissertation. In Leningrad, during the years 1959–63, graduate theses were submitted in four divisions of the Department of Psychology: general, child, and educational psychology; industrial and engineering psychology; social psychology and psychology of creativity; and psychopathology, defectology (a segment of abnormal psychology, in American usage), and psychopharmacology.

As regards specific branches of psychology, Professor A. A. Smirnov expressed his satisfaction regarding the rapid growth of Soviet engineering psychology, with specific reference to the interest of the young people in the field, development of effective co-operation with technical establishments, and participation in space-flight research (cosmonautics). Good progress was reported in educational psychology, closely integrated with the day-to-day activities of the classroom. While fundamental research on the teaching methods is in progress, with programmed learning receiving serious attention, psychologists through their research on work training in schools have contributed to the realization of the program calling for the integration of "school and life". By contrast, social psychology is making its first, uncertain steps. One of the general features of recent years, stressed by Smirnov, is a further decentralization of psychological research in the Soviet Union, with a growth of research centers outside the metropolis of Moscow and Leningrad.

While there was a delay in holding the Second Congress of the Psychological Society, due in part to the death of the organizing chairman, M. V. Sokolov, Soviet psychologists participated between 1959 and June of 1963 in no less than twenty-eight special conferences. While Leningrad was the leading city as far as the number of conferences held in one place is concerned, conferences attended or organized by psychologists were held also in such faraway places as the Transcaucasian territories. Significant progress was made, the speakers felt, in strengthening international scientific co-operation through participation of Soviet psychologists in the governing bodies of the international scientific organizations and in international congresses.

But neither Smirnov nor Anan'ev limited their comment to the positive side of the ledger. There were failures and disappointments as well. The society did not succeed in its endeavors to launch an information bulletin and a second psychological journal. Not as much progress has been made as was hoped for in establishing new psychological laboratories and in improving the training of psychologists. The project to establish an Institute of Industrial Psychology in the framework of the U.S.S.R. Academy of Sciences was not realized. There is room for improvement in the co-ordination of research in psychology. The Central Council of the Society with its fifty members was an awkward body. It met only once since 1959, its functions were not clear, and it simply did not work. It was proposed, and the proposal was, I believe, accepted to reduce the number of the members of the Presidium of the Society to twenty-one.

Some aspects of the psychology of personality were considered to be poorly developed. The principles of social psychology have been discussed at length; now it must be developed in regard to its content. The contact between psychological specialties should be strengthened. This applies also to the mathematical treatment of psychological data, contacts with the psychologists of socialist countries, and the functioning of regionally organized psychological associations in the U.S.S.R.

Growth and aging deserve further attention and should be viewed in reference to the total life cycle. In regard to psychogenesis, the interrelations between heredity and environment must be taken into account. There are challenging opportunities to expand activities in applied psychology. Anan'ev noted, as an example, problems of architecture for human living and urged the participants: Get involved in the problems of real life! This involves, sharing in the "education of the (Soviet) new man" (*vospitanije novogo cheloveka*).

A number of discussants and commentators asked to be heard. In some ways, this was for me the most interesting part of the congress. Curkovski (Lvov) emphasized the need for a team approach to the problems of human factors in industry. Morozovo (Moscow) expressed the view that child psychology, with its developmental point of view, has important contributions to make to general-theoretical psychology. M. I. Smirnov (Kirov) stressed that personality should be treated as psychology's central topic, not as an appendage. Another speaker, not clearly identified in my notes, made a plea that psychology should be introduced (or reintroduced) into the middle schools ("high schools" in American terminology) and into other institutes of higher education than those concerned with the training of teachers. Kost'yuk (Kiev), in identifying the areas and points of view which deserve more attention noted, among others: objective, quantitative methods; mathematical analysis of the data, specifically mentioning factor analysis; psychophysiological research; research on programmed learning; and psychology of personality and emotions. E. S. Kuz'min added, forcefully, that psychology of personality must be closely linked with social psychology, otherwise it remains abstract and sterile. The emergence of social psychology in the Soviet Union, documented by a symposium on the subject held in the framework of the Second Congress, is a telling symptom of ongoing changes in Soviet psychology which make predictions of future development hazardous.

"Ideological", politico-philosophical differences between "East" and "West" persist. In some fields, ideology still hampers the forward movement of psychology in the U.S.S.R. This probably will not change in the visible future. However, the present trend toward a reduction of the East–West differences in research methods is likely to continue and grow—with important benefits to scientific, world-wide psychology. In principle and at the stage of maturity, science has no place for "nationally (or internationally) advertised brands".

References

ALEKSEENKO, N. YU. (1963) *Vzaimodeistvie Odnovremennykh Uslovnykh Reaktsii u Cheloveka* [*Interaction of Simultaneous Conditioned Reactions in Man*]. Moscow: U.S.S.R. Acad. Sci. 151 pp.

ANAN'EV, B. G. (1963) I. M. Sechenov's *Cerebral Reflexes and Contemporary Psychology. Zh. Vyssh. Nerv. Deyat.* **13** (5), 772–9.

ANAN'EV, B. G. and B. F. LOMOV (Eds.) (1963) *Problemy Obshchei i Industrial' noi Psikhologii* [*General and Industrial Psychology*]. Leningrad: Leningrad University. 156 pp.

ANOKHIN, P. K. (Ed.) (1963) *Vysshaya Nervnaya Deyatel'nost'* [*Higher Nervous Activity*]. Joint Pavlovian Conference of the New York Acad. Sci. and Acad. of Med. Sci. of U.S.S.R. Moscow: Medgiz. 336 pp.

BASHILOV, V. I. DZHIGAR'YAN, I. A., MAKAROV, N. I. and PLATONOV, K. K. (1963). Research on the personality of the worker from the point of view of social psychology. *Congr. Psychol. Soc.* **5**, 228–33.

BEREZINA, G. A. and LYUBIMOVA, E. D. (1964) Ukazatel' literatury po psikhologii, opublikovannoi v 1963 g. [Index of psychological literature published in 1963]. *Vop. Psikhol.* **5**, 153–86.

BIRYUKOV, D. A. (Ed.) (1963) *Problemy Fiziologii i Patologii Vysshei Nervnoi Deyatel'nosti* [*Problems of the Physiology and Pathology of Higher Nervous Activity*]. Leningrad: Medgiz, **2**. 194 pp.

BROŽEK, J. (1961a) Recent Russian books in psychology. *Contemp. Psychol.* **6**, 62–63.

BROŽEK, J. (1961b) Nutritional research in the Soviet Union. Part I. Some general aspects. Part II. Some specific aspects. *Nutrition Rev.* **19**, 129–32 and 161–4.

BROŽEK, J. (1962a) Recent Russian books in psychology. *Contemp. Psychol.* **7**, 37–38.

BROŽEK, J. (1962b) Current status of psychology in the U.S.S.R. *Ann. Rev. Psychol.* **13**, 515–66.

BROŽEK, J. (1962c) Soviet studies on nutrition and higher nervous activity. *Ann. N.Y. Acad. Sci.* **93**, Art. 15, 665–714.

BROŽEK, J. (1963a) Recent Russian books in psychology. *Contemp. Psychol.* **8**, 252–5.

BROŽEK, J. (1963b) Soviet psychology. In: M. H. Marx and W. A. Hillix, *Systems and Theories in Psychology.* New York, McGraw-Hill, pp. 438–55.

BROŽEK, J. (1964a) Recent Russian books in psychology. *Contemp. Psychol.* **9**, 294–7.

BROŽEK, J. (1964b) Current status of psychology in the U.S.S.R. *Ann. Rev. Psychol.* **13**, 515–66.

BROŽEK, J. (1964c) Recent developments in Soviet psychology. *Ann. Rev. Psychol.* **15**, 493–594.

BROŽEK, J. (Ed.) (1964d) Selected aspects of contemporary psychology in the U.S.S.R.: a symposium. *Medical Reports, Fordham Univ., Institute of Contemp. Russian Studies* **6** (1), 1–21.

BROŽEK, J. (1964e) Various Soviet psychologies (a review of N. O'Connor, Ed., *Recent Soviet Psychology*; B. G. Anan'ev *et al.*, Eds., *Psychological Science in the U.S.S.R.*; R. A. Buoer, Ed., *Some Views on Soviet Psychology*). *Contemp. Psychol.* **9**, 100–3.

BROŽEK, J., CHAPMAN, C. B. and KEYS, A. (1948) Drastic food restriction: Effect on cardiovascular dynamics in normotensive and hypertensive conditions. *J. Am. Med. Assoc.* **137**, 1569–74.

BROŽEK, J. and SIMONSON, E. (1962) Russian research on aging. *Geriatrics* **17**, 464–76.

BROŽEK, J. and VAES, G. (1961) Experimental investigations on the effects of dietary deficiencies on animal and human behavior. *Vitamins & Hormones* **19**, 43–94.

BROŽEK, J., WELLS, S. and KEYS, A. (1946) Medical aspects of semi-starvation in Leningrad (siege 1941–1942). *Am. Rev. Soviet Med.* **4**, 70–86.

FEDOSEEV, P. N. (Ed.-in-chief) (1963) *Filosofskie Voprosy Fiziologii Vysshei Nervnoi Deyatel'nosti i Psikhologii.* U.S.S.R. Acad. Sci. 771 pp.

FILATOV, F. S. (1963) Social psychology and ideology. *Congr. Psychol. Soc.* **5**, 206–12.

GAMBARYAN, L. S. (1963) *Fisiologicheskie Metodiki Issledovaniya Vysshei Nervnoi Deyatel'nosti* [*Physiological Methods for the Study of Higher Nervous Activity*]. Erevan: Acad. Sci. Armenian S.S.R. 259 pp.

GROUP OF AUTHORS (1963a) *Nervnye mekhanizmy uslovnoreflektornoi deyetel'-nosti* [*Nervous mechanisms of conditioned reflex activity: A collection of studies*]. Moscow: U.S.S.R. Acad. Sci. 320 pp.

GROUP OF AUTHORS (1963b) *Psikhologicheskoe Nasledstvie K. D. Ushinskogo* [*The Psychological Heritage of K. D. Ushinskii.*] Rad'yans'ka Shkola. Kiev.

GROUP OF AUTHORS (1963c) Tezisy dokladov nauchnoi konferentsii psovyashchennoi 100- letiyu truda I. M. Sechenova *Refleksy Golovnogo Mozga* [*Abstracts of papers presented at a scientific conference dedicated to the centenary of I. M. Sechenov's Cerebral Reflexes*]. Odessa.

IVANOV-SMOLENSKII, A. G. (1963) *Opyt ob Ektivnogo Izucheniya Raboty i Vzarimodeistviya Signal'nykh Sistem Golovnogo Nozga (v norme i patologii)* [*Methods for an Objective Study of the Normal and Disordered Activity of the Signal Systems of the Cerebrum and their Interaction*]. Moscow: Medgiz. 703 pp.

LEVITOV, N. D. (1963) *Psikhologiya Truda* [*Industrial Psychology*]. Min. of Educ. R.S.F.S.R. 340 pp.

LOMOV, B. F. (1963) *Chelovek i Tekhnika* [*Man and Technology: outlines of engineering psychology*]. Leningrad: Leningrad Univ. 266 pp.

LURIA, A. R. (1963) *Mozg Cheloveka i Psikhicheskie Protsessy* [*Human Brain and Mental Processes: Neuropsychological studies*]. Moscow: R.S.F.S.R. Acad. of Pedag. Sci. 478 pp.

LURIA, A. R. (1964) Review of R. A. Bauer (Ed.), *Some Views of Soviet Psychology*. *Contemp. Psychol.* **9**, 103–4.

MAIZEL', N. I. (1963) Some problems of psychological selection of personnel. *Congress Psychol. Soc.* **3**, 59.

MAIZEL', S. O. (1963) *Transformatsiya Luchistoi Energii v Setchatke Chelovecheskogo Glaza* [*Transformation of Radiant Energy in Human Retina, Central Vision*]. *Gosenergoproizdat.* Moscow, Leningrad. 266 pp.

MYASISHCHEV, V. N. and TONKONOGII, I. M. (1963) Report on the conference on methods of investigations in pathological physiology of man's higher nervous activity and medical psychology. *Vop. Psikol.* **3**, 176–80.

PAVLOV, B. V. and LANGE K. A. (1963) 20th conference on problems of higher nervous activity. *Zh. Vyssh. Nerv. Deyat.* **13** (5), 946–50.

PETROVSKAYA, A. P. *et al.* (1963) *Metodike Issledovaniya Vysshei Nervnoi Deyatel'nosti Cheloveka* [*Methods of Research on Man's Higher Nervous Activity: Bibliography of Soviet Literature, 1900–1960.*] U.S.S.R. Acad. of Sci. 91 pp.

PRANGISHVILI, A. C. and KHODZHAVA, Z. I. (Eds.) (1963) *Eksperimental'nye Issledovania po Psikhologii Ustanovki* [*Experimental Psychological Investigations on Set*]. Acad. Sci. Georgian S.S.R. Tbilisi. **2**, 389 pp.

PSYCHOLOGICAL SOCIETY (1963a) *Programma S"ezda abshchestva Psikhologov* [*Program of the Second Conference of the Psychological Society*]. Moscow: R.S.F.S.R. Acad. Pedag. Sci. 47 pp.

PSYCHOLOGICAL SOCIETY (1963b) Tezisy dokladov na s"ezde obshchestva psikhologov [The theses of papers presented at the Second Meeting of the Psychological Society]. Vol. 1. *General Psychology; History of Psychology.* 216 pp. Vol. 2. *Child and Educational Psychology.* 295 pp. Vol. 3. *Engineering Psychology; Symposium on Reception and Processing of Information by Man.* 127 pp. Vol. 4. *Mental Diseases (Psychopathology). Handicaps (Defectology). Comparative Psychology.* 114 pp. Vol. 5. *Other Symposia.* 329 pp. Moscow: R.S.F.S.R. Acad. Pedag. Sci.

RAZRAN, G. (1964a) Growth, scope and direction of current Soviet psychology: The 1963 All-Union Congress. *Amer. Psychologist* **19**, 342–9.

RAZRAN, G. (1964b) Soviet studies on higher nervous activity and psychology in 1952, 1962 and 1972. *I.C.R.S. Med. Rep.* **6** (1), 13–17.

REITMAN, W. R. (1964) Soviet aspirations and attainments in research on thinking and problem solving. *I.C.R.S. Md. Rep.* **6** (1), 10–13.

ROZENTAL', I. S. (1963) *Pavlov*. Moscow: Medgiz. 147 pp.

SARKISOV, S. A. and SHOROKHOVA E. V. (Eds.) (1963) *Strukurnye i Funktsional'nye Osnovy Psikhicheskoi Deyatel'nosti* [*Structural and Functional*

Basis of Mental Activity: Proceedings of a symposium]. Leningrad: U.S.S.R. Acad. Sci.

SHOROKHOVA, E. V. (Ed.) (1963) *Sovremennaye Psikhologiya v Kapitalistich-eskikh Stranakh* [*Contemporary Psychology in the Capitalist Countries*]. Moscow: R.S.F.S.R. Acad. Pedag. Sci. 406 pp.

SVANCARA, J. (1963) Review of Bluma V. Zeigarnik, *Disturbances of thought in mentally ill individuals. Contemp. Psychol.* **8,** 209–10.

TEPLOV, B. M. (Ed.) (1963) *Tipologicheskie Osobennosti Vysshei Nervnoi Deyatel'nosti Cheloveka* [*Typological Characteristics of the Higher Nervous Activity in Man*]. R.S.F.S.R. Acad. Pedag. Sci. 3, 275 pp.

VYGOTSKY, L. S. (1962) *Thought and Language*. Transl. by E. Hanfmann and G. Vakar. M.I.T. Press, Cambridge, Mass., and Wiley, New York. 163 pp.

ZHINKIN, N. I. and SHEMYAKIN, F. N. (Eds.) (1963) *Myshlenie i Rech* (*Thinking and Speech*). Moscow: R.S.F.S.R. Acad. Pedag. Sci.

ZOTOVA, O. I. (1963) Personal interrelations in worker collectives. *Congr. Psychol. Soc.* **5,** 233–6.

Index